Talking Beyond the Page

Talking Beyond the Page shows how different kinds of picturebooks can be used with children of all ages and highlights the positive educational gains to be made from reading, sharing, talking and writing about picturebooks.

With contributions from some of the world's leading experts, chapters in this book consider how:

- children think about and respond to visual images and other aspects of picturebooks
- children's responses can be qualitatively improved by encouraging them to think and talk about picturebooks before, during and after reading them
- the non-text features of picturebooks, when considered in their own right, can help readers to make more sense out of the book
- different kinds of picturebooks, such as wordless, postmodern, multi-modal and graphic novels, are structured
- children can respond creatively to picturebooks as art forms
- picturebooks can help children deal with complex issues in their lives

Talking Beyond the Page also includes an exclusive interview with Anthony Browne who shares thoughts about his work as an author illustrator.

This inspiring and thought-provoking book is essential reading for teachers, student teachers, literacy consultants, academics interested in picturebook research and those organising and teaching on teacher education courses in children's literature and literacy.

Janet Evans is a Senior Lecturer in Education at Liverpool Hope University.

Talking Beyond the Page

Reading and responding to picturebooks

Edited by Janet Evans

Routledge
Taylor & Francis Group

LONDON AND NEW YORK

First published 2009
by Routledge
2 Park Square, Milton Park, Abingdon, Oxon, OX14 4RN

Simultaneously published in the USA and Canada
by Routledge
270 Madison Ave, New York NY 10016

Routledge is an imprint of the Taylor & Francis Group, an informa business

Transferred to Digital Printing 2010

© 2009 editorial and selection, Janet Evans; individual contributions,
the contributors.

Typeset in Garamond by Saxon Graphics

British Library Cataloguing in Publication Data
A catalogue record for this book is available from the British Library

Library of Congress Cataloging-in-Publication Data
Talking beyond the page : reading and responding to picturebooks /
edited by Janet Evans.
    p. cm.
    Includes bibliographical references and index.
    1. Group reading. 2. Children—Books and reading. 3. Picture
books for children. I. Evans, Janet.
    LC6631.L35 2009
    372.41'2—dc22   2008050345

ISBN 10: 0–415–47695–X (hbk)
ISBN 10: 0–415–47696–8 (pbk)

ISBN 13: 978–0–415–47695–9 (hbk)
ISBN 13: 978–0–415–47696–6 (pbk)

Cover illustration by 11-year-old Matthew Dempsey, for a written description see page xxvii.

To Les, my husband

Les has supported me unconditionally through all of the stages of writing this book, from the early tentative steps right through to the frenetic, rushed end. He has given me moral support, urging me on when things were difficult, as well as physical support in the form of technological expertise, which is essential if one is a technophobe!

He is a star and I could not have written this book without him. Thank you Les.

Contents

Acknowledgements

Writing a book is an extremely time-consuming and demanding task; however, I have had the pleasure of working with some very professional writers, each and every one of whom has contributed willingly to this edited volume. They have shared their knowledge and expertise in relation to picturebook research, and for this I thank them all. I hope you will enjoy and benefit from reading about their ongoing work.

A specific mention goes to David Lewis, who has been kind enough to come out of retirement to write the foreword for this book. Many thanks for this David; your thoughts and opinions are much appreciated.

Finally I would particularly like to thank the children and staff at Gilded Hollins County Primary School, Leigh, Lancashire who were, as always, willing to talk with me and share their ideas when asked. In particular I think 11-year-old Matthew Dempsey deserves a special thanks as it is his illustration that forms the cover for this book – thank you Matthew.

Janet Evans
January 2009

Permissions

Chapter 1
Three images from *Voices in the Park* by Anthony Browne, published by Doubleday. Reprinted by permission of The Random House Group Ltd.
One image from *Hansel and Gretel*, two images from *Gorilla*, one image from *Into the Forest* and one image from *Piggybook*. Reprinted by permission of Walker Books Ltd.

Chapter 2
Image and text from *Home* by Narelle Oliver. Text and illustrations © Narelle Oliver, 2006. First published by Omnibus Books, a division of Scholastic Australia Pty Limited, 2006. Licensed by permission of Scholastic Australia Pty Limited.

Chapter 3
Four double-page spreads from *Who's Afraid of the Big Bad Book* by Lauren Child. Reprinted by permission of Hodder & Stoughton Ltd.

Chapter 4
Sipe, L. & McGuire, C. (2006). 'Picturebook Endpapers: Resources for Literary and Aesthetic Interpretation'. *Children's Literature in Education* 37(4): 291–304. Reproduced with kind permission from Springer Science and Business Media.

Chapter 5
Cover and one double-page spread from *Little Mouse's Big Book of Fears* by Emily Gravett, reprinted with permission from and with thanks to Macmillan Children's Books, London, UK.

Chapter 6
Cover and one double-page spread from *Katie's Picture Show* © James Mayhew. Permission granted by Orchard Books, a division of Hachette Children's Books.

Chapter 7
Cover and one double-page spread from *The Frog Prince Continued* by Jon

Scieszka, illustrated by Steve Johnson (Puffin, 1991, 1992, 1994). Text © Jon Scieszka, 1991. Illustrations © Steve Johnson, 1991.

Chapter 8

Blethertoun Rovers poem from *Blethertoun Braes*, edited by Matthew Fitt and James Robertson, illustrated by Bob Dewar (Itchy Coo). Illustration © Bob Dewar. Reproduced by permission of Itchy Coo.

Image from *Traction Man* by Mini Grey, published by Jonathan Cape. Reprinted by permission of The Random House Group Ltd.

Image from *The Incredible Book Eating Boy* by Oliver Jeffers. © Oliver Jeffers, 2007. Reprinted by permission of HarperCollins Publishers Ltd.

Image from *Janet Reachfar and the Kelpie* by Mairi Hedderwick is reproduced by permission of Birlinn Ltd. www.birlinn.co.uk

Chapter 9

Cover and one double-page spread from *Archie's War* by Marcia Williams. © Marcia Williams, 2007. Reproduced by permission of Walker Books Ltd.

Cover and two images from *Going West* by Martin Waddell and Phillipe Dupasquier (Picture Puffin). © Martin Waddell & Phillipe Dupasquier, 1985. Reproduced by permission of The Random House Group Ltd.

Cover from *The Arrival* © Shaun Tan. Permission granted by Hachette Children's Books.

Chapter 10

One image from *My Dad* and one image from *Voices in the Park* by Anthony Browne, published by Doubleday. Reprinted by permission of The Random House Group Ltd.

Four images from *Little Beauty* by Anthony Browne. Reprinted by permission of Walker Books Ltd.

One image from *You and Me*, as yet unpublished, with permission from Anthony Browne.

Foreword

David Lewis

Most adults who become interested in picturebooks first become hooked when they start to read them with young children. Whether this is done at home with one's own offspring or in school or nursery with the children of others, there is something both pleasurable and fascinating about this act of sharing – the adults get to enjoy the enormous privilege of 'lending consciousness' to the youngsters, who in turn get to experience some of the magic of reading. Sooner or later, if the adults are curious enough, they begin to wonder how it is that such young minds manage to conjure meaning from these odd, twin-barrelled texts. The words tell you something and the pictures show you something; the two somethings may be more or less related, but they may not. Back and forth you must go, wielding two kinds of looking that you must learn to fuse into understanding. How does the alchemy work? Where does it begin? Not content with sharing, some adults take the books away with them so that they can read them in private. These are the people who want to know what role the texts play in bringing about the transformations inside the heads of the children. So another set of questions begins to take shape: Why are they constructed as they are? What does the way these pictures are framed tell us? How do the illustrations guide our looking?

It is now very clear that picturebooks for children are far from the simple nursery texts they were often supposed to be. It is true that there are many poor examples lined up on the shelves of bookshops, but that has always been true and is true of books produced for adult readers as well. Here we are concerned only with the best, and the best examples of even the simplest picturebooks have a sophistication born of an art that disguises art.

In the first place there is what might be termed a 'first order' complexity that arises simply from the text being shared between two different forms of communication – words and pictures. This has nothing to do with artistry, it is simply in the nature of things; most picturebooks (though not all) are in fact 'picture-and-word-books'. This first-order level of complexity can be found in even the briefest of board books for babies, and suggests to me that such books do not receive the attention that they should.

Next, there is what might be considered a second-order level. Pictures are not all the same: for example, there are issues of modality, or lifelikeness, to be considered, and whether images are framed or not, and how they are framed when they are. Recent studies in the semiotics of visual imagery can be helpful here in sorting out the multifarious ways in which the illustrators of picture-books manipulate what is to be looked at and interpreted. The words too can vary enormously. They may be plain and unadorned, perhaps no more than a single word on each page or a simple sentence extending through an entire book; they might be elaborated into several voices woven together or a single voice telling a story that happened long ago. There may be no story at all, the words being arranged into the pattern of a song, a poem or a well-known chant. The words may do whatever they please, or rather whatever the writer pleases.

A third-order level of sophistication arises when the pictures and words, however they are formed, begin to drift apart from one another, sometimes to the point where they seem to be referring to entirely different events or circumstances. Again, a degree of such variance can be found in the simplest of books, but now the reader begins to experience a certain amount of cognitive stretch. You have to work a bit harder to get the point, to see where the author and illustrator are leading you. You might have to suspend comprehension for a while until the penny drops or your more experienced co-reader guides you towards understanding. Irony? Well, yes; you can never begin too soon.

At a fourth and higher level still are the books where the things you might expect to happen are turned around or disappear entirely: books that lead you to a topsy-turvy world where characters from one story pop up in another or step outside the story altogether to look the reader in the eye and tell him or her how it really is. These last are books that fascinate adults as well as children, and it is not difficult to see why. They are almost always ingenious; cunning contraptions that can trip up the unwary and the unprepared. They frequently resemble games and possess a playfulness that recruits the child reader's wide experience of play. If they work for children it is because their audience has already played many a game of peek-a-boo, laughed at many a nonsense rhyme, built towers with bricks or dominoes and then knocked them down, pretended to be an astronaut, a princess or a racing driver, and held many an absorbing conversation with dolls and teddy bears.

If picturebooks are really as sophisticated as this then they are well worth examining closely. Those of us who have tried to do this usually end up being utterly captivated by their charm, their wit and often their sheer beauty. Delving into the question of what children make of them is a tougher business altogether. Even quite young children have the ability to guess what it is they are expected to say. Asked a question they will provide an answer and will probably have worked out what will best satisfy the questioner. This can make research into reader response very difficult indeed; sometimes it feels like tickling for trout – holding back and angling gently, letting the reader run on so that he or she reveals something of what is going on inside. The authors whose work is gathered together here in *Talking Beyond the Page* are experienced researchers who have addressed these problems and sought ways of finding solutions. Some are primarily interested in the talk, the interchange between adult and child; some are more preoccupied with the books themselves, at least insofar as this collection is concerned. Quite rightly, the final word goes to a master of the art itself. *Talking Beyond the Page* is a stimulating read that provides many insights, provokes thought and, time and again, turns us back to the picturebooks themselves.

Notes on contributors

Michèle Anstey and Geoff Bull run ABC: Anstey and Bull Consultants in Education (www.ansteybull.com.au). They were formerly Associate Professors at the University of Southern Queensland, where they taught literacy and children's literature at undergraduate and postgraduate level. Michèle was Director and Principal Adviser to the Literate Futures Project for Education Queensland, and a teacher in Victoria, New South Wales and Queensland. Geoff was national President of the Australian Literacy Educators' Association and founding member of the Australian Literacy Federation (ALF) as well as a teacher and teacher-librarian. Michèle and Geoff are interested in literacy teaching practices, multiliteracies and children's literature: particularly visual literacy, speculative fiction and postmodern trends in children's literature. Together they have published *Teaching and Learning Multiliteracies: Changing Times, Changing Literacies* (International Reading Association, 2006), *The Literacy Landscape* (Pearson, 2005), *The Literacy Labyrinth* (Pearson, 2004), *The Literacy Lexicon* (Prentice Hall, 2003), *Reading the Visual: Written and Illustrated Children's Literature* (Harcourt/Nelson, 2000), and *Crossing the Boundaries* (Pearson, 2002).

Evelyn Arizpe is a Lecturer in Children's Literature at the Faculty of Education, University of Glasgow. She has taught and published widely in the areas of literacies, reader response to picturebooks and children's literature. She is co-author, with Morag Styles, of *Children Reading Pictures: Interpreting Visual Texts* (Routledge, 2003) and *Reading Lessons from the Eighteenth Century: Mothers, Children and Texts* (Pied Piper Press, 2006). She has a particular interest in Mexican children's books and her current research involves immigrant children, picturebooks, literacy and culture. Also with Morag Styles, she has co-edited *Acts of Reading: Teachers, Texts and Childhood*, to be published by Trentham Books in 2009.

Janet Evans is a Senior Lecturer in Education at Liverpool Hope University and part-time freelance Literacy and Educational Consultant. Formerly an Early Years and primary school teacher, she has written eight books on language, literacy and maths education, along with articles on primary education and mathematics curricula, and chapters in edited books. Janet has taught in India, Nigeria, Australia, America, Canada and Spain and was awarded two research scholarships that enabled her to work and study in the USA. She has presented papers at many international conferences and has organized and taught on numerous in-service conferences. Janet ensures that she has time to work in schools, doing action-based research with young children and their educators. Her books include *What's in the Picture: Responding to Illustrations in Picture Books* (Paul Chapman Publishing, 1998), *The Writing Classroom: Aspects of Writing and the Primary Child 3–11 years* (David Fulton, 2001) and *Literacy Moves On: Using Popular Culture, New Technologies and Critical Literacy in the Primary Classroom* (Heinemann, 2005). Her ongoing research interests include reader response to picturebooks, critical literacy and interactive writing linked with children's bookmaking.

Prue Goodwin is a freelance lecturer in literacy and children's literature and works part time at the University of Reading, where she runs an MA course in Children's Books in Education and works with trainee teachers. She has edited several books, her most recent being *Understanding Children's Books* (SAGE, 2008). Others books include *The Literate Classroom* (David Fulton, 2005), *The Articulate Classroom* (David Fulton, 2001) and *Literacy through Creativity* (David Fulton, 2004). Prue regularly returns to the classroom to introduce children to a range of literature and to encourage wide, voracious reading.

David Lewis has been a teacher in primary and secondary schools, an Educational Researcher for the Inner London Education Authority, and Lecturer in Education at London University Goldsmiths College and Exeter University. He has published a number of articles on children's picturebooks, mainly in the journals *Signal* and *Children's Literature in Education*, and has recently stepped down from his position on the editorial committee of *Children's Literature in Education*. In 2001 he published *Reading Contemporary Picturebooks: Picturing Text* (RoutledgeFalmer). He now works as a freelance writer and is currently finishing a book on an entirely different subject – a history of the Italian city state of Ferrara during the Renaissance.

Caroline McGuire is a PhD candidate in the Reading/Writing/Literacy programme at the Graduate School of Education at the University of Pennsylvania. Formerly a coordinator of out-of-school literacy programs, Caroline now teaches children's literature classes to undergraduate and graduate students at Pennsylvania. She is completing her PhD dissertation on the oral responses of a small group of nine-year-old children to postmodern picturebooks and the children's use of postmodern characteristics in their own written and illustrated work.

Kate Noble is Assistant Education Officer at The Fitzwilliam Museum, Cambridge. Whilst working as an Early Years teacher specializing in Art she was one of the researchers on *Children Reading Pictures: Interpreting Visual Texts*

(RoutledgeFalmer, 2000) with Morag Styles and Evelyn Arizpe. Her doctoral study (2007) investigated the development of visual literacy in young children by analysing their drawing and communication in response to multimodal picture books. Her research interests include the relationship between visual and verbal literacy and the creative and cognitive possibilities afforded through the use of images in teaching and learning.

Sylvia Pantaleo is an Associate Professor in the Faculty of Education at the University of Victoria, Canada. She teaches undergraduate and graduate courses in language and literacy, and courses in literature for children and adolescents. Her programme of research has focused on exploring elementary students' understanding, interpretations and responses to contemporary picturebooks, specifically literature with Radical Change characteristics and metafictive devices. She has also examined how students use their knowledge of these characteristics and devices to create their own print texts. She is author of *Exploring Student Response to Contemporary Picturebooks* (University of Toronto Press, 2008), co-editor of *Postmodern Picturebooks: Play, Parody, and Self-Referentiality* (Routledge, 2008), and co-author of *Learning with Literature in the Canadian Elementary Classroom* (University of Alberta, 1999).

Frank Serafini is currently an Associate Professor of Literacy Education at Arizona State University, where he teaches courses in children's literature, reading pedagogy, and literacy assessment. Frank spent nine years as an elementary school teacher, three years as a literacy specialist and six years as Assistant Professor of Literacy Education at the University of Nevada, Las Vegas. In addition to numerous journal articles, Frank has authored six professional development books, the two most recent entitled *More (Advanced) Lessons in Comprehension* (Heinemann, 2008) and *Talking Comprehension* (Scholastic, 1997). Frank has also authored and illustrated a series of picturebooks with Kids Can Press, focusing on nature and the art of close observation.

Lawrence Sipe is an Associate Professor in the Graduate School of Education at the University of Pennsylvania, where he teaches courses in children's and adolescent literature. His research focuses on the responses of young children (five- to eight-year-olds) to picture storybooks. He is the author of *Storytime: Young Children's Literary Understanding in the Classroom* (Teachers College Press, 2008), and co-editor (with Dr Sylvia Pantaleo) of *Postmodern Picturebooks: Play, Parody, and Self-Referentiality* (Routledge, 2008). He has published extensively in handbooks of research, journals of literacy and children's literature, and edited volumes.

Vivienne Smith was a primary teacher for many years before moving into higher education. She is now a Lecturer at the University of Strathclyde, where she teaches in the Department of Childhood and Primary Studies. Her research interests include children's literature, critical literacy and the development of children as readers. For some time she has been interested in how the best picturebooks and flap books work and how they orientate children towards becoming engaged and active readers. She has published a number of articles, including, most recently, a chapter in Prue Goodwin's *Understanding Children's Books* (SAGE, 2008).

Morag Styles is a Reader in Children's Literature and Education at the University of Cambridge. She writes, lectures and organizes conferences internationally on children's literature, poetry, visual literacy and the history of reading. She is the author of *From the Garden to the Street: 300 Years of Poetry for Children* (Cassell, 1998), Advisory Editor for *The Cambridge Guide to Children's Books in English* (Cambridge University Press, 2001) and co-editor, with Evelyn Arizpe, of *Children Reading Pictures: Interpreting Visual Texts* (RoutledgeFalmer, 2003) and *Reading Lessons from the Eighteenth Century: Mothers, Children and Texts* (Pied Piper Publishing, 2006). She has organized exhibitions at the Fitzwilliam Museum Cambridge and the British Library.

Anthony Browne – personal notes. I was born in Sheffield and moved to a pub near Bradford when I was one. As I got older I apparently used to stand on a table in the bar and tell stories to customers about a character called Big Dumb Tackle (whoever he was). I spent much of my childhood playing sport, fighting and drawing with my older brother. I went to a grammar school in Cleckheaton, then studied graphic design at art college in Leeds. My father died suddenly and horrifically in front of me while I was there and this had a huge effect on me. I went through a rather dark period, which didn't sit very happily with the world of graphic design. After leaving college I heard about a job as a medical artist and thought that it sounded interesting – it was. I worked at Manchester Royal Infirmary for three years painting delicate watercolours of grotesque operations. It taught me a lot more about drawing than I ever learned at art college, and I believe it taught me how to tell stories in pictures. I thought that it was probably time to move on when strange little figures started appearing in these paintings, and so I began a career designing greetings cards. I continued to do this for many years, working for the Gordon Fraser Gallery.

Gordon Fraser became a close friend and taught me a lot about card design, which was to prove very useful when I came to do children's books. I experimented with many styles and many subjects, from snowmen to dogs with big eyes to gorillas. I sent some of my designs to various children's book publishers and it was through one of these that I met Julia MacRae, who was to become my editor for the next 20 years. She taught me much of what I know about writing and illustrating children's books.

In 1976 I produced *Through the Magic Mirror* (Hamish Hamilton), a strange kind of book in which I painted many of the pictures before I wrote the story. I followed this with *A Walk in the Park* (Hamish Hamilton, 1977), a story I was to revisit 20 years later with *Voices in the Park* (Doubleday). Probably my most successful book is *Gorilla* (Walker Books), published in 1983, and it was during this period that I was badly bitten by a gorilla whilst being filmed for television at my local zoo.

I have published 40 books, and among the awards that my books have won are the Kate Greenaway medal twice, and the Kurt Maschler 'Emil' three times. In 2000 I was awarded the Hans Christian Andersen Medal, an international award given to an illustrator for their body of work. This prize is the highest honour a children's writer or illustrator can win, and I was the first British illustrator to receive it. My books are translated into 26 languages and my illustrations have been exhibited in many countries – the USA, Mexico, Venezuela, Colombia, France, Germany, Holland, Japan and Taiwan – and I've had the pleasure of visiting these places and working with local children and meeting other illustrators.

I am currently working on my latest book, which involves Goldilocks and a family of bears.

Children's thoughts about picturebooks

> You can never be too old for picturebooks. I used to have a picturebook called *Giraffes Can't Dance* and I loved it but my mum gave it away because she said I was too old for it, but I think you can never be too old for picturebooks.
>
> Matthew, aged 11

In an attempt to find out what children's thoughts were about reading and responding to picturebooks, I talked with some 11-year-old children with whom I had been working. They came from a class of 23 boys and 7 girls, which made for interesting class dynamics and class discussions. Picturebooks had been read to these children on a regular basis throughout their seven years in school, and they were used to verbalising and visualising their thoughts in relation to quite unusual polysemic, postmodern picturebooks – some of which seemed to contain quite abstruse messages.

A variety of questions were considered:

- What are picturebooks?
- What do you think about picturebooks?
- Who are they for and why are they written?
- When you look at and read picturebooks, what happens in your head and how do you feel inside?
- How can we respond to them?
- What makes picturebooks different from other kinds of books?
- What is special/different about picturebooks?

Where I read, who with and how

The children talked about, then drew pictures of, where they read, whom they read with, and how. The individual children's personalities showed in their work, often along with their preferred genre of books.

Figure 1   Adam: I've drawn myself in Jamaica, reading whilst playing football

Figure 2   Sam: I have drawn myself reading in the garden with a character from the book. I am reading a book called *Nightmare Academy*

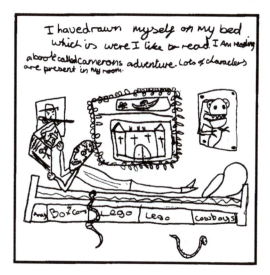

Figure 3   Cam: I've drawn myself on my bed, which is where I like to read. I am
reading a book called *Cameron's Adventure*. Lots of characters are present in my
room; some of the characters out of my book have appeared out of posters

Figure 4   Matt: I have an overwhelming imagination and as you can see I read a heck
of a lot of HORROR. I've drawn arms coming out of under the bed. There
is a face hiding under the bed, 'Teeth ground sharp and eyes glowing red.'
There are ghosts skulking around in the dark and bats flying around.
There are images of places I've seen in films and in books. Limbs of victims
hanging around. It all happens in bed. When I close the book the images
vanish, locked in the book but when it opens … they're back. The
nightmares are back!

Figure 5   Matthew: I have drawn myself reading in no particular place, but immersed in thought from the millions of tales and stories I've read in years gone by. It doesn't matter where I read, it could be absolutely anywhere in the world because I love reading.

My personal views about what makes picturebooks special /different

The children thought about what makes picturebooks special/different, before giving their reponses in illustrative and written format.

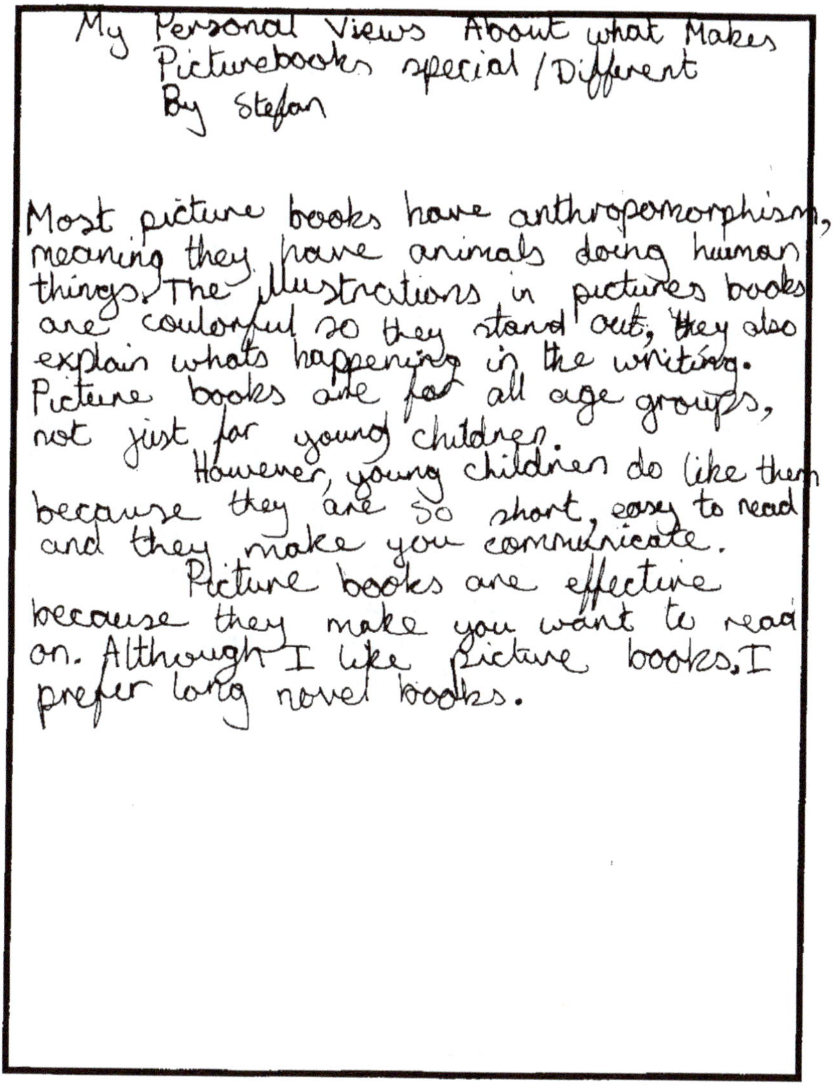

My Personal Views About what Makes
Picturebooks special / Different
By Stefan

Most picture books have anthropomorphism,
meaning they have animals doing human
things. The illustrations in pictures books
are coulorful so they stand out, they also
explain whats happening in the writing.
Picture books are for all age groups,
not just for young children.
       However, young children do like them
because they are so short, easy to read
and they make you communicate.
       Picture books are effective
because they make you want to read
on. Although I like picture books, I
prefer long novel books.

Figure 6   Stephan: Most picturebooks have anthropomorphism, meaning they have
animals doing human things. The illustrations in picturebooks are
colourful so they stand out; they also explain what's happening in the
writing. Picturebooks are for all age groups, not just for young children.
However, young children do like them because they are so short, easy to
read and they make you communicate.
Picturebooks are effective because they make you want to read on.
Although I like picturebooks, I prefer long novel books

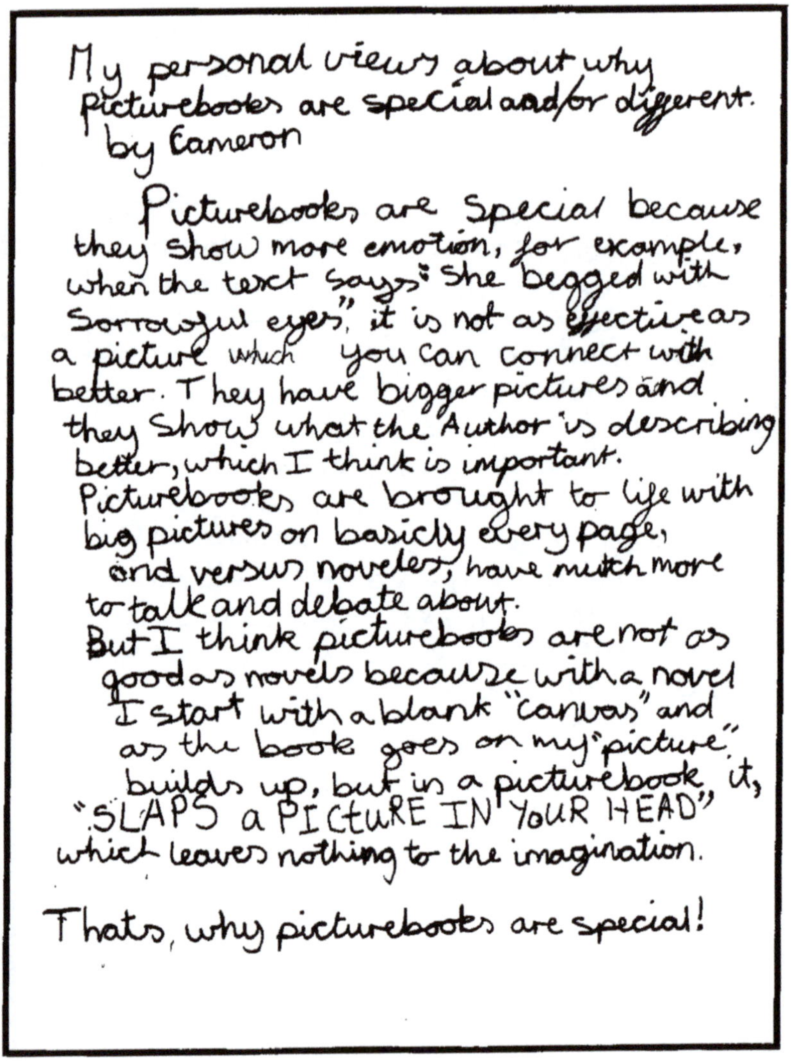

My personal views about why picturebooks are special and/or different.
by Cameron

Picturebooks are special because they show more emotion, for example, when the text says: "She begged with sorrowful eyes", it is not as effective as a picture which you can connect with better. They have bigger pictures and they show what the Author is describing better, which I think is important. Picturebooks are brought to life with big pictures on basicly every page, and versus noveles, have much more to talk and debate about.

But I think picturebooks are not as good as novels because with a novel I start with a blank "canvas" and as the book goes on my "picture" builds up, but in a picturebook, it, "SLAPS a PICTURE IN YOUR HEAD" which leaves nothing to the imagination.

Thats, why picturebooks are special!

Figure 7   Cameron: Picturebooks are special because they show more emotion, for example, when the text says, 'she begged with sorrowful eyes' it is not as effective as a picture, which you can connect with better. They have bigger pictures and they show what the author is describing better, which I think is important. Picturebooks are brought to life with big pictures on basically every page and, versus novels, have much more to talk and debate about. But I think picturebooks are not as good as novels because with a novel I start with a blank 'canvas' and as the book goes on my 'picture' builds up, but in a picturebook it 'SLAPS A PICTURE IN YOUR HEAD', which leaves nothing to the imagination. That's why picturebooks are special!

> My Personal views about what makes picturebooks special/different.
>
> I think picturebooks are special because of the huge amounts of emotion that can be fittin pictures. A picture can speak a thousand words. Even though the images aren't always realistic, in my oppinion there is always something that people can relate to in them. Picturebooks aren't always my preffered genre of book, but are origikal. The artwork is always great, each piece of artwork is almost a story of its own if you know what I mean, and only now can I really apprieciate picturebook existance. The most complex and touching things can be portrayed in a simple seeming way. There is always something real about a picturebook, and that makes them all the better to read.
>
> Matthew

Figure 8 Matthew: I think picturebooks are special because of the huge amounts of emotion that can be fitted in pictures. A picture can speak a thousand words. Even though the images aren't always realistic, in my opinion there is always something that people can relate to in them. Picturebooks aren't always my preferred genre of book, but they are original. The artwork is always great, each piece of artwork is almost a story of its own if you know what I mean and only now can I really appreciate picturebook existence. The most complex and touching things can be portrayed in a simple-seeming way. There is always something real about a picturebook and that makes them all the better to read.

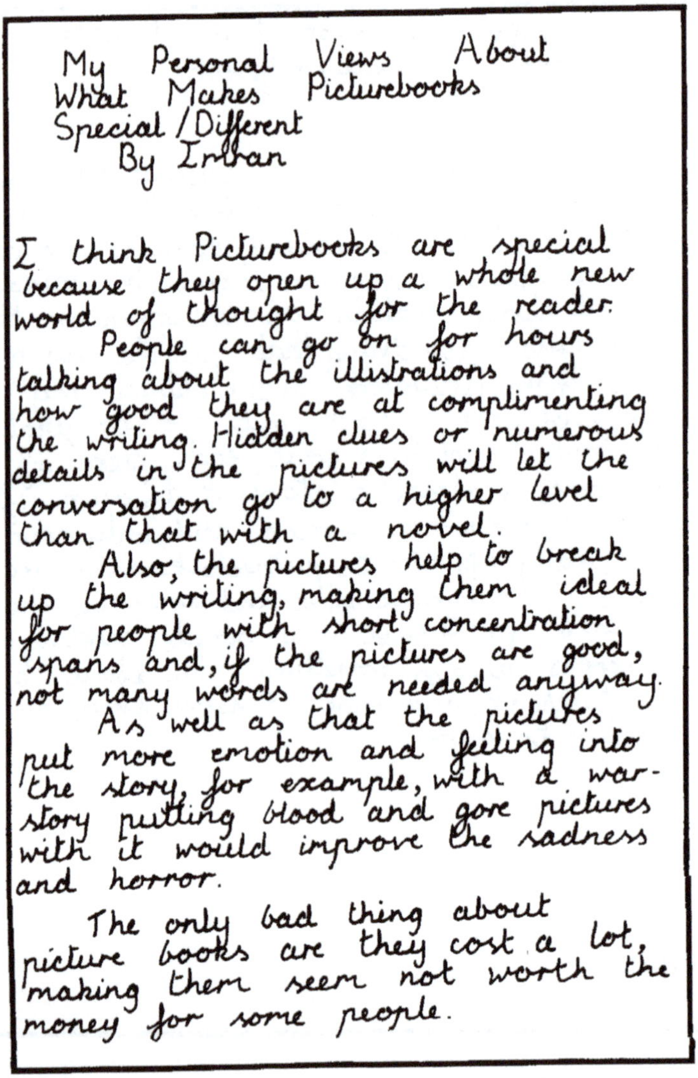

> My Personal Views About
> What Makes Picturebooks
> Special/Different
> By Imran
>
> I think Picturebooks are special because they open up a whole new world of thought for the reader. People can go on for hours talking about the illustrations and how good they are at complimenting the writing. Hidden clues or numerous details in the pictures will let the conversation go to a higher level than that with a novel.
> Also, the pictures help to break up the writing, making them ideal for people with short concentration spans and, if the pictures are good, not many words are needed anyway.
> As well as that the pictures put more emotion and feeling into the story, for example, with a war-story putting blood and gore pictures with it would improve the sadness and horror.
> The only bad thing about picture books are they cost a lot, making them seem not worth the money for some people.

Figure 9   Imran: I think picturebooks are special because they open up a whole new
world of thought for the reader. People can go on for hours talking about
the illustrations and how good they are at complementing the writing.
Hidden clues or numerous details in the pictures will let the conversation
go to a higher level than that with a novel. Also, the pictures help to break
up the writing, making them ideal for people with short concentration
spans and, if the pictures are good, not many words are needed anyway. As
well as that the pictures put more emotion and feeling into the story, for
example, with a war story putting blood-and-gore pictures with it would
improve the sadness and horror.
The only bad thing about picturebooks is that they cost a lot, making
them seem not worth the money for some people.

Talking beyond the page

When you look at and read picturebooks, what happens in your head and how do you feel inside? How would you depict the idea of 'talking beyond the page'?

Figure 10 Matthew: In my picture, I'm walking down the yellow brick road searching for treasure. I'm holding a map in my hand, but it is really a book. The book guides the way – as I read every word, the way to go becomes clearer. Characters from many genres of story are following me in the search, such as dinosaurs, ghosts, aliens, characters from traditional tales, characters from Star Wars like C3PO and R2D2. All these characters live in one huge imaginary world. I cannot really see them, as the images are just my imagination forming as I read the picturebook.

Figure 11 Nicole: I have drawn myself reading outside in my garden, drifting off
into my own world with all the characters from different genres like
mysteries and horror and for example, the yellow brick road from a
traditional tale, *The Wizard of Oz*. When I read I think at the same time, I
think about what is happening and I add characters to my own little
world.

Figure 12   Matt: My picture has no plot. It is completely based on things I like and things I've seen and things I've read. The book is spewing the images out. I have tried to separate the strange from the simple, for example, the black (outer space) at the top contains the aliens and space ships, whilst the blue (sky) at the bottom contains planes, ships and helicopters and the earth. (The F22 Raptor strayed over the boundary line. It shouldn't have done, ignore that.) My preferred styles of books are science fiction, fantasy and horror.

Figure 13   Rauman: I've drawn a character reading a book and he fell into a dream of the past where his mum has died from murder. There are strangers trying to strangle and kidnap him and animals trying to kill him and then eat him. The ghosts and skeleton represent nightmares. I've read a novel but in my mind I have visualised a picturebook instead.

Talk is crucial

Talk is crucial. These children had listened to and talked about stories over a period of years and were able to think and talk about picturebooks as a genre, that is, not any picturebook in particular, but picturebooks in general. They were part of a community of readers who knew their responses would be totally accepted and considered without ridicule or disrespect. In fact, they knew their ideas would often be the starting point for more discussion, frequently moving off at a tangent from the original focus of conversation on to a variety of different responses that regularly included drawings, writing, bookmaking, drama and more discussion.

Part One

What to respond to? Attending to aspects of picturebooks

Introduction

It isn't enough to just read a book, one must talk about it as well

Janet Evans

Figure 14 Cameron, aged 11: In my picture a teacher is reading a book to her class (some children are hidden at the side of the picture). All are thinking different things but one child, actually me, is thinking of different genres of picturebooks, for example: sci-fi, fantasy, adventure, historical, horror/spooky, traditional. I am thinking of questions directly related to the book, such as 'Who is the person in the book?'

Some books are easy to read and do not seem to need much interpretation or deep thought to understand them. However, many books are more complex and some readers find them difficult to understand. This may be because of the plot itself, the complexity of the characters, conflict within the storyline, or the resolution (or lack of resolution); or it could even be a reader's differing background knowledge and cultural dissonance with what the text is saying. Such difficulties may apply to narratives in general, but they also apply when we focus on picturebooks in particular. Just because picturebooks are shorter, have fewer words and of course have illustrations, does not necessarily make them easier to read; in fact many are extremely complex multimodal texts that often make great intellectual and cognitive demands on the reader.

If books can sometimes be difficult to understand, how can we help readers to unpick, comprehend and of course enjoy what they read? The answer that emerges again and again is responding to texts through collaborative talk. A body of research has developed, focusing on how children learn through talk, (Corden, 2002; Goodwin, 2001; Jarrett, 2006; Myhill, 2006). In addition, there is an increasing body of research focusing specifically on how talk helps children to respond to and understand texts. (Baddeley & Eddershaw, 1994; Chambers, 1993; Evans, 1998; Graham, 1990; Reedy, 2006; Sipe, 2008; Styles & Bearne, 2003; Watson & Styles, 1996).

Sharing and responding to books

When reading picturebooks I frequently feel the need to have someone to share them with, someone with whom I can enjoy the books – enjoyment being one of the principal reasons that most people read narrative picturebooks – but also someone with whom I can feel comfortable about asking tentative questions or sharing some of my thoughts, observations and queries in relation to the meaning of the book. The analogy of a journey has been used many times to represent this notion of reading and understanding, but it is a pertinent analogy: reading a book from beginning to end *is* like a journey, and it is good to have someone to share the journey with you – someone to guide you and go with you as you travel through the book and as you read the story. Metzger seems to be in accordance with this journey idea, and he gives us some indication of how easy and at the same time how difficult the understanding of narrative books can be:

> Stories go in circles. They don't go in straight lines. So it helps if you listen in circles because there are stories inside stories and stories between stories and finding your way through them is as easy and as hard as finding your way home. And part of the finding is the getting lost. If you're lost, you really start to look around and listen. Moral: be prepared to take risks.
>
> Metzger (1979)

So, just reading the book itself is hardly ever enough! It is the shared oral responses and the ensuing discussions that allow fuller and maybe differing understandings to take place. Think about the reasons that book clubs and reading circles, where people read books alone prior to discussing them, are so successful. It is the enjoyment of talking about and responding to what has been read in a comfortable, unthreatening environment with like-minded people that is one of their main successes.

Talking about books ... collaboratively

How could this way of talking about and responding to books with others be emulated with young children without the discussion becoming a mere question-and-answer session? Kathy Short (1990) looked at the importance of book talk with children between the ages of 5 and 11. She later stated (1997: 64) that 'Children should enter the story world of fiction and non-fiction to learn about life and make sense of their world, not to answer a series of questions.' Short gave the name 'literature circles' to the way of responding to and talking about books in small group, literature-based discussions. Daniels (1994) further developed this concept and showed how such groups could be used by teachers to encourage children to respond to books. Literature circles provide a very effective way of enabling teachers and children to respond to picturebooks, but they are still not used enough in classrooms! Many children read books alone without sharing them or talking about them; this is hardly ever enough to enable in-depth, meaningful understandings to take place.

Shirley Brice Heath shared this sentiment when, in her seminal text, *Ways With Words* (1985), she stressed the importance of talk by stating that 'For those groups of individuals who do not have occasions to talk about what and how meanings are achieved in written materials, important cognitive and interpretive skills which are basic to being literate do not develop.' Similarly, Smith (2005: 22) in her minibook *Making Reading Mean*, stated that an approach to reading that focuses on the process and not just the product is needed. She emphasized that we have to 'get inside children's minds as they read, so we can see and guide the thought process.' She went on to say that the best way to do this is through talk. In commenting that children will emulate what they see and experience in their classrooms, she noted that 'Children who experience talk used in an exploratory and reflective way to think about texts and reading will begin to use that sort of talk themselves. Participating in talk can induct children into new ways of literacy thinking.' (2005: 23).

Talking about and responding to books in differing ways can include written responses (Hornsby & Wing Jan, 2001), drawings and illustrated responses (Anning & Ring, 2004; Arizpe and Styles, 2003), role play, dramatic enactments and Readers' Theatre (Dixon *et al.*, 1996), and non-verbal responses including gestures, eye movements and touch (see Chapter 7, and Mackey, 2002). These differing ways of responding to reading all enable fuller understanding to take place; however, it is sometimes the time between readings that allows fuller understanding to develop – this is where our brains are given opportunities to process information. Arizpe and Styles (2003) noted this and found that much of the understanding that children make of books goes on in the thinking and the talking about books, often between re-readings of the same book. Of course, we have to recognize the rights of the reader to not respond at all and to read a book quietly and without inter-ruption (Pennac, 2006). Many people prefer to read silently, but there are also many readers who relish the opportunity to talk about what they have read during and after their read.

Who are picturebooks for?

Talking and responding to picturebooks with other interested readers is one way to develop fuller understanding. However some picturebooks are *so* complex, *so* convoluted, and *so* seemingly difficult to understand, sometimes with subject matter that is deemed by some to be unsuitable for children, that I have often found myself asking who such picturebooks are written for. Would young children make sense of them? Would older, fluent readers dismiss them immediately without taking a second look simply because they have pictures? (see Chapter 5). Are they bought and read by adults as works of art as opposed to being simply books with pictures and narrative storylines? (see Chapter 6). Exactly who is the audience for this kind of picturebook?

In writing about a very early Edward Ardizzone book, one which was published in 1937 and which courted much controversy as a result of its subject matter, perceived at the time as being unsuitable for children, Rebecca Martin posed this exact same question. She asked 'Who is the audience of children's books – children, adults or both? How are these audiences different? Is the picture book today just for small children?' (2000: 243) The Ardizzone book about which Martin was writing was *Lucy Brown and Mr Grimes* (Ardizonne, 1937). In brief, the story is about a friendship that develops between an orphan girl (who lives with her aunt) and a lonely old man. They meet in the park and he gives her presents when she asks for them. Eventually, after the orphan girl helps him to recuperate from an illness, he formally adopts her and she lives with him and his housekeeper in a beautiful country house. This was Ardizonne's second title and, in contrast to his first, provoked outrage amongst American librarians, who censored it at the time. The book went out of print and was not reissued for 33 years. The censorship was based on perceived issues of stranger danger (the little orphan girl goes away with an old man – Mr Grimes), potential paedophilia (even in the thirties), and being rewarded for exhibiting bad manners (Lucy is adopted and is showered with gifts of every imaginable kind by her new parent, Mr Grimes). However one reacts to *Lucy Brown*, the fact is that it was originally written for children.

These kinds of reactions raise questions about picturebooks that challenge the child reader (by dealing with subject matter such as sex, death, adoption, suicide, disability, etc.). Should such books be read alone by children or should adults be available to discuss and respond to the kind of questions that will inevitably be asked? Martin (2000: 249) asks 'Do small children need more help distinguishing between fact and fantasy? Are they likely to do whatever they see or read about in books, such as talking to strangers?' There is evidently still much debate about whether children should be protected from such issues in books, but the fact remains that such sensitive and emotional issues can be dealt with if adults are available to discuss any questions or queries that may arise. The importance of responding to books is crucial to enable children to make sense of books at all levels of complexity; whether *Lucy Brown* was 'ill-conceived' or not is immaterial to the fact that children need to be given the opportunity to talk about and respond to texts.

In considering the different ways in which picturebooks can be responded to, Frank Serafini (2007), in a conference paper, proposed four 'So What?' points to focus our thoughts. He suggests that:

1. The complexity of picturebooks should not be underestimated.
2. Teachers need a theoretical foundation and vocabulary to talk about images.
3. There are numerous perspectives that one can bring to picturebooks.
4. Picturebooks offer a connection between school-based literacies and multiliteracies.

The structure of this book

Some of the four points listed above, as well as many others, are considered in the ten chapters in this book. The book is organised into three parts. In the first part are five chapters that, broadly, look at the aspects of picturebooks that can be focused on to enable the reader to explore, interpret and make sense of the text. These chapters consider:

*   how readers can begin to understand visual images
*   how readers can respond in many different, multiliterate ways
*   an exploration of some children's responses to a particular, postmodern text
*   how the endpapers in picturebooks can be used to determine what a book might be about
*   how the frames used by picturebook illustrators affect the way we 'see' and consequently respond to the book itself.

The second part takes a closer look at the responses that come from different picturebooks. These chapters consider:

*   responses to books as art forms in relation to fine art
*   children's differing responses to multimodal picturebooks

- some immigrant children's responses to picturebooks and other kinds of visual texts
- how children develop different kinds of understandings through picture-books.

The third and final part comprises just one chapter, an interview with Anthony Browne. This is a sequel to the first interview he gave over ten years ago in *What's in the Picture? Responding to Illustrations in Picturebooks* (Evans, 1998). In this latest interview, Browne shares some of his thoughts about how his work has developed over the last ten years, and we get a glimpse of some illustrations from his next picturebook, *You and Me.*

Each of the chapters relates to the overall title and, when taken together, they show that we really do need to 'talk beyond the page'. As Hannah, aged 11, says, 'When we start to talk about a book in a group I love it because we start with one thing and then end on something totally different. We turn the pages and really start to think about different things. I really like that and I always ask myself, "How did we get on to this from that?"'

References

Anning, A. & Ring, K. (2004). *Making Sense of Children's Drawings.* London: Open University Press

Arizpe, E. & Styles, M. (2003). *Children Reading Pictures: Interpreting Visual Texts.* London: RoutledgeFalmer

Baddeley, P. & Eddershaw, C. (1994). *Not So Simple Picture Books.* Staffordshire: Trentham Books

Chambers, A. (1993). *Tell Me: Children, Reading and Talk.* Stroud: Thimble Press

Corden, R. (2002). *Literacy and Learning Through Talk.* Buckingham: Open University Press

Daniels, H. (1994). *Literature Circles: Voice and Choice in the Student Centred Classroom.* Maine: Stenhouse Publishers

Dixon, N., Davies, A. & Politano, C. (1996). *Learning With Readers Theatre: Building Connections.* Winnipeg, Manitoba: Peguis Publishers

Evans, J. (ed.) (1998). *What's in the Picture?: Responding to Illustrations in Picture Books.* London: Paul Chapman Publishing

Goodwin, P. (2001). *The Articulate Classroom: Talking and Learning in the Primary School.* London: David Fulton

Graham, J. (1990). *Pictures on the Page.* Sheffield: National Association for the Teaching of English

Heath, S. B. (1985). *Ways With Words: Language, Life and Work in Communities and Classrooms.* New York: Cambridge University Press

Hornsby, D. & Wing Jan, L. (2001). 'Writing as a Response to Literature' in Evans, J. (2001) *The Writing Classroom: Aspects of Writing and the Primary Child.* London: David Fulton, pp.46–65

Jarrett, P. (2006). 'Time to Talk Sense'. *The Primary English Magazine* 12(2)

Mackey, M. (2002). *Literacies Across Media: Playing the Text.* London: RoutledgeFalmer

Martin, R. (2000). 'Edward Ardizzone Revisited: Lucy Brown and the Moral Editing of Art'. *Children's Literature in Education* 31(4): 241–57

Metzger, D. (1979). 'Circles of Stories'. *Parabola* IV(4): 104–5

Myhill, D. (2006). 'Talk, talk, talk: teaching and learning in whole class discourse'. *Research Papers in Education* 21(1), March 2006: 19–41

Pennac, D. (2006). *The Rights of the Reader.* London: Walker Books

Reedy, D. (2006). 'Effective Talk in Reading Lessons: Having Proper Conversations with Children'. *English 4–11* 28, Autumn 2006: 21–3

Serafini, F. (2007). 'Expanding Students' Interpretative Repertoires'. Conference paper. International Reading Association International Convention, Toronto, May 2007

Short, K. (1990). *Talking About Books: Creating Literate Communities.* Portsmouth: Heinemann

Short, K. (1997). *Literature as a Way of Knowing.* Maine: Stenhouse Publishers

Sipe, L. (2008). 'Young children's visual meaning-making in response to picture-books' in Flood, J., Heath, S. B. & Lapp, D. (eds) *Handbook of Research in Teaching Literacy through the Visual and Communicative Arts* Vol 2. London: Lawrence Erlbaum

Smith, V. (2005). *Making Reading Mean.* Royston: UKLA Publications, Minibook 20

Styles, M. & Bearne, E. (2003). *Art, Narrative and Childhood.* Stoke-on-Trent: Trentham Books

Watson, V. & Styles, M. (1996). *Talking Pictures: Pictorial Texts and Young Readers.* London: Hodder & Stoughton

Children's literature

Ardizonne, E. (1937). *Lucy Brown and Mr Grimes.* London: Oxford University Press

1 Understanding visual images in picturebooks

Frank Serafini

Visual systems of meaning in picturebooks offer different resources and potentials for constructing meanings from written language. Because of this, readers need to familiarize themselves with a variety of differing ways of making sense and reading the images. This chapter draws upon theories of semiotics and visual grammar to present a framework for approaching, analysing and comprehending the visual images in contemporary picturebooks. Drawing on some of Anthony Browne's picturebooks to illustrate the concepts presented, readers are provided with vocabulary and concepts necessary for supporting children's understandings of picturebooks.

In an oft-quoted definition of the picturebook, Bader (1976: 1) states that 'a picturebook is text, illustrations, total design; an item of manufacture and a commercial product; an art form; a social, cultural and historical document; and foremost, an experience for the child. It hinges on the interplay of illustrations and written text, the simultaneous display of two facing pages and the drama of the turning page.' This definition, and the compound word 'picturebook' has been used by various researchers and literary theorists to connote the unified nature of the written language and visual images of this literary form (Kiefer, 1995; Lewis, 2001). The picturebook is a unique literary experience, where meaning is generated simultaneously from written text, visual images and the overall design. Sipe (1998a) has described the relationship between written text and visual images in the picturebook as 'synergistic', suggesting that what is constructed from the combination of the two sign systems is greater than the potential meanings offered by either written text or visual image in isolation.

Although picturebooks, used extensively in many reading programmes and instructional resources, convey meanings through the use of two sign systems – written language and visual image – the primary focus in contemporary reading education has been on the strategies and skills necessary for understanding written language. While numerous pedagogical resources are available that focus on strategies for reading and comprehending written text (Harvey & Goudvis, 2000; Owocki, 2003; Snow & Sweet, 2003), pedagogical approaches focusing on strategies for comprehending visual images, in particular those included in contemporary picturebooks, are only just emerging.

This lack of pedagogical attention to visual images and visual systems of meaning presents serious challenges to teachers at a time when image has begun to dominate the literate lives of their children (Fleckenstein, 2002; Kress, 2003). Unsworth and Wheeler (2002) suggest that 'if children are to learn how to analyse the ways images make meanings, they need to gain knowledge of the visual meaning-making systems deployed in images.' In addition, due to its multimodal nature, the picturebook may provide a bridge from the traditional text-based literacies of the past with the multiliteracies necessary in the future (Anstey & Bull, 2006). Evidently the contemporary picturebook has a great deal to offer.

Picturebooks represent a traditionally accepted, ubiquitous literary format that continues to play a significant role in elementary reading curricula. In addition, picturebooks are multimodal, meaning they draw upon multiple modes of expression – namely, written language, visual image and graphic design – to tell a story or offer information. Although the relationship or interplay between visual image and written language may vary across picture-books (Nikolajeva & Scott, 2000), in order to construct meaning in trans-action with picturebooks, and to fully experience what contemporary picturebooks have to offer, children need to attend to both systems of meaning.

In general, written language has been the dominant system of meaning used in educational contexts, with visual image often relegated to the role of supporting written text rather than as a system of meaning in its own right (Kress & van Leeuwen, 2001). The two systems of meaning contained in picturebooks are governed by distinct logics: written language is governed by the logic of time or temporal sequence, whereas visual image is governed by the logic of spatiality, organized arrangements and simultaneity (Kress & van Leeuwen, 1996). The temporal sequence or the order in which words appear in a sentence or phrase is important for understanding written language. For example, 'The dog chased Morgan,' is very different from 'Morgan chased the dog.' In visual images, the positioning, size and composition of the contents of an image affect the meanings conveyed. The visual and textual meaning systems in picturebooks require readers to attend to both temporal and spatial elements to make sense of these multimodal texts.

Because visual systems of meaning inherent in picturebooks offer different resources and potentials for constructing meanings compared with written language, teachers need to familiarize themselves with various approaches for analysing and understanding visual images, in addition to the strategies they use for comprehending written language. Sipe (1998b: 66) suggests that 'when it comes to the visual aspects of picturebooks, many teachers may feel they lack the artistic and aesthetic training necessary to talk with children and to guide their understanding.' If teachers are going to be able to help children make sense of the visual images and written language of the picturebook, they need first to be able to analyse and comprehend these multimodal texts themselves. Once teachers have a more extensive knowledge base concerning various strategies for approaching and understanding visual images, they will be better positioned to help children construct meaning for themselves with these texts.

This chapter draws upon theories of semiotics and visual grammar, in particular the work of Kress and van Leeuwen (1996), to present a framework for approaching, analysing and comprehending the visual images in contemporary picturebooks. In order to help the reader of this chapter make sense of the strategies, theories and approaches being discussed, I use a limited number of picturebooks from the noted artist and children's author Anthony Browne to illustrate the concepts presented. All examples in this chapter are taken from the following picturebooks: *Voices in the Park* (2001), *Zoo* (1992), *Gorilla* (1983), *The Tunnel* (1989), *Hansel and Gretel* (1981), *Into the Forest* (2004) and *Piggybook* (1986). Many of these books are unnumbered, so the page being referred to is described as a particular 'opening', meaning the number of the double-page spread counted from the beginning of the book. The description of the image being considered will also help ensure we are sharing and discussing the same image. If you familiarize yourself with these picturebooks, or have them as references while reading this chapter, I believe your experience will be greatly enhanced.

Visual grammar and picturebooks

This is not the first account of how semiotics and visual grammars can be used to understand the images contained in contemporary picturebooks. Lewis (2001) discussed how Kress and van Leeuwen's work in visual grammar related to visual images contained in fictional picturebooks, and used their work as a framework for understanding how images in narrative picturebooks were used in conjunction with text to tell the story. In addition, Unsworth and Wheeler (2002: 68) drew upon Kress and van Leeuwen's work to suggest that critical reviews needed to attend more systematically and carefully to the images contained in picturebooks. They stated that 'most reviews of children's picturebooks give a brief synopsis of the story with an evaluative comment, but usually mention the illustrations only briefly and superficially.'

For the purposes of this chapter, I will focus on four important elements of visual grammar that should be considered when approaching and interpreting an image or series of images in or across picturebooks: narrative processes, visual symbolism, composition and perspective. These four elements, along with other elements and components described by Kress and van Leeuwen, are considered important aspects of an image's structural organization or composition. Although the elements are presented and discussed separately, in a picturebook image they work in concert to narrate the story and provide the viewer with information in visual form.

1. Narrative processes: actors, vectors, demands and offers

Images in picturebooks depict characters, actions and relationships between participants and viewers. Various narrative processes are used to represent action in the story and the relationships between objects and characters. Any character in the story, whether human, animal or an animated object, is considered a participant when placed in the image. These participants act and react to one another, to inanimate objects, and to the circumstances in the scene depicted; in other words, images often depict something happening to someone, that is, one participant doing something to an object or another participant. Lewis (2001: 118) writes that 'picturebooks are full of action processes, for they are primarily concerned to represent, in words and sequences of pictures, doings and happenings, most often in the form of narrative.'

When considering an image with participants doing something, it is necessary to begin by considering who is doing what to whom or what object. An actor may be physically interacting with another actor or object, may be simply looking at an actor or object, or may be looking directly at the viewer. Each of these interactions form what Kress and van Leeuwen call a 'vector'. Vectors are imaginary lines formed between actors, objects and viewers. When one actor stares at another or points a finger at another actor, it constitutes a vector. Considering the possible vectors in an image can alert us to the narrative aspects of an image.

For example, in *Voices in the Park*, in the second opening of the third voice (see Figure 15), there is an image where Smudge and Charles are sitting on a park bench looking directly at each other. This particular vector runs from one participant to another in this image. These participants are focused on one another and seem to be disregarding their parents who are seated almost out of view on the ends of the bench. In this image, the two characters are making an important connection. They are becoming friends despite their class distinctions and their parents' differences. When a vector runs between two participants in an image it is considered an 'offer', meaning the viewer of the image is considered an outsider looking in on the actions being depicted. In this image, we are being offered something to consider. As readers we are positioned as observers, focusing on the actions and relationships among the characters in the visual image.

A very different type of vector occurs when a participant in the image looks directly at the viewer rather than into the scene. This is called a 'demand'. By gazing directly at the viewer, the character is demanding that we respond directly to their gaze. We are drawn into their appeal and must consider what they are requesting. For example, in *Voices in the Park*, in the second and last opening of the fourth voice (see Figure 16), Charles stares directly at us, the viewer. His gaze requires that we consider Charles's stare, his predicament, and his situation. In both images, Charles seems to want to leave his mother's side and continue to play with Smudge, suggesting he regrets his mother's decision to leave and her need to control him and have him sit close by her on the park bench.

Figure 15 Voices in the Park: Smudge and Charles on park bench

In both sets of images described above, the image would have taken on extremely different meanings if the characters of Smudge and Charles looked away from one another when they were seated on the bench, or if Charles looked at his mother rather than directly at the viewer. Numerous books on art history and film discuss the concept of 'gaze' (Arnheim, 1986; Sturken & Cartwright, 2001; van Leeuwen & Jewitt, 2001).

2. Visual symbolism: bars, street lamps and park benches

Visual symbols are used to represent ideas that are conventionalized through their use in socio-cultural contexts: for example, offering a red rose as a sign of love or caring, the golden arches of a particular fast food chain, the use of a cross for Christian values, or the colour red for anger or violence. Visual symbols are constructed in social settings and used by artists to convey meanings beyond the literal level. In addition, a motif is a recurring pattern or use of a visual component that refers to a theme or particular meaning. The three motifs or visual symbols that I would like to consider in this section, bars, street lamps and park benches, are used by Anthony Browne across

I got talking to this boy. I thought he
was kind of a wimp at first, but he's
okay. We played on the seesaw and
he didn't say much, but later on he
was more friendly.

Figure 16 Voices in the Park: Charles stares at the viewer

several of his picturebooks. I have found that Browne uses these visual symbols in various images to convey particular meanings, and they become more meaningful when considered across texts as well within their role in one particular picturebook image.

Browne uses vertical bars, whether actual bars, shadows or vertical objects such as trees and bed posts, to suggest internment, lack of freedom, or personal space, captivity and imprisonment. Whether physical imprisonment, for example in several of the images in *Zoo*, or psychological imprisonment, for example in *Hansel and Gretel* or *Gorilla*, Browne draws the reader into the plight of particular characters and the power structure of a group of participants by positioning them on various sides of these vertical bars. Throughout the story of *Hansel and Gretel*, from the image on the title page depicting a bird in a cage, the bed posts drawn in various backgrounds, window panes, vertical lines in the trees, smokestacks, and the print on the children's bed pillows, to the actual bars that imprison Hansel later in the book (see Figure 17), the motif of bars suggests the overarching theme of internment and psychological captivity that haunts Browne's characters throughout this story.

Figure 17 Hansel and Gretel: behind bars

In the second opening of *Gorilla*, the vertical lines of the father's chair and the vertical lines in the drapery foreshadow the young girl's isolation and lack of freedom that emerge later in the story. In the third opening, we see this motif continued in the wainscoting on the wall behind the father and the vertical stripes in the wallpaper (see Figure 18). In the fourth opening, in what is one of the most revealing images for me, the young girl is depicted sitting in bed, and the viewer is positioned to see her through the bars of the bed posts. This image further connotes the isolation that eventually forces her to find solace in her stuffed gorilla. Browne uses vertical lines as a symbol of imprisonment or isolation in several other books, in particular *Zoo*, where he uses bars to separate the humans from the animals. One begins to wonder throughout this unusual book who is on the inside and who is on the outside of the bars.

Two additional visual symbols that Browne uses quite extensively are the street lamp, to separate characters, settings and emotions; and the park bench, to bring these elements together. In general, we find that vertical lines, in particular street lamps and bars, are used by Browne to suggest particular themes of isolation and separation, while horizontal lines, in particular the boards used in park benches, are often used as a bridge to bring elements and

Figure 18 Gorilla: girl in light

characters together. For example, in the image mentioned earlier from the third voice in *Voices in the Park*, where Smudge and Charles are sitting on a park bench, there is a street lamp used to separate the worlds and perspectives of the two characters. However, the street lamp does not cut the image all the way through. Instead, the boards of the park bench stretch across the bottom of the image connecting the two characters. These horizontal lines in the park bench suggest a coming together of the two perspectives, as does the blending of the two dogs depicted in the image.

In another image in *Voices in the Park*, the third opening of the first voice, where Smudge's father is positioned on the left and Charles's mother is pictured on the right, they are separated by a street lamp (see Figure 19). However, this time the vertical line of the street lamp cuts the image completely into two sections, the mother's side being larger and somewhat cleaner and tidier. The street lamp here is used as a metaphor for the separation of the two social classes represented by the two adult characters. The fact that the street lamp goes all the way from top to bottom may suggest that their differences may be irreconcilable. In other images in *Voices in the Park*, Browne uses the street lamp to suggest a change from the desolation of winter to the rebirth of spring, and the dominance of Charles's mother on his life.

In *The Tunnel*, Browne uses a street lamp to separate the mother from her two children as she tires of their fighting and sends them out into the world.

I was just planning what we should have to eat
that evening when I saw Charles had
disappeared. Oh dear! Where had he gone?

Figure 19 Voices in the Park: Smudge's father and Charles's mother at park bench

The vertical lines suggest themes of isolation and separation whilst the horizontal lines serve to bring disparate elements and characters together. These themes and visual symbols become more obvious when we see them throughout Browne's work, not just employed in a single image.

3. Composition: salience, positioning and framing

The way things are organized and positioned in an image is called composition: the arrangement and placement of various objects determines their relative importance and how they interact with other elements in an image.

Three important aspects of composition are:

- **salience** – what is depicted as being important and significant in an image
- **positioning** – where objects and actors are located in an image
- **framing** – how lines and negative space are used to frame particular objects and participants in an image.

Each of these compositional elements adds to the overall image and offers clues to its meaning and how it might be considered and interpreted.

Salience

Salience is the degree to which an artist or illustrator is trying to catch your eye and place importance on a particular object or participant in an image; in addition, it creates a hierarchy of importance among the visual elements of an image. Some entities are positioned and depicted to have more importance or prominence than others. There are numerous ways of drawing the viewer's attention to particular elements of an image, and several of these are discussed here.

Salience does not necessarily relate directly to meaning, but it does suggest what an artist wants the viewer to attend to. We can look at an image and know what the artist is trying to make us look at without knowing exactly what it might mean. Salience is a compositional process of calling attention to certain features in an image.

Three techniques that artists and graphic designers employ to call attention to particular aspects of an image are:

- the use of colour and contrast
- the use of foregrounding and focus
- the relative size of the participant or object.

Learning to attend to what is made salient can help us to understand what an illustrator of picturebooks is trying to say and mean. The process of interpreting exactly what a particular compositional element of an image means is a bit more complex.

Whether a character or object is bigger than another character or object, whether it is in the foreground of an image, depicted in bright colours or in sharp focus, can make that character or object stand out. Anthony Browne uses each of these techniques throughout the picturebooks mentioned to draw readers' attention to various objects and characters. For example, in *Into the Forest*, Browne uses the colour red in the little boy's jacket to catch the readers' attention and as a visual symbol or possible metaphor for Little Red Riding Hood. Against the monochromatic grey background, his red jacket really catches one's eye. The little boy is foregrounded in several of the images to increase his salience, and drawn with precise details so the viewer attends more readily to his image.

The use of colour and contrast

From the title page of *Voices in the Park*, Browne uses the colour red, negative or white space, and a central position to call the reader's attention to the mother's hat. Throughout this story we begin to attend to her red hat, and soon realize how the hat is used as a symbol of the mother's dominance over Charles and others throughout the story. Before we can interpret what the hat possibly stands for, we need to attend to this visual element. Calling one's attention to particular elements of an image is the first step in making sense of what one sees.

The use of foregrounding and focus

Both focus and contrast can also be used to push things into the background and make them seem less important. Throughout *Piggybook*, the mother's face is drawn with little or no details, and is depicted in sepia tones and muted colours to suggest her lowly position in the family hierarchy. At the same time, the boys, Simon and Patrick, and their father are depicted in sharp focus, full colour and more detail. The mother is simply part of the background until the final few pages of the story, when she emerges to claim her rightful place in the family and is depicted in full colour, smiling at us.

The relative size of the participant or character

This can call one's attention to a character's importance in an image or his or her circumstances in the story. Throughout various images in his books, Browne uses large trees and relatively small children to depict issues of isolation, anxiety and impending doom. For example, in the fourth opening of *Into the Forest*, the young boy is drawn very small in comparison with the dark forest he is entering (see Figure 20), thereby making the reader aware of his anxieties. What a different story this image would tell if he was heading out of the woods rather than into it. In addition, in *Hansel and Gretel*, the two children are drawn small in scale when compared with the trees, the adults and the surroundings in which they find themselves.

In numerous images throughout *Voices in the Park*, Charles is drawn much

Figure 20 Into the Forest: boy walking in the forest

smaller than his mother and partially hidden from view. His relative size and position in the image relates to the subordinate role he plays, while his mother's domineering role is represented by her larger size and foregrounded position. Browne uses size, focus, colour and position to offer the reader ways to interpret the characters and objects throughout his images.

Positioning

The positioning of objects and characters determines their importance and how viewers react to them. Kress and van Leeuwen (1996) have detailed what they refer to as 'information zones' in their framework. Information zones refer to the placement of entities in the upper and lower halves of the image, the left and right sections, or the centre and periphery. In general, things placed in a central position are given more importance than those on the periphery, as in the placement of the red hat in *Voices in the Park* mentioned previously. Additionally, objects and participants placed in the upper half of an image are considered the 'ideal' while those in the lower half are considered the 'real'. By 'ideal' and 'real', Kress and van Leeuwen are referring, respectively, to things that are more spiritual than earthly, more ethereal than factual, and more idealized or essential than practical.

For example, in the opening spread of *Gorilla* (see Figure 21), the father is

Figure 21 Gorilla: father and daughter at breakfast

positioned as the ideal and the daughter as the real. The father is placed in the upper section, well above the girl, looking down at his newspaper, oblivious to the happenings in the real world around him. In the second opening of the fourth voice in *Voices in the Park*, Smudge is positioned on a see-saw high above Charles. She represents what Charles wants to be able to do, the freedom that he lacks and the fun that he believes he should be having: in other words, his ideal.

The left and right halves of an image also have different meanings. In our culture, where we read from left to right, we also tend to view images from left to right. This means that the left half suggests what is old and given, while the right half suggests what is new or possible. In 'before and after' images, the 'before' image is almost always placed on the left, so we read the images from old to new. For example, in the third opening of *The Tunnel*, the mother's hand is placed in the upper-left quadrant pointing in the direction she is sending her children. We have no trouble understanding that the children are moving from left to right, from where they have been, the old, to where they are headed, the new. Throughout *In the Forest*, the boy is positioned on the left side of the image when Browne wants us to realize he is headed into the woods and impending trouble. The left side represents where the boy has been, a safer environment, and the right side represents where he is headed, a more dangerous setting.

Framing

The last compositional element referred to here is called 'framing'. Framing is created by the use of borders, negative space or lines around an object or participant to draw readers' attention to what is in the frame, or how the frame separates certain entities. In *Piggybook*, when the mother returns to find her husband and children rooting around for scraps in the living room, her shadow is framed in the doorway, setting her apart from the ravaged house. The frame accentuates her posture and her return. On the opening page of *Zoo*, Browne depicts each member of the family in his or her own frame, suggesting a separation among family members. In the third opening of *Gorilla*, Browne uses shadows to frame a character. In this instance, he uses the light from a television to frame the little girl and to emphasize her isolation. Framing can be achieved in a number of ways; attending to what is included within frames and how they emphasize and separate elements of an image is an important consideration. Framing is covered in more detail in Chapter 5.

4. Perspective: looking up and down; being near or far

The last element of visual grammar that I will describe is that of perspective, or point of view established between the viewer and the objects and participants included in an image. How close up or how far away we are positioned relative to the objects and participants in an image changes the sense of intimacy in our relationship to those elements. When the characters in a story are portrayed in an image from a close social distance, we feel closer to them. In contrast, the farther away they are positioned, the less we are able to connect with them. In addition, an artist may depict a particular character or object from straight on, or above or below a viewers' point of view. When we are positioned to look up at a character, or other characters in an image are positioned to do so, we imbue the character being looked at with power. When we look down on an object or character, or when another character does so, they tend to have less standing or power.

Browne uses these elements of visual grammar to draw us into the lives, emotions and circumstances of the characters, and to suggest their relative status in his stories. For example, in the fourth voice in *Voices in the Park*, when Smudge encounters Charles's mother, she is portrayed from a very close distance and Smudge is positioned to look up at her. She seems very powerful. In the same way, when the mother returns from her self-imposed exile in *Piggybook*, she is positioned well above her husband and sons as they root around for scraps and beg her forgiveness (see Figure 22). They are portrayed

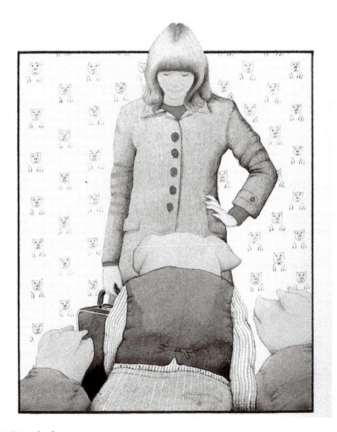

Figure 22 Piggybook: mother returns

as pigs grovelling at her feet, and so the change in the power structure is demonstrated.

In much the same way, throughout the first voice in *Voices in the Park*, Charles is portrayed in the shadow of his mother, hidden behind her in many of the images, and smaller in size and from a farther distance away than his mother. In *Gorilla*, after the gorilla has grown to full size, we look up at his character throughout the story. We are positioned as the little girl looking up at her new-found hero and saviour. Finally, in the closing spread of *In the Forest*, we are drawn into the arms of the mother as she welcomes the boy home from his adventures. By portraying some characters from above or below, near or far, we are invited to interact and understand them in different ways.

Concluding remarks

Each of the compositional elements and artistic techniques discussed here is used to help the artist and illustrator share meanings and tell the story through visual images. Knowing even the basics of these techniques can help teachers and readers of picturebooks appreciate the richness of these visual components and understand how they are used to convey meaning. As a reader and admirer of Anthony Browne's work, it has taken me time and careful examination to see how he draws upon various visual symbols, motifs, perspectives and elements of visual design to construct deeper layers of meaning in his picturebooks. Readers approaching his work for the first time should not be overwhelmed by his images, nor by the analysis presented here.

Consider Browne's work an adventure, an exploration into the world of visual meanings and grammars. By considering the visual components used within and across his books over a period of time, we are able to make connections that are more meaningful and revealing than by considering just one image or book for a single reading or viewing. It is through close inspection of the components and visual design of images, together with a theoretical understanding of art criticism and visual semiotics, that we are able to extend our understanding of contemporary picturebooks and other visual images we may encounter on a day-to-day basis. This exploration into the compositional and other visual elements of picturebooks provides us with a solid foundation from which to expand children's interpretive repertoires.

References

Anstey, M. & Bull, G. (2006). *Teaching and Learning Multiliteracies: Changing Times, Changing Literacies*. Newark, Delaware: International Reading Association

Arnheim, R. (1986). *Art and Visual Perception: A Psychology of the Creative Eye*. Berkeley, California: University of California Press

Bader, B. (1976). *American Picturebooks from Noah's Ark to The Beast Within*. New York: Macmillan

Fleckenstein, K. S. (2002). 'Inviting imagery into our classrooms' in K. S. Fleckenstein, L. T. Calendrillo & D. A. Worley (eds) *Language and Images in the Reading-Writing Classroom*. Mahwah, New Jersey: Erlbaum, pp.3–26

Harvey, S. & Goudvis, A. (2000). *Strategies that Work: Teaching Comprehension to Enhance Understanding*. Portland, Maine: Stenhouse Publishers

Kiefer, B. Z. (1995). *The Potential of Picturebooks: From Visual Literacy to Aesthetic Understanding*. Englewood Cliffs, New Jersey: Prentice-Hall

Kress, G. (2003). *Literacy in the New Media Age*. London: Routledge

Kress, G. & van Leeuwen, T. (1996). *Reading Images: The Grammar of Visual Design*. London: Routledge

Kress, G. & van Leeuwen, T. (2001). *Multimodal Discourse: The Modes and Media of Contemporary Communication*. London: Edward Arnold

Lewis, D. (2001). *Reading Contemporary Picturebooks: Picturing Text*. London: RoutledgeFalmer

Nikolajeva, M. & Scott, C. (2000). 'The dynamics of picturebook communication'. *Children's Literature in Education* 31(4): 225–39

Owocki, G. (2003). *Comprehension: Strategic Instruction for K-3 Students*. Portsmouth, New Hampshire: Heinemann

Sipe, L. (1998a). 'How picture books work: A semiotically framed theory of text-picture relationships'. *Children's Literature in Education* 29(2): 97–108

Sipe, L. (1998b). 'Learning the language of picture books'. *Journal of Children's Literature* 24(2): 66–75

Snow, C. & Sweet, A. (2003). *Rethinking Reading Comprehension*. New York: Guilford

Sturken, M. & Cartwright, L. (2001). *Practices of Looking: An Introduction to Visual Culture*. Oxford: Oxford University Press

Unsworth, L. & Wheeler, J. (2002). 'Re-valuing the role of images in reviewing picture books'. *Reading* 36(2): 68–74

van Leeuwen, T. & Jewitt, C. (2001). *Handbook of Visual Analysis*. London: SAGE Publications

Children's literature

Browne, A. (1981). *Hansel and Gretel*. London: Julia MacRae Books

Browne, A. (1983). *Gorilla*. London: Julia MacRae Books

Browne, A. (1986). *Piggybook*. London: Julia MacRae Books

Browne, A. (1989). *The Tunnel*. London: Julia MacRae Books

Browne, A. (1992). *Zoo*. London: Julia MacRae Books

Browne, A. (2001). *Voices in the Park*. New York: DK Publishing

Browne, A. (2004). *Into the Forest*. Cambridge, Massachusetts: Candlewick

2 Developing new literacies

Responding to picturebooks in multiliterate ways

Michèle Anstey and Geoff Bull

In this chapter we explore how the increasing pace of change in contemporary society, together with technological innovation, has hastened the development of new forms of literacy that have become known as the New Literacies. We examine how these new literacies have changed the way that literature, particularly children's literature, is written (produced) and read (consumed). We then discuss the characteristics of postmodern picturebooks and how they can be used to support the new literacies. Finally, we argue the case for a new perspective on response to picturebooks that we believe is required with the advent of the new literacies.

The New Literacies and technological change

Change is one of the overarching trends of the later twentieth and early twenty-first centuries, and will continue to be so. The world of the twenty-first century is characterized by an increasing pace of change in technological, social and economic ways. This has led to the proposition that change is the new constant and will affect all aspects of teachers' and children's lives, from the global to the local.

The texts that are currently available, particularly children's picturebooks, have adapted to these new circumstances. Concepts of literacy, literacy knowledge, skills and processes have been modified as purposes and contexts for literate activity have been influenced by these new conditions (see Freebody & Luke, 1990, 2003; Hawisher & Selfe, 2000; Kress, 2003; Kress & van Leeuwin, 2001; Lankshear, Gee, Knobel & Searle, 1997; Lankshear & Knobel, 2004; Luke, 1995; Luke & Freebody, 1999, 2000).

As we have written elsewhere (see Anstey, 2002a, 2002b; Anstey & Bull, 2006), we believe that to be literate an individual must now be able to incorporate existing and new literacy knowledge, processes and skills into new contexts – for new purposes – using new technologies. Given these new conditions, we adapted the definition of literacy suggested by Luke & Freebody (2000: 9) (see Anstey 2002a: 15):

> Literacy is the flexible and sustainable mastery of a repertoire of practices with the texts of traditional and new communication technologies via spoken, print and multimedia, and the ability to use these practices in various social contexts.

This definition is useful because it identifies the characteristics of a literate person and focuses on literate practices. The concentration on practices can then be logically extrapolated to develop appropriate pedagogy. The linking of literacy, literate practices and pedagogy is particularly useful when considering the implications of new literacies for educational purposes. As we have stated elsewhere (see Anstey & Bull, 2006: 19), in terms of this definition, to be literate one has to be:

- **flexible**: positive and strategically responsive to changing literacies
- able to **sustain mastery**: have developed the ability to reformulate current knowledge or access and learn new literate practices
- in possession of a **repertoire of practices**: have a range of knowledge, skills and strategies to use when appropriate
- able to **use traditional communication technologies**: paper and live (e.g. face-to-face encounters, plays and other dramatic performances)
- able to **use new communication technologies**: digital-electronic (using multiple modes, often simultaneously).

This definition recognizes that literacy must encompass the new communication technologies such as those employed by mobile phones and computers. Because these new technologies often use texts that are not limited to the print-based forms that many people grew up with, questions arise about whether the literacies of traditional texts are adequate for digital-electronic technologies. In order to understand a print text, children need access to knowledge about language and to shared ways of making meaning. The study of linguistics has enabled us to build up knowledge of how language is constructed and how it works. The study of semiotics has led us to understand how particular groups in society share ways of making meaning. We contend, therefore, that children need to acquire knowledge about the linguistic semiotic system if they are to learn how to construct and interpret print texts.

However, many texts contain material in both print and visual form, so clearly knowledge of the linguistic semiotic system alone is not sufficient. Nevertheless, a significant proportion of what has been going on in schools in literacy teaching and learning since the invention of the printing press in 1484 (when William Caxton printed the first children's book, *Fables of Aesop*) has focused on the interpretation of print only. This is somewhat surprising given that most books, including the *Fables of Aesop*, contain some graphic or visual information in the form of illustrations, charts or diagrams. Clearly, children need to acquire knowledge about the visual semiotic system if they are to make meaning from paper texts. This is particularly the case for picturebooks, where the images increasingly play a role in the construction of meaning. However, the visual semiotic is just as important in the interpretation of mathematics, science and geography books, since these often contain significant numbers of photographs, diagrams, graphs and maps. Most print texts are therefore multimodal – they contain both print and visual elements. Kress (2000: 184) suggests that all texts can be viewed as multimodal rather than monomodal, since even those texts without any visual material contain punctuation marks that give direction as to how the text should be read (e.g. through intonation, pause or stress). For Kress, such texts have audio elements that accompany the print.

In the case of live and digital technologies, texts such as plays, cartoons, videos and films can be conveyed by the internet, DVDs or mobile phones. Here the audio elements are more noticeable and play a more central role in meaning-making through such things as dialogue, music and sound effects. These elements make up the audio semiotic system. These texts also contain a lot of gestures that convey meaning, which can be augmented by how characters appear in relation to one another (their position) and their proximity (how close or far away they are). In live and digital technologies, moving images as well as still images play a critical role in constructing meaning. In these texts the gestural and spatial semiotic systems are used. Table 1 below (from Bull & Anstey, in press) presents a summary of the five semiotic systems we have been discussing.

Table 1 Overview of the five semiotic systems

Semiotic system	Some examples of signs and symbols that convey meaning within them
Linguistic: oral and written language	vocabulary, generic structure, punctuation, grammar, paragraphing
Visual: still and moving images	colour, vectors, line, foreground, viewpoint
Gestural: facial expression and body language	movement, speed, stillness, body position
Audio: music and sound effects	volume, pitch, rhythm, silence, pause
Spatial: layout and organization of objects and space	proximity, direction, position in space

It is important to realize that there needs to be a balance between the new literacies and the more traditional views of what some have termed the 'old literacies'. Referring to old and new literacies could produce a false dichotomy that would, in our view, be counterproductive. There is still a need to be concerned about the knowledge, skills and processes of oral and written language (the linguistic semiotic system). Children still need to know about such things as plot, theme and characterization, and they still need to be aware of the grammar of the linguistic system. However, the linguistic should not take precedence over the other semiotic systems. The late twentieth and early twenty-first centuries have ushered in an unparalleled shift towards the visual and a concentration on the still and moving image. Kress (2003: 140) characterizes this shift as a move from text *'telling the world* to *showing the world'* (his emphasis). With the advent of the new literacies, both readers and writers now have to be knowledgeable about the following developments. They must be:

- fluent in the five semiotic systems (see Table 1)
- aware of the nature and variety of multimodal texts
- able to understand the differences between paper, live and digital electronic technologies
- conversant with the vast array of texts that are now available in the three technologies
- conscious of the changes in various texts brought about by the hardware of technology (e.g. the shift away from paper to screen)
- cognizant of the changes in linguistic text brought about by such things as email, SMS messaging and the screen (writing in these situations is becoming less formal and more speech-like and screen-like, and spelling is becoming more unconventional)
- aware that readers of multimodal text need to understand the grammar and conventions for reading visual and audio text (for example, the use of line to lead the eye or silence to force a pause or emphasize).

Of course technological change by itself has not produced all the changes in literacy discussed here. There have also been advances in our knowledge about literacy, particularly in the area of multiliteracies. Multiliteracies can be defined as the range of literacies and literate practices used in all sectors of life. This means being literate in multiple modes (live, paper and digital electronic), being able to use appropriate literate practices in many different contexts, and being critically literate. It is important to realize that multiliteracies are not merely about technologies (see Anstey & Bull, 2006). Technological change and multiliteracies have contributed to the move away from a reliance on print only to a more detailed focus on live and digital electronic communication technologies. This change in focus has drawn attention to the range of multimodal texts and the variety of semiotic systems that operate in contemporary teaching and learning contexts. The new literacies, while still based on the more traditional, look quite different from the old and require a whole new range of knowledges, skills and processes. It may be that these changes generate even more fundamental differences by changing the way we talk about literacy. It may perhaps be more accurate to think of writing as 'production' and to construct reading as 'consumption'. While it is still appropriate to think of writing and reading a linguistic text, it is somewhat incongruous to talk of writing and reading a moving image.

Technological change and the picturebook

Just as technological change has impacted upon literacy, so it has transformed the production of picturebooks. During the 1960s, in addition to many social and cultural changes, there were great advances in the printing of picture-books. The optimism and experimentation of this decade brought changes in attitudes, people began to value picturebooks more highly, and advances in colour printing revolutionized the format. Martin (1996: 233) identified this period as the time of cross-over from black and white to full colour printing through the advent of more refined photographic lithography. Kiefer (2008: 19) also points out that this period saw a streamlining of book production through the use of laser printing. These new technologies enabled almost perfect colour reproduction as well as the qualities and textures of a range of media such as paint, collage, pastel and crayon. In Australia the added problems of a small, local market and high production costs were not overcome until the late 1960s, when a quality printing industry was established in Asia.

Joseph and Lulu and the Prindiville House Pigeons (1972), written and illustrated by Ted Greenwood, and two picturebooks written by Jenny Wagner and illustrated by Ron Brooks, *The Bunyip of Berkeley's Creek* (1974) and *John Brown, Rose and the Midnight Cat* (1977) were turning points in the Australian scene. In the UK the books of Charles Keeping, *Black Dolly* (1966) and *Shaun and the Cart-Horse* (1967), and Brian Wildsmith, *ABC* (1962) and *Birds* (1967), were groundbreaking, while in the US Maurice Sendak led the way with *Where the Wild Things Are* (1963). All of these picturebooks are outstanding examples of the use of colour, texture and media. In Table 2 below (adapted from our earlier work, Anstey & Bull 2000: 79–82) we have summarized some of the major turning points in picturebooks brought about by the development of new technology.

Colour, texture and media continue to be one of the focuses in modern picturebook production, allowing contemporary illustrators the opportunity for experimentation and flexibility with new styles and techniques. The watercolour techniques in *Where in the World* (2005), written by Marie-Francine Hébert from Canada and illustrated by Janice Nadeau; the digital colouring of the graphite pencil illustrations in *The Arrival* (2006), by Shaun Tan from Australia; and the black-and-white pencil drawings in *The Invention of Hugo Cabret* (2007), by Brian Selznick from the US, are testament to the continuing, international focus on illustration and book production.

New technologies have also allowed further developments, such as cut-outs, in book production. In *The Viewer* (1997) by Gary Crew (illustrated by Shaun Tan), the designers have used cut-outs to show the views through a viewmaster or kaleidoscope. Similarly, in *Little Mouse's Big Book of Fears* (2007) by Emily Gravett, cut-outs have been used to show evidence of where little mouse has been. In *Home* (2006) by Narelle Oliver, actual photographs have been combined with collage, linocut rubbings, pastel, pencil and watercolour to produce an innovative approach to illustration. These three examples demonstrate the continuing role that technological progress plays in the broader development of the picturebook.

Technological progress can be seen to have changed the nature of texts, and of literacy itself, as well as advancing the development of book production. However, these changes have not taken place in a vacuum. As can be seen from Table 2 below, these transformations have been accompanied by social and cultural changes that have influenced the plots, themes and audiences of picturebooks as well as how they are constructed. An almost parallel development has occurred during this period of technological change, where authors and illustrators have self-consciously constructed both the visual and the print texts in picturebooks to create multiple meanings through the use of techniques such as different narrator positions and points of view. We have termed this type of book a 'postmodern picturebook' (see Anstey & Bull, 2000).

The postmodern picturebook

In our review of the picturebook in the twentieth and twenty-first centuries (Anstey & Bull, 2004), we found that the postmodern picturebook was itself a product of changing times and technologies, and incorporated characteristics that were particularly suited to teaching of the new literacies. Since the late twentieth century this type of picturebook has been commonly referred to as a postmodern picturebook (see Lewis, 1990, 2001; Grieve, 1993; Watson & Styles, 1996, and more recently Arizpe & Styles, 2003). We suggest that the narrative in a postmodern picturebook is realized through the illustrative text (i.e. the images) and through the written text (i.e. the words). Therefore an individual needs to be both a reader and a viewer in order to engage with this type of picturebook. In this sense the postmodern picturebook can be described as a multimodal text.

Because postmodern picturebooks use particular metafictive elements to create multiple meanings, they question established plots, characters and even the setting out of books. The result is a blend of illustrative and fictional styles that is to be read and viewed quite differently. They are therefore particularly suited to the pedagogies associated with the new literacies. There are a number of devices that are commonly incorporated into picturebooks to introduce postmodern elements that support the teaching and learning of the new literacies. They include (Anstey & Bull, 2000; Anstey, 2002b):

- **non-traditional ways of using plot, character and setting** that challenge reader/viewer expectations and require different ways of reading and viewing (as in *Wolves*, 2005, by Emily Gravett)
- **unusual uses of the narrator's voice** to position the reader/viewer to read the book in particular ways and through particular characters' eyes. This can be achieved by the written or visual text (as in *Grandad's Gifts*, 1992, written by Paul Jennings and illustrated by Peter Gouldthorpe)

Table 2 Change in picturebooks brought about by the development of new technology

	United Kingdom	Australia	United States
1960	• During the 1960s and 1970s refinements in off-set litho printing occurred. • 1962. Oxford University Press decided to experiment: Wildsmith's *ABC* published. Printed in Austria where the colour and painterly quality could be reproduced best. • Charles Keeping explored issues of death, urban environments and single-parent families in *Shaun and the Cart-Horse* (1967) *Charley, Charlotte and the Golden Canary* (1967) and *Joseph's Yard* (1970) • 1967 Brian Wildsmith's *Birds* published. • 1968 Wildsmith's *Fishes* published – first use of double-page spread for illustration.	• During the 1960s partially illustrated novels were more prolific than picturebooks. This was attributed to the difficulty of competing with UK & US imports, the small population and the expense of production. • 1969. *Sly Old Wardrobe*, written by Ivan Southall and illustrated by Ted Greenwood, drawn from the eye level of a child, with caricatured faces and multiple scenes on a page. Forerunner to major changes of the 1970s.	• Craft of colour separation developed to a high level in US. • In the 1960s Leo Lionni continued to write and illustrate his fables in mixed media (*Inch by Inch*, 1960, *Frederick*, 1967 and *Swimmy*, 1968). All used the whole page and double-page spreads. • 1963. Maurice Sendak trilogy commenced with publication of *Where the Wild Things Are*. Portrayed childhood fears and emotions.
1970	• John Burningham moved to line and watercolour in *Mr Gumpy's Outing* (1970). • Cartoon-style figures and comic-strip-style design and layout rose in popularity through the work of Quentin Blake (*Mind Your Own Business*, 1974) and Raymond Briggs (*Father Christmas*, 1973).	• 1970s was a period of great change and boom in picturebooks in Australia. Now able to compete economically due to the ability to print cheaply in Asia. • 1972. *Joseph and Lulu and the Prindiville House Pigeons* by Ted Greenwood had sophisticated text, adult appeal, and unusual format and layout.	• *In the Night Kitchen*, the second of Sendak's trilogy on childhood fears, was published in 1970. It was the most controversial in layout, using cartoon-style sequences across double spreads and because it featured the main character, Mickey, nude, flying through the bakery and city at night.

	United Kingdom	Australia	United States
1970	• Some return to 'period detail' with subtle colour use of fine line and miniatures style seen in the work of Nicola Bayley (*Nursery Rhymes*, 1975). • In the late 1970s John Burningham explored children's fantasy worlds, with the humdrum of parents in *Come Away from the Water Shirley* (1977) and *Time to Get Out of the Bath Shirley* (1978).	• 1974. *The Bunyip of Berkeley's Creek* written by Jenny Wagner and illustrated by Ron Brooks. Seen as turning point in the Australian picturebook: abstract and philosophical concept of 'Who am I?', multi-layered, adult and child appeal, unusual format and style of illustration, and multiple meanings in both text and illustrations. • 1977. *John Brown, Rose and the Midnight Cat* by Wagner and illustrated by Brooks, regarded as a groundbreaking book: multiple readings, adult and child appeal, symbolism, intertextuality, abstract concepts of loneliness, jealousy and relationships.	• 1976. Margot Zemach wrote and illustrated *It Could be Worse*. Caldecott Honor book. Unusual use of watercolour inks, design and layout to create atmosphere and movement. Lots of byplay in the illustrations.

- **indeterminacy** (indefinite or nebulous detail) in written or illustrative text, plot, character or setting, which requires the reader to construct some of the text and meanings (as in *Jumanji*, 1981, by Chris Van Allsburg)
- **a pastiche of illustrative styles** that requires the reader/viewer to employ a range of knowledge and grammars to read (as in *Black and White*, 1990, by David Macaulay)
- **change to traditional book formats** with new and unusual design and layout, which challenge the reader/viewer's perception of how to read a book (as in *When the Wind Blows*, 1982, by Raymond Briggs)
- **contesting discourses** (between illustrative and written text), requiring the reader to consider alternate readings and meaning (as in *Drac and the Gremlin*, 1988, written by Allan Baillie and illustrated by Jane Tanner)
- **intertextuality**, which requires the reader/viewer to access and use background knowledge from other texts in order to access the available meanings (as in *The Frog Prince Continued*, 1991, written by Jon Scieszka and illustrated by Steve Johnson)
- **the availability of multiple readings and meanings** for a variety of audiences (as in *The Rabbits*, 1998, written by John Marsden and illustrated by Shaun Tan).

Some additional points about technology

In summarizing the case that we have made so far, we would suggest that technological change has necessitated the development of new literacies. These literacies have changed the focus of literacy teaching and learning: away from an emphasis on the linguistic only; towards alternative ways of sharing and making meaning (the visual, audio, gestural and spatial semiotic systems) through the print, live and digital electronic communication technologies. All texts should be regarded as multimodal, and the postmodern picturebook is an ideal tool for exploring multimodality. We would suggest that technology has made a significant impact on literacy, literacy pedagogy and the way we talk about text. Before we move on to the question of response, there are some further points that we would like to make about technological change and its effects on learners.

- Children's worlds are saturated by technology, multimodal texts and the communication technologies of the digital age (see Gee, 2003; Carrington, 2006; Henderson, 2008)
- Children's experiences with the digital world outside of school may be vastly different from their in-school experiences
- While we, as adults, talk about the new technologies, to children they are a given and are seen as everyday
- The new technologies and the new literacies require a new and different set of knowledges, skills and processes (see Jewitt, 2002 and Kinnane, 2008) that are often not accessible in print-only classrooms.

Responding to multimodal texts in classrooms incorporating the new literacies

Children are often asked to respond to a story as part of the discussion that goes on in and around a text. This is sometimes directed towards comprehension of the story and sometimes towards encouraging enjoyment. Traditionally, with children aged 4 to 12, these responses are enacted in literacy lessons and involve such activities as orally retelling the plot; a dramatic portrayal of part, or all, of the narrative; changing the ending of the story; reinterpreting a character; writing a diary or reflection journal; constructing a plot profile or drawing a picture. We would suggest that, if the new literacies require new knowledges, skills and processes, then the tasks that we ask children to engage in need to be re-examined.

This does not mean that traditional ways of responding are no longer of any value. They are, and will continue to be, important ways of responding to text. However, these responses have been designed for classrooms that are print-focused. These more traditional ways of responding to text are necessary but not sufficient in the digital age in which we live. We have argued in this chapter that classrooms now need to focus on print, live and digital electronic technologies that incorporate all five semiotic systems. There also needs to be a focus on multimodal texts rather than just print-only texts – hence we have suggested that postmodern picturebooks are ideal vehicles for consolidating the new literacies. We would now like to take an alternative look at some of the traditional ways of responding to narratives. Our suggestions draw on the developments brought about by changes in technology and the new literacies, and capitalize on the special qualities of postmodern picturebooks.

Alternative ways of responding

1. Using storyboards as a response to narrative

Definition of term

A storyboard is a device used to retell, or plan, the sequence of a narrative. It is a tool used by authors and illustrators to plan the layout and organization of the visual and linguistic texts (e.g. the placement of double-page spreads, or the viewpoint for an illustration, such as bird's eye or bottom-up). A series of small illustrations, called frames, are used to map or shape the plot. Each of the frames is very basic in design and often uses cartoon-like figures. While teachers traditionally use the storyboard to focus on retelling, an alternative is to use it to examine the relationship between visual and linguistic text in the narration of the story and the development of theme and characterization.

Description of activity

Children can be asked to construct storyboards either before they begin to write a story (as a rehearsal) or after they have read one (as a retelling). Initially this can be a tool for the construction of a narrative, completed before writing begins, or as a deconstruction or reconstruction, if is it done after the narrative has been written or read. Once children have mastered this more traditional use of the storyboard, they can use it to focus on aspects of design and layout of illustrative and written text. For example, they can draw the frames of the storyboard (in art lessons) or construct them using photos from a digital camera.

Regardless of the technology used, the focus should be on how best to portray the events in the plot and the characters' involvement in, and reaction to, them. Children would focus on posture, body position, organization of objects in the illustrations, point of view, etc. They would make decisions about what to portray through illustration and what should be left for the reader to imagine from the written text. In this way the focus is on how the visual and linguistic text work together to make meaning.

Nature of response

In such an activity children are still involved in the process of telling or retelling, but they are also using the linguistic and visual semiotic systems to construct the frames of the storyboard. This means that they reflect upon the role of each semiotic system in telling the story and the relationship between the visual and linguistic text. They are also engaging with print communication technology. If they use a digital camera to construct scenes then they are involved with the gestural and spatial semiotic systems as well as digital electronic communications technology. The storyboard can, in addition, be used to develop the theme of a narrative and will assist in planning the shape of the story through a focus on initiating events, climax and resolution and how these relate to particular frames. Engaging in these types of activities will also provide children with experiences of the codes of still images such as line, colour and shape. The important point here is that storyboarding promotes a different kind of response, examining all semiotic systems and incorporating the new technologies and new literacies.

Use of postmodern picturebooks

The use of picturebooks presents teachers with a threefold advantage. First, the books are a highly interesting way of exploring literature that motivates children to read further. Second, picturebooks introduce children to both print and visual text and the need to 'read' both. Third, with the variety of picture-books now available, it is possible to find books that are suitable for all ages, for example *The Rabbits* (1998, by John Marsden, illustrated by Shaun Tan) and *The World According to Warren* (2007, by Craig Silvey, illustrated by Sonia Martinez).

Postmodern picturebooks add a number of important dimensions. Because these books have been specifically designed to tell the story through both print and illustration, they focus the reader's attention on both word and image. This allows for an easy introduction into the linguistic and visual semiotic systems for children of any age. Particular devices that are employed in postmodern picturebooks (such as non-traditional ways of using plot, character and setting; indeterminacy; contesting discourses; pastiche of illustrative styles and multiple meanings) all focus on plot, theme and character. The storyboard promotes investigation of how these devices have been employed.

Extension activities

We have discussed the use of storyboarding with still images found in traditional picturebooks and postmodern picturebooks. Children can also be encouraged to construct a storyboard for a video clip (a moving image) they have watched or are about to construct.

If they choose to construct a moving image as part of their response then they will also use the audio, gestural and spatial semiotic systems, and live and digital communication technologies. This will involve them in learning about the codes of moving images (such as lighting, point of view and framing). For further discussion of the codes and conventions of still and moving images see Anstey & Bull (2006).

2. Using colourscripts to investigate mood, time and context

Definition of term

A variation on the storyboard idea is the colourscript. It can take the form of a number of frames (as in a storyboard) that contain the colours that are to be used in various scenes from a narrative. Animators originally used it when planning animated films. It focuses on how colour and colour schemes portray theme, mood, passages of time and context.

Description of activity

Children can use this technique to help them in the construction of a story or in the analysis (deconstruction) of a story they have written or in a picturebook that they are reading. A colourscript can be used to develop the context of a story by illustrating the passage of time through the seasons of the year or by showing details of the setting of the story. Colour can also show mood – for example, by using blues and greens for sadness and yellows and oranges for happiness. The colourscript focuses children's attention on how the illustrative text and particular colour has a role to play in telling the story, whereas the storyboard concentrates more on the written text or layout and organization of the visual and written texts.

Nature of response

In such an activity, children are still involved in the process of construction or deconstruction but they are also using the visual semiotic system to construct the frames of the colourscript. They are engaging with print communication technology because they have to consult the written story to check on details such as plot, theme, setting, passage of time and characterization. They may use a computer to generate the colourscript, and if so then they are also involved with digital electronic communication technology.

Use of postmodern picturebooks

Postmodern picturebooks are very useful in developing the concept of the colourscript because many of them are constructed in a particular way to show the inter-relatedness of the written and illustrative text (see Anstey & Bull, 2000, for more detail). Devices commonly used in the postmodern picturebook, such as a pastiche of illustrative styles (to explore colour) and non-traditional ways of using plot, character and setting (to investigate mood and setting) can be explored using colourscripts. An excellent example of a postmodern picturebook that has a very clear colourscript linked to the narrative and theme is *The Red Tree* by Shaun Tan (2001).

Extension activities

Children can also be encouraged to construct a colourscript for a video clip (a moving image) they have watched or are about to construct. If they choose to construct (or review) a moving image as part of their response then they will engage with the audio, gestural and spatial semiotic systems and digital communication technologies.

3. Character development through modelling and sculpture

Definition of term

Characters can be developed by constructing models using paper, wood or metal, or by using materials such as potatoes or clay for sculpting.

Description of activity

Children can explore various body attitudes, poses, points of view or facial expressions through modelling and sculpting to see how characterization can be expressed. These activities involve children with the visual, gestural and spatial semiotic systems. Once they understand how character can be constructed, children can then apply what they have learned to the analysis of character.

Nature of response

Variations on these activities can involve the use of cameras to photograph the models and sculptures from different points of view for inclusion in stories, or the use of lighting to modify poses or expressions. A series of different shots can also be used to illustrate character change or development. Models and sculptures can be juxtaposed in relation to one another to redefine character. Cameras can be employed during drama lessons to photograph character development, with either still or moving images. All the activities described that use a digital camera can be collated on computer.

Use of postmodern picturebooks

The postmodern picturebook is particularly useful in investigating non-traditional ways of developing character. *Zoo* (Anthony Browne, 1992) is an excellent postmodern picturebook through which to examine characterization as portrayed through body position, posture, facial expression and gesture.

Extension activities

There are also computer programs available that use modelling and sculpture (e.g. Claymation) that can be employed even with very young children. Many of these activities will involve children in the exploration of live and digital electronic technologies. Once children have engaged with a number of these activities designed to explore the construction of character, it is much easier for them to deconstruct character in picturebooks.

4. Using photography

Photography can be used to show development of plot, theme, mood, passage of time, context and characterization. Apart from the benefits of using other semiotic systems and communication technologies, photography enables children to construct images quickly without having to spend inordinate amounts of time drawing. It also means that children do not have to be confident artists or illustrators in order to create images for picturebooks. Photography is now being used more frequently by 'real' illustrators to supplement other images that they have created using more traditional media. An excellent example of this is *Home*, written and illustrated by Narelle Oliver (2006), who combined photography with elements of collage, linocut rubbings, pastel, pencil and watercolour. In Figure 23 below, photography has been combined with other media to show a peregrine falcon that is preparing to nest amongst city buildings.

Some final comments

There are a number of general points we would like to make about our suggested activities for alternative ways of responding.

The falcons have not eaten for days.
At sunrise the male leaves the new nest
in search of food.

He soars between sheer towering cliffs
that gleam like water. There is no smoke or fire.
There must be birds to catch.

Figure 23 From *Home*: photography is combined with other media

1. In this chapter we have limited ourselves to a discussion of response with picturebooks only. Many of the suggestions we have made can be applied, with some modification, to the study of narratives with few illustrations.
2. The use of picturebooks, particularly postmodern picturebooks, is not limited to young children. Although we have kept in mind an age range of 4 to 12, we strongly believe that all primary/elementary and secondary children can benefit from a close study of postmodern picturebooks suitable for their level of development. We are a long way away from the period when picturebooks were suitable for the under-8s only.
3. We, or the teachers we have worked with in classrooms, have used all of the suggested activities with children from 4 to 12 years old. We are firmly of the belief that the use of all the communication technologies and semiotic systems is not something that should be delayed until children are older. Many children have been steeped in these areas well before they arrive in our schools.
4. Some children arriving at school will be very technologically and digitally literate but will not have the background in print literacy that we have come to expect. They can be regarded as both literate and non-literate. We

should not be surprised at this, given the range of new literacies that are now a part of children's everyday lives. The investigations we have recommended enable these children to use their digital literacies to explore and enhance their print literacies.

5. It may be that some of the children in school who are seen to be 'at risk' in literacy development may have a problem with the linguistic semiotic system but not with literacy in general. The investigations we have recommended enable children to be successful using literacies with which they are more familiar (e.g. using the visual to augment the linguistic).

6. Many teachers with whom we have worked in multiliterate classrooms tell stories of at-risk children making great progress in literacy once they are given access to a range of semiotic systems.

7. Postmodern picturebooks have often been described as being deliberately self-conscious about the way in which they are developed and produced. The investigations we have recommended enable children to investigate the devices used in postmodern picturebooks and how they shape meaning.

In our view, the teaching and learning of the new literacies is not so much a challenge for children's learning but a challenge for teachers to construct suitable learning contexts. We hope that some of the ideas we have presented will assist teachers with this challenge.

References

Anstey, M. (2002a). 'It's not all black and white: Postmodern picturebooks and new literacies'. *Journal of Adolescent and Adult Literacy* 45(6): 444–57

Anstey, M. (2002b). *Literate Futures: Reading.* Coorparoo, Australia: State of Queensland Department of Education

Anstey, M. & Bull, G. (2000). *Reading the Visual: Written and Illustrated Children's Literature.* Sydney: Harcourt

Anstey, M. & Bull, G. (2004). 'The picturebook: Modern and postmodern' in Hunt, P. (ed.) *International Companion Encyclopaedia of Children's Literature* 2nd edition Vol 1. London: Routledge, pp.328–39

Anstey, M & Bull, G. (2006). *Teaching and Learning Multiliteracies: Changing Times, Changing Literacies.* Newark, Delaware: International Reading Association

Arizpe, E. & Styles, M. (2003). *Children Reading Pictures: Interpreting Visual Texts.* London: RoutledgeFalmer

Bull, G. & Anstey, M. (in press). *Reading and Writing in a Multiliterate World: The Consumption and Production of Multimodal Texts.* Melbourne: Curriculum Corporation

Carrington, V. (2006). *Rethinking Middle Years: Early Adolescents, Schooling and Digital Culture.* New South Wales: Allen & Unwin

Freebody, P. & Luke, A. (1990). 'Literacies programmes: Debates and demands in cultural context'. *Prospect: A Journal of Australian TESOL* 11: 7–16

Freebody, P. & Luke, A. (2003). 'Literacy as engaging with new forms of life: The four roles model' in Anstey, M. & Bull, G. (eds) *The Literacy Lexicon* 2nd edition. Sydney: Pearson, pp.51–66

Gee, J. P. (2003). *What video games have to teach us about learning and literacy.* New York: Macmillan

Grieve, A. (1993). 'Postmodernism in picturebooks'. *Papers,* 4(3): 15–25

Hawisher, G. E. & Selfe, C, L. (2000). *Global Literacies and the World-Wide Web.* London: Routledge

Henderson, R. (2008). 'It's a digital life! Digital literacies, multiliteracies and multi-modality'. *Literacy Learning: the Middle Years* 16(2), June 2008: 11–15

Jewitt, C. (2002). 'The move from page to screen: The multimodal reshaping of school English'. *Visual Communication* 1(2): 171–96

Kiefer, B. (2008). 'What is a picturebook, anyway?' in Sipe, L. & Pantaleo, S. (eds) *Postmodern Picturebooks: Play, Parody and Self-Referentiality.* New York: Routledge, pp.9–21

Kinnane, A. (2008). 'Who are we teaching again?: Teaching in a digital world'. *Literacy Learning: the Middle Years* 16(2) June 2008: 32–3

Kress, G. (2000). 'Multimodality' in Cope, B. & Kalantzis, M. (eds) *Multiliteracies: Literacy Learning and the Design of Social Futures.* Melbourne: Macmillan, pp.182–202

Kress, G. (2003). *Literacy in the New Media Age.* London: Routledge

Kress, G. & van Leeuwin, T. (2001). *Multimodal Discourse: The Modes and Media of Contemporary Education.* London: Edward Arnold

Lankshear, C. & Knobel, M. (2004). 'Text-related roles of the digitally "at home"'. Paper presented at the American Education Research Association Annual Meeting, San Diego. http: //www.geocities.com/c.lankshear/roles.html

Lankshear, C. with Gee, P., Knobel, M. and Searle, C. (1997). *Changing Literacies.* Buckingham: Open University Press

Lewis D. (2001). *Picturing Text: The Contemporary Children's Picturebook.* London: Taylor & Francis

Lewis, D. (1990). 'The constructedness of texts: Picturebooks and the metafictive'. *Signal* 62: 131–46

Luke, A. (1995). 'When basic skills and information processing aren't enough: Rethinking reading in new times'. *Teachers College Record* 97(1), Fall: 47–62

Luke, A. & Freebody, P. (2000). *Literate Futures: Report of the Review for Queensland State Schools.* Brisbane: Education Queensland

Luke, A. & Freebody, P. (1999). 'Further notes on the four resource model'. http: //www.readingonline.org/research/lukefreebody.html

Martin, D. (1996). 'Children's book design' in Hunt, P. & Ray, S. (eds) *International Encyclopaedia of Children's Literature.* London: Routledge, pp.461–77

Watson, V. & Styles, M (1996). *Talking Pictures: Pictorial Texts and Young Readers.* London: Hodder & Stoughton

Children's literature

Baillie, A. (1988). *Drac and the Gremlin* (illustrated by J. Tanner). Melbourne: Viking Kestrel

Bayley, N. (1975). *Nursery Rhymes.* Publisher unknown

Blake, Q. (1974). *Mind Your Own Business.* Publisher unknown

Briggs, R. (1973). *Father Christmas.* London: Hamish Hamilton/Coward

Briggs, R. (1982). *When the Wind Blows.* London: Penguin

Brown, A. (1992). *Zoo*. London: Random House

Burningham, J. (1970). *Mr Grumpy's Outing*. London: Jonathan Cape

Burningham, J. (1977). *Come Away from the Water, Shirley*. London: Jonathan Cape

Burningham, J. (1978). *Time to Get Out of the Bath, Shirley*. London: Jonathan Cape

Crew, G. (1997). *The Viewer* (illustrated by S. Tan). Melbourne: Lothian

Gravett, E. (2005). *Wolves*. London: Macmillan

Gravett, E. (2007). *Little Mouse's Big Book of Fears*. London: Macmillan

Greenwood, T. (1972). *Joseph and Lulu and the Prindiville House Pigeons*. Sydney: Angus and Robertson

Hébert, M.-J. (2005). *Where in the World* (illustrated by J. Nadeau). Montreal: Bonappétit & Son

Jennings, P. (1992). *Grandad's Gifts* (illustrated by P. Gouldthorpe). Melbourne: Viking

Keeping, C. (1966). *Black Dolly*. London: Brockhampton Press

Keeping, C. (1967). *Shaun and the Cart-Horse*. London: Oxford University Press

Keeping, C. (1967). *Charley, Charlotte and the Golden Canary*. London: Oxford University Press

Keeping, C. (1970). *Joseph's Yard*. London: Oxford University Press

Lionni, L. (1960). *Inch by Inch*. New York: Astor-Honor Inc.

Lionni, L. (1967). *Frederick*. New York: Pantheon

Lionni, L. (1968). *Swimmy*. New York: Random House

Macaulay, D. (1990). *Black and White*. Boston: Houghton Mifflin

Marsden, J. (1998). *The Rabbits* (illustrated by S. Tan). Melbourne: Lothian

Oliver, N. (2006). *Home*. Malvern, South Australia: Omnibus Books

Sendak, M. (1963). *Where the Wild Things Are*. London: Harper Collins

Sendak, M. (1970). *In the Night Kitchen*. US: Harper & Row

Selznick, B. (2007). *The Invention of Hugo Cabret*. New York: Scholastic Press

Scieszka, J (1991). *The Frog Prince Continued* (illustrated by S. Johnson). Melbourne: Puffin

Silvey, C. (2007). *The World According to Warren* (illustrated by S. Martinez). Fremantle: Fremantle Press

Southall, I. (1969). *Sly Old Wardrobe* (illustrated by T. Greenwood). Sydney: Cheshire

Tan, S. (2006). *The Arrival*. Melbourne: Lothian

Tan, S. (2001). *The Red Tree*. Melbourne: Lothian

Van Allsburg, C. (1981). *Jumanji*. Boston: Houghton Mifflin

Wagner, J. (1974). *The Bunyip of Berkeley's Creek* (illustrated by R. Brooks). Melbourne: Penguin

Wagner, J. (1977). *John Brown, Rose and the Midnight Cat* (illustrated by R. Brooks). Melbourne: Penguin

Wildsmith, B. (1962). *ABC*. London: Oxford University Press

Wildsmith, B. (1967). *Birds*. London: Oxford University Press

Wildsmith, B. (1968). *Fishes*. London: Oxford University Press

Zemach, M. (1976). *It Could be Worse*. New York: Farrar, Straus and Giroux

3 Exploring children's responses to the postmodern picturebook *Who's Afraid of the Big Bad Book?*

Sylvia Pantaleo

During the past 20 years in the world of picturebooks there has been a pronounced trend towards a particular type of picturebook that many label as 'postmodern'. The picturebook *Who's Afraid of the Big Bad Book?* (Child, 2002) exhibits numerous postmodern characteristics as it blurs boundaries, subverts literary traditions and conventions and exhibits the use of several metafictive devices in both text and illustration. As well as discussing the playful nature of Child's picturebook, this chapter explores the responses and interpretations of eight, nine and ten year old children to *Who's Afraid of the Big Bad Book?* Child's text, like other postmodern picturebooks with metafictive devices, contributes to readers' aesthetic appreciation of literature, visual literacy competence, and literary and literacy understandings.

In the world of picturebooks there has been a pronounced trend during the past 20 years towards a particular type of picturebook that many label as postmodern. Several scholars (Coles & Hall, 2001; Lewis, 2001; Sipe & Pantaleo, 2008; Yearwood, 2002) have noted how the features of many contemporary picturebooks reflect characteristics of the broader historical, social, and cultural movement referred to as postmodernism. As discussed elsewhere (Pantaleo & Sipe, 2008), 'postmodernism' is a term used to describe the tendencies, changes and/or developments that have occurred in architecture, literature, art, music and philosophy during the last half of the twentieth century.

There is much agreement amongst those scholars and researchers who have identified particular features of postmodern picturebooks. Some of the common characteristics of postmodern picturebooks include multiple viewpoints, intertextuality, indeterminacy (i.e. indefinite or uncertain detail), eclecticism, collage, playfulness, parody and pastiche (i.e. art that imitates the style of other art; or a dramatic, musical or artistic piece composed of fragments or techniques of other works), as well as the breaking of genre boundaries, the abandonment of linear chronology, and the emphasis on the constructedness of texts (Pantaleo & Sipe, 2008). Some postmodern characteristics are more encompassing (e.g. metafiction, blurring) and could subsume some of the specific postmodern features (e.g. parody). However, it is difficult to identify with certainty the particular characteristics that are compulsory in order for a picturebook to be classified as postmodern. Furthermore, by doing so, one would create a binary situation (postmodern–not postmodern), which would be antithetical to the character of postmodernism itself. Therefore, given the multiplicity of postmodern characteristics, it seems logical to think of picture-books as located along a continuum of postmodernism (Pantaleo & Sipe, 2008).

Many individuals (Coles & Hall, 2001; Grieve, 1993; McCallum, 1996; Nikolajeva, 1998; Watson, 2004) have described postmodern fictions as inherently metafictive: that is, the use of particular devices or techniques undermine expectations or reveal 'the fictional nature of fiction' (Lewis, 2001: 94). According to Lewis, metafictive devices have become more prevalent in light of the postmodernist attack on authoritative order and unity. Waugh (1984: 2) described metafiction as 'fictional writing which self-consciously and systematically draws attention to its status as an artefact in order to pose questions about the relationship between fiction and reality.' Metafictive texts draw attention to their status as fiction and text through the use of a number of devices or techniques. In picturebooks, 'the specific strategies through which metafictions play with literary and cultural codes and conventions' (McCallum, 1996: 400) can be employed with both the verbal and the visual text.

During the past several years I have been exploring primary children's processes of reading and understanding postmodern picturebooks and examining how they use their knowledge of Radical Change characteristics (Dresang, 1999) and metafictive devices to create their own texts (Pantaleo, 2002, 2004, 2006, 2007a, 2007b, 2007c, 2008). Dresang (2005) has further developed her theory. Succinctly, Radical Change describes how the digital principles of 'connectivity, interactivity and access' (Dresang, 1999: 14) can be used to explain three types of fundamental changes taking place in contemporary children's and young adult literature.

- Type One Radical Change characteristics, **changing forms and formats**, incorporates one or more of the following characteristics: 'graphics in new forms and formats, words and pictures reaching new levels of synergy, nonlinear organization and format, nonsequential organization and format, multiple layers of meaning [and] interactive formats' (Dresang, 1999: 19).
- Type Two Radical Change characteristics, **changing perspectives**, refers to 'multiple perspectives, visual and verbal, previously unheard voices, [and] youth who speak for themselves' (Dresang: 24).
- Type Three Radical Change characteristics, **changing boundaries**, is where books include characteristics such as 'subjects previously hidden, settings previously overlooked, characters portrayed in new complex ways, new types of communities, [and] unresolved endings' (Dresang: 26).

Neither the three types of Radical Change nor the characteristics of each type are mutually exclusive. Several Type One Radical Change characteristics are parallel to some of the metafictive devices that have been identified in the research literature. Elsewhere (Pantaleo, 2006, 2008) I have described the interrelationships between postmodern fiction, metafiction and Radical Change characteristics.

Who's Afraid of the Big Bad Book? (hereafter referred to as *Who's Afraid?*) (2002), by Lauren Child, is one of the picturebooks that eight-, nine- and ten-year-old children have read and discussed during some of my research projects. The semiotic playground – that is, the visual and verbal sign systems – of *Who's Afraid?* blurs boundaries, subverts literary traditions and conventions and exhibits the use of several metafictive devices in both text and illustration. This chapter focuses on the ludic, playful nature of *Who's Afraid?* and explores children's responses to and interpretations of some of the metafictive devices in this postmodern picturebook.

A closer look at *Who's Afraid of the Big Bad Book?*

Readers familiar with Lauren Child's *Beware of the Storybook Wolves* (hereafter referred to as *Storybook Wolves*) (2000) will appreciate how she reverses certain plot elements in *Who's Afraid?* In *Storybook Wolves*, Big Wolf and Little Wolf exit Herb's bedtime storybook. With the assistance of characters from Herb's book of fairy tales, he avoids being consumed by these lupine foes; furthermore the wolf duo is both transformed and vanquished. In *Who's Afraid?*, Herb accidentally falls asleep reading his book of fairy tales and, when he awakens, he discovers that *he* has fallen into his book.

The peritextual elements (Pantaleo, 2003) of *Who's Afraid?* include inter-textual connections (Little Wolf, Miss Goldilocks, a green caterpillar who is the transformed Big Wolf from *Storybook Wolves*) and the illustrative framing device of mise-en-abyme, whereby a visual or verbal text is 'embedded within another text as its miniature replica' (Nikolajeva & Scott, 2001: 226). The verso (left-hand side of the page) of the first opening of the book is text and the recto (right-hand side of the page) is a full-page illustration of Herb reading his book and eating his supper. Herb's book is also open to the same first opening. Thus, readers are reading about Herb who is reading about himself. Readers learn that Herb loves storybooks and he reads his books everywhere, including when he eats … as a result, evidence of Herb's dietary history is found in his books in the form of bits of squashed food!

On the second opening, readers view Herb and his friend Ezzie, who is staying overnight, sleeping in their beds. Herb falls asleep with his head on a page in his book of fairy tales and when readers turn the page to the third opening, they see that Herb has woken up in the same double-page spread that he fell asleep on. He is awakened by a 'high-pitched shrieking noise' (unpaginated) and quickly realizes that he is in a bed that is huge and lumpy, unlike his own bed that is 'just right' (unpaginated). An ill-tempered Goldilocks addresses Herb in large capital letters and informs him that he is in HER story.

On the fourth opening (see Figure 24), Herb scampers down the stairs and

Figure 24 Fourth opening of *Who's Afraid of the Big Bad Book?* by Lauren Child

meets three mild-mannered bears that offer him some porridge. The petulant and self-centered Goldilocks reminds the polite bears that 'this story is called "Goldilocks and the Three Bears" not "The Little Show-off in Pyjamas has Breakfast!"' (unpaginated). Herb exits that story, escaping from Goldilocks, and on the fifth opening (see Figure 25) readers view Herb hurrying along a path through a forest. As he dashes along the trail, Herb warns two children not to nibble on a gingerbread house, overhears a woman in a tower complaining about the pain she is enduring as a man climbs her braid of yellow hair, and sees a feline dressed in black boots and a feathered hat. The little green caterpillar (aka Big Wolf) at the end of the pathway on the recto is overlooked by Herb as he hastens along the path.

The sixth opening of *Who's Afraid?* is a double gatefold with an enormous door in the centre of the double-page spread. When Herb opens the doors of the palace, and readers open the flaps of the gatefold (the seventh opening), Herb interrupts the royal ball. In the bottom right-hand corner of the far recto, the Little Wolf makes his guest appearance. On the extreme left-hand page of the gatefold, the typeface resembles a script that would be used for an invitation to a fancy party. The music ceases once the partygoers become aware of Herb; the King and Queen, who are loudly discussing the whereabouts of Prince Charming and the Queen's throne, are not impressed when they learn the identity of the intruder. The Queen chastises Herb for how he has defaced and changed her story. Herb has drawn moustaches, glasses and tattoos on various characters; added telephone stickers to every room; and removed the royal thrones and Prince Charming (for his mother's birthday card) from the book.

Fortuitously, on the next opening Herb's pencil case is lying on the ballroom floor and so he draws a new throne for the Queen. But when Herb attempts to erase her moustache, he inflicts pain on her Highness and she orders him to be seized. Using the scissors from his pencil case, Herb cuts a hole in the floor/page and escapes to the next story. However, on the subsequent opening he finds himself on the ceiling of a room because when he was 'younger' he tore out a few pages of Cinderella's story and glued them back in upside down. As Herb speaks with Cinderella's cruel stepmother and stepsisters on the next page, the telephone rings and it is the Queen informing the stepmother of Herb's identity. The infuriated stepmother wants revenge, but quick-thinking Herb draws a door on the wall and escapes to the next opening and to a very dusty kitchen ... with Cinderella (and some of Herb's crumbs).

Cinderella retells the events of her embarrassing experience: she went to the ball but the Prince was late, her dress transformed into rags, and her carriage turned back into a pumpkin. Herb guiltily explains the Prince's tardiness at the ball and states that he can locate the Prince if he can only get out of the book. Using one of Herb's phones, Cinderella calls her Fairy Godmother (the same character who assisted Herb in *Storybook Wolves*). When the Fairy Godmother materializes on the next page she reluctantly, after reprimanding Herb for defacing the book, agrees to rescue him. However, on the next opening the kitchen door flies opens and an angry Goldilocks and Cinderella's stepmother

He ran past two children nibbling a house made of ginger biscuits. 'I wouldn't do that' called Herb.

'**Oh, get lost!**' shouted the children.

He ran past a man climbing up what looked like a long plait of hair.

'*Ouch!*' cried the voice belonging to the hair.

And when he saw a cat wearing a feathered hat and high-heeled boots,

Herb ran a bit faster.

Herb ran all the way through the forest...

Figure 25 Fifth opening of *Who's Afraid of the Big Bad Book?*

appear searching for Herb, the perpetrator of the fairy-tale chaos. Following the Fairy Godmother's advice, Herb ascends the text in order to escape his pursuers. On the subsequent opening, the piercing scream of Goldilocks shakes the book so forcefully that it falls off Herb's bed and he lands on his bedroom floor.

Ezzie is awakened by Herb's unceremonious homecoming and, after Herb explains his textual excursions, he and Ezzie spend the night restoring the book to its original state, except for a few minor disfigurements. Herb draws a padlock on the front door of the Three Bears' cottage and Ezzie glues a mousy brown wig on Goldilocks. The verso of the last opening depicts an infuriated, wig-wearing girl attempting a break and enter!

Contextualizing the research: working with the children

As stated previously, *Who's Afraid?* was one of the postmodern picturebooks used for my research. As both researcher and teacher in these studies, I worked with eight- to ten-year-old children and the classroom teachers for approximately 80 minutes each morning for nine weeks. I began the projects by talking about the notion of 'response' and used a variety of activities to demonstrate how humans are constantly responding to multiple stimuli in their lives, and that there are various kinds of responses and ways to respond. Teacher modelling, as well as other various instructional activities, was used to develop the children's understanding of the qualities of a 'good' aesthetic response. Time was also devoted to talking about small group discussions, with the goal of developing a communal understanding of the expectations, etiquette and protocol of 'successful' discussions.

Willy the Dreamer (Browne, 1997) was used to introduce the children to the semiotic notion of intertextuality and to underscore the importance of thoughtfully viewing the illustrations in picturebooks. The sequence of other picturebooks used during the research reflected an increasing complexity of the use of literary and illustrative devices (see Pantaleo, 2009, 2008, 2007a, 2007b, 2007c, 2006). The children read each picturebook independently, completed at least one written response, and participated in discussions in small groups that were peer-led and mixed-gender. Following the audio-recorded small-group discussions, the Radical Change or metafictive devices were explicitly taught and/or reviewed during various whole-class activities that involved the children discussing and examining the picturebooks. During each research project, the children read *Storybook Wolves* before reading *Who's Afraid?*, but most classes did not write a response to the former text nor discuss it formally in either a small-group or whole-class context.

Throughout the studies the children were also encouraged to make connections between the devices or characteristics that they were learning about in the literature and the existence of these features in other print and digital texts. As well as the required texts, I brought other postmodern picturebooks into the classrooms for the children to peruse. Finally, as the culminating activity of each research project, the children created their own print texts that incorporated the characteristics and devices that they had learned about during the studies.

Responding to the metafictive in *Who's Afraid of the Big Bad Book?*

I believe that Child's picturebook features many metafictive devices, including the following:

a) multistranded narratives, that is, 'two or more interconnected narrative strands differentiated by shifts in temporal and spatial relationships, and/or shifts in narrative point of view' (McCallum, 1996: 406)
b) stories within stories
c) disruptions of traditional time and space relationships in stories/narratives
d) nonlinear plots including narrative discontinuities
e) intertextuality
f) parodic appropriations
g) typographic experimentation
h) mixing of genres, language styles or speech styles, and/or ways of telling stories
i) pastiche of illustrative styles
j) new and/or unusual layout and/or design
k) illustrative framing, including mise-en-abyme
l) indeterminacy.

The data analysed for this chapter were responses written by 78 eight-, nine- and ten-year-old children. Spelling has been conventionalized in the children's responses and all names are pseudonyms. Content analysis of the children's work revealed that the children wrote about more than one central idea, as is evident in the responses to *Who's Afraid* written by Jerry and Kathleen.

> It was like a sequel to *Beware of the Storybook Wolves* but instead of characters coming out of the story, Herb went in. The illustrations were a bit different this time, there were more photographs and a gatefold in it and a squashed pea and a hole and an upside-down page and a missing prince. As well as the worm and the Little Bad Big Wolf there were lots of intertextual connections. This time Herb interacted with the words like in *The Three Pigs* [Wiesner, 2001] and there were some mise-en-abyme pictures and some illustrated rips too on the end pages. The fonts changed too like when Goldilocks screamed so loudly that the book fell off the bed, the words went in a spiral.
>
> Jerry, aged ten

> This book had Herb in it like the other book. It also had characters from the other book with Herb. In this book I spotted the wolf from *Beware of the Storybook Wolves* at some parts such as the ball wearing his dress. I also

spotted the caterpillar like in the forest when Herb was running. The book had a lot of pastiche used like the dresses had real fabric and the food was real food. There was also typographic experimentation like on the second last page when Goldilocks screamed. I think that this book was funny because Herb was going in the story and talking to the characters. Also I thought it was funny because they were all looking for Prince Charming and Herb had cut him out and glued him on his mom's birthday card. I also noticed mise-en-abyme because Herb had the book that we were reading and then Herb went into the book.

Kathleen, aged nine

Data analysis revealed that although the children wrote about several metafictive devices in their responses to *Who's Afraid?*, the following six devices were written about most frequently:

1. intertextuality
2. pastiche of illustrative styles
3. parodic appropriations
4. new and/or unusual layout and/or design
5. typographic experimentation
6. mise-en-abyme.

1. Intertextuality

Approximately two-thirds of the 78 children identified intertextual connections in *Who's Afraid?* Allen (2000: 2) states that 'intertextuality is one of the most commonly used and misused terms in contemporary critical vocabulary'. In my work, I use the term 'intertextuality' to refer to connections between texts. I embrace an expanded notion of 'text' and consider textual and/or illustrative connections to other kinds of texts, such as books, movies, characters, cultural knowledge and artifacts, television, video, works of art, advertisements and 'sayings'. Some children wrote about general connections to fairy tales, such as 'Herb went into the book and wanted to find a way out so he travelled through a lot of fairy tales' (Mark, aged ten); whilst others identified specific characters from fairy tales, such as Goldilocks, the Three Bears, Rapunzel, Hansel and Gretel, and Puss in Boots. Many children commented on the intertextual connections to characters from *Storybook Wolves* (Cinderella, the Fairy Godmother, Big Wolf/green caterpillar, and Little Wolf).

Shecara, aged ten, commented:

I found tons of connections between *Beware of the Storybook Wolves* and *Who's Afraid of the Big Bad Book?* For instance the Fairy Godmother and the wicked witch were in both stories, the wolf was also in the dress that the Fairy Godmother put him in the first book. I am really interested in the real pictures and thinking about using them in my own story. I found TONS of intertextual connections with all of the fairy tales such as Puss in Boots, Hansel and Gretel and Rapunzel.

Nolan, also aged ten, said:

> I really liked how in the pictures she [Child] made some of it realistic and the rest cartoony. It was also neat when Herb was in the evil stepmother's house, his words were one side up and the evil Stepmother's words were the other side up. When he was in the ballroom the stuff that he drew on the people looked like pen but in the end it says they rubbed it off with erasers. When Herb is running through the forest did you notice the Big Bad Wolf as a caterpillar? It said on the back that there was a special guest appearance from the Little Bad Wolf and I saw him in the ballroom. On the dedication page there is sticker that is stuck on Baby Bear. I liked this story more than *Beware of the Storybook Wolves* because there were more characters from other fairy tales and how they kind of made fun of them and they had lots more intertextual connections.

2. Pastiche of illustrative styles

Child's pastiche of illustrative style complements and symbolically reflects the fragmented and intertextual nature of the multiple tales in the book. The collage artwork can be described as synergistic in nature, due to the combined effects of the medium used to create the illustrations. Child's pastiche of illustrative style includes pictures and photographs cut and combined; colourful fabric; ink drawings; textured, watercolour and patterned paper; and concrete objects such as bits of food, sequins and stickers. Over half of the 78 children commented on Child's exuberant illustrative style in *Who's Afraid?* In Sydney's response below she identifies several different media used in the illustrations.

> I think this book is sort of funny because the words go up and down and around. I noticed what looked like photos of sequins, clay and feathers. When I was finished reading the book I felt dizzy. It was probably from the upside-down text. I saw the wolf from *Beware of the Storybook Wolves*. I also like how the personality of the characters changed, such as Cinderella's stepsisters, Goldilocks, and the Fairy Godmother. I like it because unlike other stories, when the characters act the same way in this book they're like real people. I also saw what looks like a photo of grass taped on. I saw lots of hidden things, for example the caterpillar and sequins. This book is excellent because of the all the detail.
>
> Sydney, aged nine

3. Parodic appropriations

Approximately one-third of the children identified parodic appropriations in the picturebook. Although not all intertextual connections are parodies, all parodic appropriations are intertextual in nature. According to Hutcheon (1985), parody is 'repetition with difference' (p.32), 'a bitextual synthesis' that 'incorporates the old into the new' (p.33). Lukens (1999: 224) writes that 'a parody reminds us of something known, then gives fresh pleasure by duplicating form that contrasts to new and humorous meaning.' Although writers, illustrators and artists may create texts that are intertextual and parodic in nature, it is the reader and/or viewer who interprets the texts; further, interpretation of text as intertextual or parodied is dependent on recognition or knowledge of the original text (Pantaleo, 2004). Nearly all of the children who wrote about parodic appropriations in *Who's Afraid?* commented on the transformed personality of one particular character: Goldilocks. Mason and Sabrina both made insightful comments:

> The book I just read was a good book. I never thought that Goldilocks was so whiny. It's very creative when you have to read upside down in this book. I didn't really like the Fairy Godmother. She was pretty strict and it was a parody of how they switched Goldilocks around and the Fairy Godmother and the other characters. In this book I like the happily-ever-after part because Herb gets away and Goldilocks has to wear a wig and gets locked out of the Bears' house.
>
> Mason, aged nine

> When I read this book I thought it was funny because the fairy-tale characters had different personalities than they normally would have. For example, Goldilocks was all bossy and stubborn and the Fairy Godmother was a little strict. The book was also funny because Herb drew a moustache on the queen in ballpoint pen and he flipped a page upside down. The text sometimes made me dizzy because it went round and round and up and down. I like Lauren Child's books because they're always funny. This book was like *Beware of the Storybook Wolves* because of the characters diving in and out of their stories.
>
> Sabrina, aged eight

4. New and/or unusual layout and/or design

Over one-third of the children commented on Child's use of unusual layout in *Who's Afraid?* A few of the features that can be described as unusual with respect to layout include the upside-down text/pages, the hole on the recto of one page in the book (see Figure 26), and the double gatefold. Many children simultaneously experienced puzzlement and amusement when they reached the upside-down pages.

Figure 26 Child uses unusual layout features in *Who's Afraid of the Big Bad Book*, such as a hole in one page

Once again I loved the illustrations in this book. I never get tired of their collage-like appearance. I loved how the author/illustrator made the words part of the picture. For example when the Fairy Godmother commanded Herb to climb the stairs and it showed the type all disordered to make steps – it was very imaginative and different. I thought it was very helpful how it showed the guest appearance, The Little Bad Wolf, in his (so-called) dress at the ball. The endpapers were very creative because it looks like Herb had to cut his way into the book. I probably enjoyed this book better than her other book because I think she used a little more imagination in this book than the other one. I thought Goldilocks had the spirit of a spoiled, normal little girl. One of my favourite pages was the dedication page because I think that the pictures told a silent story.

Nicky, aged ten

5. Typographic experimentation

One-third of the children included comments about some aspect of typographic experimentation in their responses. They noted how Child varies the appearance, placement and orientation of the typed matter in the book to complement and communicate meaning about events and characters. For example, 'fairy tales' is written in a medieval-like script on the second opening. When Goldilocks initially speaks to Herb, she speaks in upper-case letters, some of her phrases are bolder than others for emphasis, and her text is arranged in five horizontal lines, resembling a megaphone. Several children wrote about how the text on the recto of the twelfth opening is arranged like a ladder so that Herb can escape from Cinderella's stepmother and Goldilocks (see Figure 27). Ethan and Hunter both wrote detailed responses to this part of the book:

This book is one of my favourites we have read because of all of the intertextual connections such as the Little Bad Wolf. I was constantly thinking about the connections to the other book (*Beware of the Storybook Wolves*) and to fairy tales. I do not think that you could read and understand this book without reading the other book. There were a lot of little funny things about it like the squished peas. The book had different text fonts to describe the mood or express the meaning of what he/she was saying/doing. When Herb went to the ball the text was that of royalty and represented the class element. Up to the point where he enters the ball the text is a bold face to represent normality with the touch of change. And from the ball on the text represents mayhem and evil for the evil stepmother. All in all, the book is very funny and emotional. It was a great book.

Ethan, aged ten

I thought the book *Who's Afraid of the Big Bad Book?* was really funny and good. I thought it was really funny when the prince got cut out of the book and Herb had to tape him back in. I also thought that it was funny

'What shall I do?' flustered Herb.

'Quick! Climb up the text!' said the fairy godmother.

Herb grabbed hold of the letters and scrabbled up letters the sentences. Some of the words were a bit weak and the whole lot started to wobble.

At that moment the door flew open.

'HE'S IN YOUR KITCHEN, LOOKING FOR MORE FOOD!'

It was the unmistakably ear-piercing voice of Goldilocks. Right behind her was the wicked stepmother and she was not in a pretty mood, having snagged her stockings climbing a ladder out of the upside-down room.

Figure 27 One example of typographic experimentation in *Who's Afraid of the Big Bad Book?*

when the Queen had a moustache. I noticed that there was a lot of pastiche in the book. For example she [Child] used photographs, collage and her own drawings. I also noticed that there was some mise-en-abyme in the book. I also noticed that when the Three Bears are talking they all had their own font. The Papa Bear had a really BIG sized font and the Mother Bear had a medium-sized font and the Baby Bear had a small-sized font, which is an example of typographic experimentation.

Hunter, aged eight

6. Mise-en-abyme

As described earlier, the cover of *Who's Afraid* contains an example of mise-en-abyme. In art, mise-en-abyme is a technique in which an image contains a miniature replica of itself. Mise-en-abyme is also a type of narrative framing device.

One-quarter of the children wrote about Child's use of visual mise-en-abyme in the book. When they were introduced to the term, concrete examples such as Russian stacking dolls assisted the children in understanding the replication process of mise-en-abyme. In the bottom right-hand corner of the front dust jacket and cover (which are identical) of *Who's Afraid?*, Herb is reading a book, holding it open so that readers can view both the front and back cover. Readers see that they and Herb are reading the same book and several children made comments:

> I noticed that on the front cover it was mise-en-abyme because we were looking at the same book that Herb was looking at. I thought it was humourous when on the first page it's mise-en-abyme but it didn't have the little boy because he was not in the book yet. I thought some of the characters were the same as the ones in *Beware of the Storybook Wolves*. For example the Fairy Godmother and Little Bad Wolf (he didn't find his prince).

Monique, aged eight

> This is definitely my favourite book so far! I think it's great how she [Child] uses real things in the book, like the wigs are hair cut out from magazines. I love how she cut a hole in the book and had the two pages upside down. She uses mise-en-abyme three times in the book. On the front cover, on the page with the monsters (basically) and the page with the Three Bears' house (the book Herb is reading is on the bed). And I think that's really cool! I think it's neat how the stories changed because of the things Herb had done. Also I noticed an intertextual connection. On the page when he's running through the forest there is a small green caterpillar, like the Big Bad Wolf from the other story *Beware of the Storybook Wolves*. I really enjoyed this book.

Katherine, aged ten

Discussion

Nearly half of the children wrote about aspects that reflected how Herb's actions, both outside (e.g. adding moustaches, tattoos, wigs and phone stickers; removing the Queen's throne and Prince Charming; gluing in pages upside down) and inside the fairy-tale book, contributed to the process of creating the story. Herb's adventures in the fairy-tale book constantly remind readers of the fictional nature of the story, of 'the artifice of what they are reading' (Georgakopoulou, 1991: 6). Like Mackey (1990), Georgakopoulou (1991: 9) writes that metafictive texts require simultaneous reader involvement and 'critical detachment'. As a reader of his fairy-tale book, Herb definitely became involved and took on a co-author role as he physically changed the text and illustrations in the book. When Herb fell into the book, he again participated in constructing the story as he travelled through the fairy tales. However, his involvement in the diegetic – the fictional world in which the events and situations that are narrated occur – taught him lessons about the importance of critical detachment.

According to McCallum, metafictive devices contribute to the aesthetic reading experience, as 'underlying much metafiction for children is a heightened sense of the status of fiction as an elaborate form of play, that is a game with linguistic and narrative codes and conventions' (1996, p.398). As author and illustrator, Lauren Child engaged in multiple forms of play when she created *Who's Afraid?* – she played with intertextual connections, parodic appropriations, synergistic stories, art styles, typography, types of discourse, jokes, and picturebook form and format. The children's responses communicated their understanding and appreciation of Child's playful use of metafictive devices. Indeed, Herb's transformations of his fairy-tale book, his textual excursions in the book, Child's pastiche style of illustration, as well as the overall book design and layout, contribute to the game-playing with codes and conventions in *Who's Afraid?*

As well as being humorous, *Who's Afraid?* teaches many lessons about illustrative and literary elements and devices, about how literature works, and about book elements and design. The range of semiotic systems conveying meaning in both the visual and verbal text contributes to the game-playing and ludic nature of the book. Postmodern picturebooks such as *Who's Afraid?* extend thought and discussion about this sophisticated and flexible art form. Child's text, like other postmodern picturebooks with metafictive devices, contributes to readers' aesthetic appreciation of literature; visual literacy competence; and literary and literacy understandings, including the development of a repertoire of narrative structures and the facilitation of higher-level thinking skills. The children's responses in this chapter also reveal their development of a metalanguage to discuss the metafictive devices. The children acquired a discourse, a language to talk about the postmodern picturebooks, as a result of their engagements with particular kinds of texts in a particular context.

References

Allen, G. (2000). *Intertextuality*. New York: Routledge

Coles, M. & Hall, C. (2001). 'Breaking the line: New literacies, postmodernism and the teaching of printed texts'. *Reading: Literacy and Language* 35(3): 111–14

Dresang, E. (1999). *Radical Change: Books for Youth in a Digital Age*. New York: The H. W. Wilson Company

Dresang, E. (2005). 'Radical change' in Fisher, K., Erdelez, S. & McKenzie, L. (eds) *Theories of Information Behavior: A Researcher's Guide*. Medford, New Jersey: Information Today, pp.298–302

Georgakopoulou, A. (1991). 'Discursive aspects of metafiction: A neo-oral aura?' *Edinburgh Working Papers in Linguistics* 2: 1–13

Grieve, A. (1993). 'Postmodernism in picture books'. *Papers: Explorations into Children's Literature* 4(3): 15–25

Hutcheon, L. (1985). *A Theory of Parody: The Teachings of Twentieth-Century Art Forms*. London: Methuen

Lewis, D. (2001). *Reading Contemporary Picture Books: Picturing Text*. New York: RoutledgeFalmer

Lukens, R. (1999). *A Critical Handbook of Children's Literature* 6th edition. New York: Addison-Wesley Educational Publishers Inc.

Mackey, M. (1990). 'Metafiction for beginners: Allan Ahlberg's *Ten in a bed*'. *Children's Literature in Education* 21(3): 179–87

McCallum, R. (1996). 'Metafictions and experimental work' in Hunt, P. (ed.) *International Companion Encyclopedia of Children's Literature*. New York: Routledge, pp.397–409

Nikolajeva, M. (1998). 'Exit children's literature?' *The Lion and the Unicorn* 22(2): 221–36

Nikolajeva, M. & Scott, C. (2001). *How Picturebooks Work*. New York: Garland Publishing

Pantaleo, S. (2002). 'Grade 1 children meet David Wiesner's three pigs'. *Journal of Children's Literature* 28(2): 72–84

Pantaleo, S. (2003). '"Godzilla lives in New York": Grade 1 children and the peritextual features of picture books'. *Journal of Children's Literature* 29(2): 66–77

Pantaleo, S. (2004). 'Exploring Grade 1 children's textual connections'. *Journal of Research in Childhood Education* 18(3): 211–25

Pantaleo, S. (2006). 'Readers and writers as intertexts: Exploring the intertextualities in student writing'. *Australian Journal of Language and Literacy* 29(2): 163–81

Pantaleo, S. (2007a). 'Writing texts with Radical Change characteristics'. *Literacy* 41(1): 16–25

Pantaleo, S. (2007b). '"Everything comes from seeing things": Narrative and illustrative play in Black and White'. *Children's Literature in Education: An International Quarterly* 38(1): 45–58

Pantaleo, S. (2007c). 'Exploring the metafictive in elementary children's writing'. *Changing English* 14(1): 61–76

Pantaleo, S. (2008). *Exploring Student Response to Contemporary Picturebooks*. Toronto: University of Toronto Press

Pantaleo, S. (2009). 'An ecological perspective on the socially embedded nature of reading and writing'. *Journal of Early Childhood Literacy*

Pantaleo, S. & Sipe, L. (2008). 'Postmodernism and picturebooks' in Sipe, L. & Pantaleo, S. (eds) *Postmodern Picturebooks: Play, Parody, and Self-Referentiality*. New York: Routledge, pp.1–8

Sipe, L. & Pantaleo, S. (2008). Postmodern Picturebooks: *Play, Parody, and Self-Referentiality*. New York: Routledge.

Watson, K. (2004). 'The postmodern picture book in the secondary classroom'. *English in Australia* 140: 55–7

Waugh, P. (1984). Metafiction: *The Theory and Practice of Self-Conscious Fiction*. New York: Methuen

Yearwood, S. (2002). 'Popular postmodernism for young adult readers: *Walk Two Moons, Holes* and *Monster*'. *The ALAN Review* 29(3): 50–3

Children's literature

Browne, A. (1997). *Willy the Dreamer*. Cambridge, Massachusetts: Candlewick Press

Child, L. (2000). *Beware of the Storybook Wolves*. New York: Scholastic Inc.

Child, L. (2002). *Who's Afraid of the Big Bad Book?* New York: Hyperion Books for Children

Wiesner, D. (2001). *The Three Pigs*. New York: Clarion Books

4 Picturebook endpapers

Resources for literary and aesthetic interpretation

Lawrence Sipe and Caroline McGuire

This chapter focuses on one element of picturebooks that is often over-looked – the front and back endpapers. Although all hardcover books have endpapers, in picturebooks they assume a special semiotic signifi-cance, as part of the integrated design of the entire book. Illustrators, editors and designers use endpapers in various ways, including helping children predict what will happen in the book, introducing major characters or events, or gesturing toward the major theme of the story. A typology is presented: a picturebook may have (1) front and back endpapers that are the same plain colour, (2) front and back endpapers that are two different colours, (3) endpapers with an illustration that is the same on the front and back endpapers, and (4) endpapers with illus-trations that are different on the front and back endpapers. Numerous examples of these four patterns are discussed, along with children's interpretations of them.

In addition to illustrations for every page of text, contemporary picturebooks have other features and conventions that have evolved to add to the richness of the form. In the field of children's publishing, illustrators, authors, editors, and book designers have paid special attention to the ways in which the front and back covers, dust jacket, endpapers, half-title and title pages, and dedi-cation page all work together with the text and accompanying illustrations to produce a unified effect. These features are often referred to as the 'peritext' of the picturebook, a term first used by Gerard Genette (1987) to describe all the physical features within a book aside from the author's words.[1] Although all books obviously have some of these features, such as covers and a title page, in picturebooks all peritextual features are especially planned and designed so that there is an aesthetic coherence to the entire book (Higonnet, 1990).

---

1 Following Genette's (1997) terminology, *peritextual* components include conventions contained *within* the book, whereas the *epitext* is found *outside* the book in such forms as authorial corre-spondence and book reviews. *Paratext* refers to both peritext and epitext: 'In other words, for those who are keen on formulae, *paratext = peritext + epitext.*' (Genette, 1997: 5).

In this chapter, we explore one of the important peritextual features of picturebooks – the endpapers. Endpapers (sometimes called endpages) are pages glued inside the front and back covers of a book, and are thus the first parts of the interior of the book to be seen when the book is opened, as well as the last to be seen after the story has been read and the book is about to be closed. After describing the nature and history of endpapers, we discuss the various types of endpapers and their different purposes and semiotic significance. In presenting this typology, we use examples from many contemporary picturebooks. We also draw on Sipe's (1998, 2000; Sipe & Bauer, 2001) research for numerous vignettes of four- to eight-year-old children's responses to the endpapers as they hear picture storybooks read aloud and talk about the peritextual features of these books with their teachers.

The nature of the bookbinding process requires that all hardcover books have endpapers. In the history of European bookbinding, the first decorated endpapers seem to have been produced by the technique of marbling, with marbled endpapers becoming a standard feature of high-quality bindings by the middle of the seventeenth century (Wolfe, 1990). The first generally recognized picturebooks for children, the 'toy books' of Walter Crane and Randolph Caldecott created in the last half of the nineteenth century, did not include endpapers as they were first produced with soft board covers. It was not until the beginning of the twentieth century that children's picturebooks began commonly to include illustrated endpapers as a part of the total book design and construction. The endpapers serve to connect the book's cover to the text block, providing protection to the first and last printed leaves (Roberts & Etherington, 1982). Both front and back endpapers consist of a leaf that adheres to the inside of the cover, known as the *pastedown*, and a facing leaf (not pasted to the cover), known as the *flyleaf*. At the front of the book, the pastedown is on the left and the flyleaf is on the right, whereas at the back of the book, the flyleaf is on the left and the pastedown is on the right.

Although the endpapers, as part of the peritext, mediate the reader's transition to the interior of the book, neither they nor the peritext more generally have been considered in depth by scholars of contemporary picturebooks (Nikolajeva & Scott, 2001).[2] Empirical research on children's responses to peritextual features of picturebooks is likewise sparse, the single exception being the work of Pantaleo (2003), who examined the ways in which a class of first-grade children discussed the peritextual features of nine picturebooks. The children learned peritextual terminology (such as 'endpapers' and 'dustjacket'), and used peritextual elements to predict and to confirm their interpretations

---

2 In their standard texts about contemporary picturebooks, Stewig (1995) and Nikolajeva and Scott (2001) each devote a few pages to a discussion of endpapers within their treatments of peritextual elements. Although Kiefer (1995) mentions endpapers at several points in her text, she does not discuss them in any extended way. Neither Nodelman (1988) nor Lewis (2001) mention endpapers except in passing.

about characters, plot, setting and tone of the books. Their talk about peritextual features was found to contribute significantly to their 'aesthetic appreciation and cognitive and literary understandings of the books'.

Acting as a liminal, 'on the threshold' type of space (Turner, 1969), the endpapers constitute a 'space between', where the reader is neither outside nor yet inside the story simply because the 'real' story has not yet started. Genette (1997: 1) remarks that 'More than a boundary or a sealed border, the paratext is, rather, a threshold, or – a word Borges used apropos of a preface – a 'vestibule' that offers the world at large the possibility of either stepping inside or turning back.' Derrida (1981: 35) suggests that because of the peritext 'the text is no longer the snug airtight inside of an interiority or an identity-to-itself'. As a 'space between', the peritext is uniquely placed to draw attention to the materiality of the book and to provide a playful arena for the production of textual meaning (Higonnet, 1990), as well as presenting a rich orienting experience to the reader. Endpapers, in particular, mark a movement from the public space of the cover to the private world of the book, much as stage curtains rising and falling mark the entrance into and exit from a drama. During the reading of *The Three Little Pigs* (Marshall, 1989), for example, the teacher showed and read the front cover, which depicts the three pigs on a stage, flanked by brick-red curtains. She then opened the book and silently showed the endpapers, which have no decoration other than their brick-red colour. Brad, a first-grader, commented:

> Well, it's like a curtain, like on the front cover, the curtain's open, the curtain's red, and um, then the endpages, they're red, too, and it's like, like the curtain's closed, and you're gettin' ready for the play to start.

Brad had not been taught this idea of the endpapers as stage curtains; he constructed the idea himself. Clearly, he did not take these plain endpapers for granted. He used his knowledge of what a theatre looks like before a play begins, and linked this to the two visual experiences of the front cover and the endpapers. Although Brad's teacher had emphasized the importance of the endpapers, in our experience many teachers pay only cursory attention to certain peritextual features, namely the front cover or dust jacket and the title page, skipping over the endpapers entirely. It is our hope that, by discussing the variety of ways in which endpapers function in picturebooks, their importance will become evident to teachers, who will then invite their students to engage in meaningful interpretation of this important peritextual element.

Typology of picturebook endpapers

Like the picturebooks of which they are an integral part, endpapers represent a great variety of visual forms and perform a number of different functions. We have attempted to represent this rich diversity of form and function by constructing an orderly typology: a classification that presents, however artificially, a way of thinking about endpapers and their contribution to the aesthetics of the picturebook. This typology grew naturally from our examination of hundreds of contemporary picturebooks. We limited our study to picture storybooks, excluding informational texts in picturebook form, and created a set of categories that seemed to comprehensively describe all of the examples we encountered. At the broadest level, we noted that when we open a picturebook, we may see either endpapers of a plain colour or endpapers that contain some type of illustration. If we then compare the front endpapers to those at the back of the book, we may note that they are either identical or somehow different. Thus, there are two main dimensions of our typology – whether the endpapers are illustrated or unillustrated, or whether the front and back endpapers are identical or dissimilar. Within the four categories delineated by these two dimensions, we will further articulate the various roles that endpapers can play in the construction of meaning from picturebooks.

1. Unillustrated, identical front and back endpapers

Although we may tend to pay little attention to plain-coloured endpapers, their inclusion in picturebooks is both intentional and considered, and it is worth contemplating their semiotic significance. In some cases, the colour of the endpapers reflects the dominant colours in the palette of the illustrations that follow, contributing to the visual aesthetic coherence of the book as a whole. Norton Juster's Caldecott Medal-winning *The Hello, Goodbye Window* (2005), illustrated by Chris Raschka, exemplifies this attention to a close colour match. Raschka (2006) has explained that, in order to achieve the precise shade of ochre for the plain-coloured endpapers in this book, he produced several sample colour swatches using the mixed media he had employed in the illustrations for the story. In this case, the pleasantly bright colour of the endpapers prepares readers for the cheerful and upbeat story that follows.

Another example of consistency in the picturebook palette is Christopher Myers' (2007) intriguing interpretation of the text of Lewis Carroll's classic nonsense poem *Jabberwocky*, where the Jabberwock is represented by a gigantic basketball player with enormous hands, and the hero is a much younger and smaller player. In this provocative incarnation, the neon-green endpapers are consistent with many of the letters in the title on the front cover, coloured backgrounds for the story text, and elements of the story illustrations. The story and illustrations are rendered in an exuberant neon palette of saturated hues, like the green of the endpapers. Thus, plain-coloured endpapers are often used to indicate the overall mood or tone of the story to follow, as in *Saint George and the Dragon* (Margaret Hodges, 1984), where the endpapers are a bluish-grey, indicating the serious tone of the story as a whole, as well as suggesting a twilight atmosphere. In the two openings before the text begins (the title page and the dedication page), the sun is just beginning to rise; thus the endpapers provide an atmospheric prelude in both a literal and figurative sense. The endpapers may also set the tone in contrast to the cover of the book.

In *Faithful Elephants* (Yukio Tsuchiya, 1988), the dark maroon colour of the endpapers stands in stark opposition to the light, airy, delicate pastel tints of the front cover, signalling the sombre story of wartime tragedy to come.

In addition to setting the tone or mood of a story, plain-coloured endpapers can also refer more specifically to elements of the story, such as particular characters or events in the plot. Such an interpretation was made by four- and five-year-olds responding to *In the Rainfield: Who is the Greatest?* (Isaac Olaleye, 2000), an African folk tale in which human figures representing Wind, Fire and Rain hold a contest for supremacy. On the front cover and throughout the story, Wind and Fire are represented as men, whereas Rain is represented as a woman with lavender skin. At the end of the story, when Rain triumphs, the children discussed the significance of the lavender endpapers, with Deena suggesting that 'Maybe 'cause the lady [the illustrator, Ann Grifalconi] liked the colour purple and she put in on there because Rain was the best girl.' Here, Deena connects Rain's victory to the prominent place given to the lavender colour in the endpapers. She understands that the endpapers gesture toward the answer to the question posed in the title of the book.

The plain black endpapers in Chris Van Allsburg's *Bad Day at Riverbend* (1995) serve a more complex purpose related to the metafictive plot of the story. The tale concerns the citizens of a small Western town who are suddenly threatened by the appearance of 'shiny, greasy slime'. The illustrations of the town are executed in black outline style, as in a colouring book, and the slime, in various scribbled colours, covers parts of the townspeople, their animals and the landscape. As a posse rides out to find the cause of this affliction, the text of the story states that 'they were frozen in the bright light that suddenly filled the sky'. In the accompanying illustration, a realistically drawn hand appears from the right, holding a red crayon. Here we recognize the source of the slime and the existence of two levels within the story world: the colouring-book world of the townspeople and the artistic play of a fictional child. The story concludes with the child heading outside to play, having closed the colouring book. We understand the closing text, 'And then the light went out', in relation to the facing black flyleaf. In other words, the endpapers, in combination with the text, invite the reader to conclude that the bright light is connected to the child's opening of the colouring book and the darkness to her closure of it. The black endpapers give readers the same experience of 'lights out' as the townspeople of Riverbend, just as readers prepare to close the picturebook themselves. Thus the endpapers mediate our experience of the metafictive element in the story.

In a much lighter vein, plain-coloured endpapers may joke playfully with the reader. In David Macaulay's *Black and White* (1990), the reader first encounters the words 'Black and White' on the cover, and then opens the book to see bright red endpapers. The endpapers in this case seem to make a visual pun, making us think of the old riddle about what is 'black and white and red all over', and, indeed, newspapers have a part to play in this postmodern tour de force (Kiefer, 1995).

It is important to consider the significance of the various types of paper that are utilized as endpapers. For example, in David Wiesner's *Sector 7* (1999), the story of a voyage among clouds, the mottled beige parchment-paper endpapers suggest the texture of a cloud. Wiesner's *Flotsam* (2006) contains endpapers suggesting the colour and texture of sand, appropriate for a story that takes place on the seashore. In a similar way, the rough, almost corrugated brown paper used for the endpapers in Maurice Sendak's *We Are All in the Dumps with Jack and Guy* (1993) evokes the cardboard shelters used by the homeless children in the book. Another story about homelessness, Libby Hathorn's *Way Home* (1994), employs endpapers that resemble crumpled paper, foreshadowing both the theme of the story and the way in which street people are 'thrown away' by society. Another type of paper that is occasionally used for contemporary picturebooks, marbled paper, was extensively used during the Victorian era (Wolfe, 1990). This element of the historical tradition of bookmaking is referenced by the endpapers in *The Book that Jack Wrote* (Jon Scieszka, 1994), which plays with and subverts such conventions. Christopher Myers' *Wings* (2000), a contemporary story that draws on the classical myth of Icarus, contains blue-and-white marbled endpapers, both as a reference to its classical origins and as a means of representing the feathers of the wings so central to the story. As one eight-year-old observed of these endpapers, 'It looks like some kind of antique paper.'

2. Unillustrated, dissimilar front and back endpapers

When examining the endpapers of a picturebook, it is a good idea to attend to both the front and back endpapers, for their meaning may depend on the contrast they present. In Karen Hesse's *Come On, Rain!* (1999), for example, the vibrant red of the front endpapers suggests the scorching heat and aridity of the city during the dog days of summer. The story is centrally about the relief a rain shower brings to four pairs of mothers and daughters, who emerge from their stifling apartments to dance among the raindrops. The cool blue back endpapers provide a fitting visual closure to the story. The same transition from red to blue endpapers is used to quite different purpose in Doreen Cronin's *Duck for President* (2004). Duck's rising ambitions lead him from a successful campaign to depose Farmer Brown to a gubernatorial victory, and finally to his election to the highest office in the United States. The red front endpapers and blue back endpapers are appropriate for this American political story, and also serve to represent Duck's journey from the red barn to the White House. Red is used predominantly in the first part of the story, while the Oval Office in Washington is rendered in blue, carefully matched to the hue of the back endpapers.

Change in colour from front to back endpapers may also relate to the passage of time. In *The Napping House* (Wood, 1984), the story begins on a rainy night when 'everyone is sleeping', aptly captured by the dusky-grey front endpapers. In the course of the cumulative story, as a succession of characters crowd the granny in her bed, we see out of the window that the rain stops and the sun begins to rise. The end of the story comes with the full light of day, and the azure-blue back endpapers correspond to the clear morning sky. As six- and seven-year-old children discussed this book, they noted this change in colour and commented on its significance:

Sally: That makes sense, because it's dark when the story starts, so there's a darker endpage, and it's lighter when the story ends. So the endpage is lighter, back there.

Gordon: Yeah, that makes sense! Darker, then lighter. That's different, like most books, the endpages are the same on the front and the back.

These children are clearly aware of the endpapers' potential to contribute important interpretive information; Gordon's comment indicates his familiarity with the design convention of identical front and back endpapers. A more complex use of different coloured endpapers is represented in Barbara Lehman's *Rainstorm* (2007). A lonely boy stares out of his window on a rainy day, but by chance discovers a secret passage that leads him to an idyllic island where he makes new friends. He brings these friends back home with him, and the last illustration shows them happily playing together on a sunny day. The front endpapers are a dark purplish-grey colour, signifying both the rainy day and the boy's sad mood; by contrast, the back endpapers are a bright sky-blue, indicating both the boy's improved mood and the more pleasant weather.

In Anthony Browne's *Zoo* (1992), the front and back endpapers are a part of the serious and subtle message of the book: a meditation on the ways in which human beings oppress and imprison both animals and each other. The book's front cover presents the title as white text on a black background above a family portrait of a mother, father and two sons, which is superimposed on a background of bold black-and-white stripes. From the very beginning of this carefully designed book, the reader is alerted to the possibility of stark contrasts or reversals in the story to come. The front endpapers repeat this contrast, with the pastedown in white and the flyleaf in black. As the family tours the zoo, the father and sons demean and criticize the animals, displaying increasingly obnoxious behaviour, while the mother appears ever more distraught. These portrayals of people appear consistently on the left-hand side of the double spreads, while the zoo animals are depicted on the right-hand side. The father and sons show no compassion for the animals, which Browne casts through both text and pictures as miserable in their bare and sterile cages. Mum concludes 'I don't think the zoo really is for animals. I think it's for people.' This reversal of perspective is further emphasized on the following, final opening of the picturebook, with its illustration of one of the sons imprisoned in an empty cage, and the words 'That night I had a very strange dream.' The back endpapers are the mirror image of the front endpapers, with the flyleaf, now on the left side, black and the pastedown white. Because the design of the book has associated human beings with the left-hand side of the spread and animals with the right-hand side, the reversal of black and white on the endpapers is a visual semiotic gesture toward this crucial subtext. The endpapers echo Mum's comment, which is both about the purpose of zoos and the broader philosophical question of the nature of being human.

3. Illustrated, identical front and back endpapers

In our third major grouping, identical front and back endpapers feature various types of illustrations that relate to plot, setting, characters or visual design elements in the story. In Maurice Sendak's classic *Where the Wild Things Are* (1963), the endpapers are illustrated with overlapping shapes resembling leaves, which echo the stylized palm trees on the cover and suggest the lush foliage of a tropical forest. The somewhat muted palette and fine black cross-hatched lines, employed by Sendak throughout the book, are prefigured in the endpapers. As six- and seven-year-olds interpreted these endpapers, several children suggested what perspectives might produce the image shown. Gordon interpreted the image as 'the tops of the trees'. Jim agreed, commenting that the endpapers reminded him of 'an airplane picturing that or a helicopter'. They also suggested what might lie beyond the leaves: 'Wild things are in a forest.' The endpapers seem to function as stage curtains for the drama of Max's adventures in the land of the Wild Things. Just as Sendak's endpapers gesture to the setting of that story, the front and back endpapers of Martin Waddell's *Owl Babies* (1992) represent the bark of the tree where the three owlets anxiously await the return of their mother. The endpapers place the reader in the same secure, comfortable setting, alongside Sarah, Percy and Bill at home in a 'hole in the trunk of a tree'. Thus we as readers are prepared to identify with the babies' eagerness to be reunited with their mother and the comfort they feel at the beginning and end of the story when the family is gathered together.

David Diaz's Caldecott Medal-winning illustrations for *Smoky Night*, Eve Bunting's (1994) story of the Los Angeles race riots, include endpapers in the mixed-media collage style featured throughout the book. The endpaper collage is an embellished version of the background used on the eleventh opening of the story, where a firefighter rescues two missing cats belonging to the protagonist and his neighbour. The collage materials, including matches, a red warning reflector and representations of flames on a background of wood, hint at the physical destruction and the chaos left in the wake of the riots.

Thematic and plot elements are also present in the endpapers for *The Very Hungry Caterpillar* (Eric Carle, 1969). Carle's characteristic painted tissue-paper collage is studded with hundreds of white holes, representing the voracious appetite of the title character. The story follows the caterpillar on his gustatory adventures, with the holes appearing even more dramatically in the illustrations as a series of circular cut-outs. A third example of the connection between endpapers and story plot also features in the work of Eric Carle in Bill

Martin Jr.'s *Brown Bear, Brown Bear, What Do You See?* (1967). The structure of the story is a chain of colours and animals (brown bear, red bird, yellow duck, etc.) linked by the repeating pattern of the text. It is noteworthy that the endpapers for this book consist of a series of nine horizontal bands of torn painted tissue paper exactly corresponding to the colour sequence in the book, from the brown bear through to the goldfish.

A picturebook's endpapers can be fully understood only after the whole picturebook is studied. In these books, the front endpapers may be seen as an opportunity to speculate about the book that will follow, whereas readers may be in a position to more completely understand the significance of the same image when they encounter it on the back endpapers. Most American published versions of *Red Riding Hood* end happily, with the rescue of Red Riding Hood and her grandmother by a hunter or woodsman. In contrast, Christopher Coady's (1991) dark and sinister retelling ends with the words 'And the wolf threw himself on Red Riding Hood and gobbled her up.' This abrupt conclusion is prefigured in the dark palette and shadowy, autumnal scenes throughout the book. The endpapers show several fallen leaves lying atop a cloak, which is rendered in deep shades of red and maroon. Commenting on this image, six- and seven-year-old children identified Red Riding Hood's cloak, and wondered why it was on the ground, strewn with leaves. When the children saw the same image on the back endpapers, they realized its significance: 'She's really dead now.'

Another example of a book with endpapers that allude to the fate of the characters and repay study after the story is finished is Arthur Yorinks' *Ugh* (1990), a humorous gender-reversed variant of *Cinderella* with a setting in the Stone Age. Ugh, the Cinderella figure, lives with his two brothers and two sisters, who make him 'clean the cave and find food and wash clothes' while they go 'to the grove and watch[ed] dinosaurs eat trees'. Ugh's turn in fortunes begins when he invents the first bicycle and abandons it when he misunderstands the acclaim of the crowd as hostility. As the tribe members seek to find the creator of this marvellous invention, Ugh's siblings claim ownership, but it is only Ugh who can ride the bike around the block. Ugh is proclaimed king, while 'his brothers and sisters were so upset that they threw themselves into the ocean and were eaten by a whale'. The main events of the story, including Ugh's invention of the bicycle, the adulation of the crowd, and the fate of his brothers and sisters, are presaged in the front and back endpapers, which resemble cave paintings.

Allan Ahlberg and Bruce Ingman's *Previously* (2007) is an intertextual romp connecting several well-known fairy tales. While this approach is common enough, Ahlberg and Ingman give an interesting twist to the story by presenting the tales in a reversed chronological order, with each successive part of the story presenting what had happened *previously*. The endpapers consist of monochromatic black drawings on a forest green background, and these drawings gesture toward the various fairy tales in the story and the setting of many of them in the forest.

Illustrators may utilize a pattern of repeated images in endpapers. In Kevin Henkes' Caldecott-winning *Kitten's First Full Moon* (2004), for example, the identical front and back endpapers are completely covered by many rows of heavily black-outlined white circles on a grey background. A column of these same circles also appears on the half-title page, and throughout the book the moon is represented as a white circle with a thick black border, so this motif is sustained from cover to cover. The series of circles on the endpapers suggests that the story recounts the first of what will be many full moons for the tiny kitten. A similar repetition of circular forms comprises the endpaper art for *Knuffle Bunny* (Willems, 2004), the story of young Trixie's loss of a beloved stuffed toy rabbit at the Laundromat. Each image shows a wide-eyed Knuffle Bunny peering helplessly through the window on the circular washer door as it spins through suds in the wash cycle. Upon seeing the endpapers, Emma, a three-year-old, exclaimed 'I know what happens! I know because he is in this picture here and when he gets lost he is in the washer the whole time, but no one knows that except we know.' She then explained that she knows what will happen because 'it's in these pictures in the front', demonstrating her understanding that the repeated image lies at the centre of the plot. Willems uses the same approach in *Knuffle Bunny Too* (2007), where there are repeated images of two nearly identical knuffle bunnies, which are the object of jealousy and contention between Trixie and one of her classmates.

A fourth example of repeated illustration on endpapers is found in Tony Kushner and Maurice Sendak's *Brundibar* (2003), a retelling of a children's operetta performed by Jewish children at the Nazi concentration camp Terezin. The rose-orange endpapers are composed of repeated images of a boy sitting atop a bird in flight. Birds, representing both menace and escape, figure prominently in many of the illustrations throughout the story. Near the close of the story, the same repeated motif of the boy flying atop a bird, in sombre violet, forms the background for one of the operetta's songs, which references the flight of the blackbird and the sinister passing of time. The following double spread also depicts children astride blackbirds, who seem to be abducting them from their mourning mothers. At the end of the story, children appear on colourful orange-and-pink birds, as they end their song in triumph. Although this triumph may be understood in a tragically ironic way because of the horrific concentration-camp setting, the book's orange-rose endpapers nevertheless provide a note of hope and optimism.

Endpapers may also be illustrated with a number of images of a story character. Though Nikolajeva and Scott (2001: 247) assert that 'A common device is to depict the main character several times on endpapers, performing various actions, most often not mentioned inside the book,' we did not find this technique to be particularly widespread. One notable example is *Owen* (Kevin Henkes, 1993), the story of a young mouse and his attachment to Fuzzy, his beloved blanket. The matching front and back endpapers show Owen and Fuzzy in four different poses, with each pose repeated to form a diagonally striped pattern. In Ian Falconer's third book about Olivia the pig, *Olivia* ...

and the Missing Toy (2003), the endpapers show a 12-step process whereby Olivia secures her 'best toy' to a wall using adhesive tape, a procedure that might have prevented the traumatic toy loss recounted in the story. In both cases, the endpaper images are consonant with the stable characterization across each story: Owen's devotion to Fuzzy, and Olivia's spunk and self-reliance.

4. Illustrated, dissimilar front and back endpapers

In our final major grouping, the front and back endpapers are composed of different illustrations that frame the story in various ways. An easy but effective way of making the illustrations different is to simply reverse the illustration from the front endpapers so that it appears as a mirror image on the back endpapers. One of the most distinguished examples of this technique appears in Paul Zelinsky's Caldecott-winning *Rapunzel* (1997), with the endpapers' panoramic village scene of trees, a river and tile-roofed buildings. Zelinsky makes particularly deft use of conventions of directionality, with the front endpapers showing a peacock and a villager with his donkey facing to the right, inviting the viewer to turn the page. On the back endpapers, the reversed Italian Renaissance-style painting provides elegant closure to the story, with the peacock and villager looking left toward the final pages. A similar effect, executed horizontally rather than vertically, is the 'stupendous star-filled ceiling' depicted on the endpapers in Maira Kalman's *Next Stop Grand Central* (1999). Yet another variation on this mirroring technique is the left-to-right transposition of endpaper images. At the beginning of *Madlenka* (Peter Sís, 2000), the pastedown (left) shows the Earth, resembling a blue marble in the vastness of outer space, whereas the front flyleaf (right) zooms in for a closer view of the planet with its continents and oceans. These same illustrations are utilized at the back of the book, where the left-hand image depicts the closer view of the Earth and the right-hand image shows the Earth from farther away. The illustrations themselves, however, are not reversed; it is only their placement on the left or right that has changed.

Different front and back endpapers may also serve to represent changes that have occurred over the course of the story. Anthony Browne's *The Tunnel* (1989) tells the story of a brother and sister 'who were not at all alike'. On the left-hand page of the first opening, portraits of the two children are presented on contrasting backgrounds: the girl before an interior wall covered in flowered wallpaper and the boy before a red-brick wall. These same walls appear in the two illustrations on the right-hand page, where the girl is curled up with a book on a windowsill while her brother plays soccer outside. Though estranged at the beginning, the children grow close through a fantastic adventure in which the girl rescues her brother – a change in their relationship that is anticipated and reflected by the book's endpapers. The front endpapers show the floral wallpaper and a book on the pastedown, while the flyleaf shows an expanse of brick wall. The back endpapers maintain the orientation of the backgrounds, but now the book appears against the brick wall, alongside a soccer ball. Because both the book and the floral wallpaper have been strongly associated with the girl, and the brick wall and soccer ball with the boy, the placement of the book and the ball together against the exterior brick wall suggests both the siblings' new bond and the girl's movement from passivity to active exploration. Gordon, a six-year-old, remarked on the difference between the front and the back endpapers. As he speculated about the reason for the change, he drew a parallel with the change in the siblings' relationship: 'But when they got happy, they put the soccer ball there, they put their things together.'

Differences in the front and back endpapers may also be related to changes in story setting and the ways in which we interpret characters' feelings or emotions. In *Fox* (Wild, 2000), the same forest scene of trees and rocks is presented in strikingly different endpaper palettes, in bright orange and red at the front and verdant greens and blues at the end. The story begins as Dog and Magpie, both injured in a forest fire, band together to overcome their disabilities. Though the lonely and envious Fox tries to break apart their friendship, Magpie finally realizes that Dog's devotion is irreplaceable. The change from a palette of destruction to one of life and growth is consonant with the renewal of a forest after a fire, and also suggests that Dog and Magpie's friendship will be renewed. On a lighter note, the front and back endpapers in *A Cultivated Wolf!* (Becky Bloom, 1999; published as *Wolf* in the US) show the changes wrought in a village by the spread of reading and storytelling. In the story, a wolf, frustrated by his inability to scare a group of farm animals engrossed by books, decides to learn to read for himself and is accepted by the animals as a fellow storyteller. The front endpapers depict the wolf walking through a village full of morose and isolated inhabitants, whereas the back endpapers show the same village happily transformed by the presence of the storytelling animals. In the classic Caldecott winner *Make Way for Ducklings*, Robert McCloskey (1941) employs front and back endpapers that also suggest changes in the ducks and their island home. On the front endpapers, a series of eight images of hatching ducklings running from the upper left to lower right could be understood either as the chronological sequence of one duckling's emergence from its egg or as all eight ducklings from the story ranged in their trademark line. The back endpapers are blank, suggesting that the ducklings have left the island where they hatched and moved closer to maturity.

Another example of the endpapers reflecting changes over the course of the story is Barbara Reid's astonishing Plasticine illustrations in *The Subway Mouse* (2003), in which a mouse born and raised 'below the platforms in a busy subway station' eventually achieves his dream of reaching Tunnel's End and catches his first glimpse of the sky. The endpapers show the change in the scope of the mouse's world, from bleak grey concrete walls on the front endpapers to an expansive blue sky dotted with fluffy clouds at the back. A more abstract use of endpapers to indicate changes in a story character's mood is present in *Picturescape* (Elisa Gutiérrez, 2005), in which a young boy goes on a school field trip to an art museum. The first few openings of the book are rendered monochromatically, suggesting the quotidian quality of the boy's life, which becomes vibrant only as he goes to the museum and magically enters a series of paintings, all of which are representations of the work of famous Canadian painters. When he returns home, the bedroom scene is rendered in radiant light and colour. This change in mood is prefigured by the front and back endpapers: the front endpapers show vertical stripes in a very limited palette of grey, charcoal and black; by contrast, the back endpapers contain similar vertical stripes, now in a range of bright colours reminiscent of many of the works of art.

Some picturebooks use the endpapers both to begin and end the narrative. In Steven Kellogg's version of *Jack and the Beanstalk* (1991), for example, the front endpapers show the giant, having descended from his sky-castle in a tornado, stealing gold, the singing harp and the hen that lays the golden eggs from a pirate ship. The title page continues the story, depicting the giant's return to his castle via tornado; the sinking pirate ship; and our first sight of Jack, who is looking at a procession of a king and queen and their retainers on horseback. All of these details were noted by six- and seven-year-old children. Robert noticed that 'the story shows how the giant got the gold'. Don said 'First the giant steals the gold from the pirates, and then Jack steals the gold from the giant.' Also present on the endpapers, title page, and dedication page are images of a hot-air balloon with a bearded man in a star-studded robe. This man is also depicted on the first and second openings. On the first opening (the beginning of the verbal text), the man holds a book in which he is painting. The arrangement of golden blocks on this small book is identical to the arrangement of the large golden text blocks on the opened book we hold in our hands. The implication is that this wizard is writing the story. Don observed 'Hey, that guy is writing the book! He's probably an artist, maybe a magician, too!' Don then turned to the end of the book, pointing out that the wizard was also depicted on the back endpapers: 'He's here again at the end. And the book says "finished". [The small book the wizard is holding shows the word "finis"]. He made the book. He's the magician, the guy who made the whole entire book!' The back endpapers truly conclude the story, showing Jack and his family in a grand coach proceeding home to his castle. Thus, this is a case in which to omit discussion of the endpapers would be to ignore the beginning and ending of the story.

Two picturebook versions of *Noah's Ark*, by Peter Spier (1977) and Jerry Pinkney (2002), provide an interesting contrast in the way they utilize endpapers as a part of their retelling of the Biblical story of the Flood. In Spier's version, the front endpapers show Noah working in his vineyard on the flyleaf, while the destructive qualities of humanity, in the form of a conquering army leaving a city in flames, are depicted on the pastedown. In the background are cedars of Lebanon, the symbols of peace, righteousness and endurance. The back endpapers again depict Noah on the flyleaf, planting a vineyard in the soggy soil. Instead of the red-and-orange flames of the burning city, we see the red and orange of a rainbow, with the cedars of Lebanon flourishing under it. The images of death have been replaced by images of life and hope, and Noah is engaged in the same occupation as before. This brings the story to a satisfying closure, and is one of the principal ways Spier achieves resolution and a sense of completion. Jerry Pinkney also makes full use of the endpapers in his version, using them to set Noah's story in the broader context of the Genesis creation account. On the front endpapers, Pinkney's accomplished watercolour painting depicts the profusion of life, and includes the words 'In the beginning, God created the heaven and the earth … And God saw that it was good.' This prepares readers for the first opening, where a burning city demonstrates that human beings have spoiled the beauty and goodness of the world. At the end of the book, the last opening shows the rainbow symbolizing God's promise. The promise, 'Seedtime and harvest, cold and heat, summer and winter, night and day, shall never cease as long as the earth endures', accompanies an image of the entire planet encircled by rainbows on the back endpapers. In this way, Pinkney has framed the story of Noah as part of the ongoing story of humanity, whereas Spier begins and ends with Noah.

Our final examples of books with different illustrations on the front and back endpapers demonstrate the potential of endpapers to extend or blur the boundaries of the story. In *Don't Let the Pigeon Drive the Bus* (Mo Willems, 2003), the front endpapers provide the first indication of the pigeon's cherished dream of driving a bus. The pigeon appears on the pastedown, dwarfed by an enormous thought bubble that includes five images of the pigeon as a bus driver. The story recounts his unsuccessful quest to take the wheel, and concludes with a newfound desire to drive a truck. While the pigeon spots the truck in the last opening, it is only on the back endpapers that this new dream is represented in another thought bubble, with images of the pigeon as a truck driver. Just as the pigeon's dream on the front endpapers generated the story within the book, we are invited to interpret the dream on the back endpapers as the opening to another adventure.

Diary of a Worm (Doreen Cronin, 2003) utilizes endpapers to blur the boundaries of the story, told through the worm's diary entries. The endpapers, which appear as pages in a scrapbook, show various photos and mementos of events that are not repeated in the course of the story. For example, the front endpapers include taped-in snapshots of the worm's first day at school and 'The family vacation – on Compost Island', as well as his report card. The back endpapers include photographs of other memorable events, a scrap of paper money captioned 'Isn't this leaf awesome?!' and a comic strip drawn by the worm. The endpapers therefore present readers with alternative and additional ways of recording memories, and gesture toward events in the worm's life that may have both preceded and succeeded the story told in the diary. Likewise, in *Meerkat Mail* (Emily Gravett, 2006), a home-away-home story about a meerkat who is bored with his life in the colony and sets out for adventure, the endpapers show mementos and photos from Sunny's life. The front endpapers include a newspaper clipping about the meerkat motto ('Stay safe, stay together'), as well as photos of Sunny with his relatives and friends. The back endpapers gesture towards both his adventures and his return to the colony by representing his travel photocard, a luggage tab and another newspaper clipping, headlined 'Sunny comes home!' The back endpapers also include photos of Sunny on his adventures and when reunited with his mum.

Conclusion

The typology we have presented can be useful to educators as they talk with children about the design and aesthetic unity of picturebooks. We believe that the examples we have discussed in each category of the typology represent the major forms and purposes of endpapers in contemporary picturebooks, and that these examples demonstrate the interest and interpretive sophistication even young children can display given teachers' support. One suggested procedure in sharing picturebooks with children is to make a habit of examining both the front and back endpapers before the story is read, in order to assist children in making predictions and to speculate about the meaning of the endpapers. Special attention should be paid to whether the front and back endpapers are the same or different, and the possible significance of this choice. We have found that children rather quickly become accustomed to close examination of endpapers and that they engage in interpreting them with a great deal of enthusiasm and insight. After the story is read, the endpapers bear revisiting, because their complete semiotic significance is often not apparent until the conclusion of the story.

Once children know the conventions of picturebook design, including the various uses and purposes of endpapers, they can begin to appreciate how some books subvert these conventions. In *The Stinky Cheese Man and Other Fairly Stupid Tales* (1992), Jon Scieszka's amusing collection of postmodern fairy tales, readers are startled to see an endpaper before the end of the story. Jack the narrator explains this bizarre placement as he tries to trick his nemesis the Giant: 'Shhhhh. Be very quiet. I moved the endpaper up here so the Giant would think the book is over.' This is only one of the many violations and subversions of picturebook conventions in this amusing book. Before the teacher read Jack's explanation of his trickery, a six-year-old child recognized that the endpaper is misplaced: 'That's funny – the endpaper isn't supposed to be there.' In other words, the child had internalized the convention of the endpapers' placement, and could appreciate the ways in which *The Stinky Cheese Man* plays with this convention.

Examining endpapers isn't always straightforward. Another postmodern picturebook that makes ingenious use of endpapers is Emily Gravett's *Wolves* (2005), which uses the metafictive device of a book within a book (or a type of mise-en-abyme), and therefore has two sets of endpapers. The book itself has a red board cover, and the front endpapers, as well as the back endpapers, are a mottled brown colour overlaid with random light lines that resemble scratches. The plot of this book concerns a rabbit who borrows a book from the 'West Bucks Public Burrowing Library' about wolves – in fact, a red book precisely like the one we as readers hold in our hands, though it shows some signs of wear. The endpapers of the book that Rabbit borrows are similar to those we've already seen, but they also show some signs of wear and contain a pasted-in borrowing slip stamped with due dates as well as a pocket containing a call number card that the reader can remove (unfortunately, this feature, as well as another removable item, were excluded in the US edition of the book). As Rabbit reads his book, the illustrations depict some of the openings he sees as well as his oblivious stroll through a wolf's legs, up its tail, through its fur and on to its snout. Rabbit's moment of horrified realization accompanies the text 'Wolves eat mainly meat. They hunt large prey such as deer, bison and moose. They also enjoy smaller mammals, like beavers, voles and ...' The following opening depicts a much-scratched, bitten and torn book with a scrap of paper reading '... rabbits.' This is followed by a disclaimer by the author that 'no rabbits were eaten during the making of this book. It is a work of fiction,' and the offer of 'an alternative ending'. This alternative ending takes place against the backdrop of the inner book's endpapers and consists of a crudely pasted together Rabbit and Wolf sharing a jam sandwich; thus the illustration appears to be constructed from scraps of paper from the original book. As readers, the last thing we encounter is the unsullied back endpapers of our book, with a feeling of gratitude that we have not shared Rabbit's experience. Sipe and Pantaleo (2008) provide more information on postmodern picturebooks and their characteristics.

Although we have focused on endpapers in this chapter, it is important to examine the relationship of picturebook's endpapers to other parts of the peritext. In many of our examples, we have referred to the ways in which the endpapers relate to the front and back cover, title page and the rest of the illustration sequence. Picturebooks are aesthetic wholes, so carefully designed that everything in the book is the result of someone's choice, and we can speculate with children about why those choices were made. Sipe (2008) offers a comprehensive theory of children's literary understanding that includes their responses to peritextual features in the context of storybook readalouds. In some instances, we can be certain about the rationale for a design choice. For example, illustrator David Wiesner (2001) comments about his Caldecott-winning *The Three Pigs*: 'Then, there are the other subtle details that are so much fun to pay attention to in bookmaking. I knew early on that I wanted the binding to reflect the story. So the reddish spine represents the brick, the grey body of the binding the sticks, and the ochre endpapers the straw of the story,' (quoted in Silvey, 2001). However, if we do not know the illustrator's reasons for a design choice, we are free to speculate with children about possibilities that make sense. When we discuss picturebooks with children, we should make them aware that every element in the picturebook is meaningful and worthy of interpretation. If we communicate this clearly in our discussions with them, they will quickly adopt this stance. Gordon, a six-year-old, became particularly intrigued with the semiotic significance of endpapers. He assumed that there was always a reason for the choice of their colour or design. During a readaloud of *Changes* (Anthony Browne, 1990), Gordon speculated about the endpapers, which are painted a light tan with small, darker brown spots:

Gordon: Hmm. I wonder if they chose different kind of endpages. I wonder why they did choose this. Wait, let's look through the book, we might notice something like this. [He pages through the book, coming to an illustration of a wall that is a similar colour.] That's sort of the same texture here... . Maybe the walls are the same [turns back to the endpapers].

Teacher: So the endpages represent, maybe, the walls?

Gordon: Maybe. Dots on 'em. Probably you can't just see that stuff. All the little dots and scratches. All the little dots, rock, in the wall. Or the ground. It makes you feel like you're on the ground, or something.

Notice how Gordon uses the language of choice and intentionality, learned from his teacher, to speculate about the significance of the endpapers. He is also interested in relating the endpapers to other parts of the book. Children can also understand the use of endpapers as framing devices for stories and the various ways in which they do this. If teachers attend to the meaning of endpapers, children will too, and their literary and visual aesthetic experience will be enhanced. This kind of discussion deepens and broadens children's critical thinking abilities, their ability to make inferences, and their appreciation of picturebooks as art objects. The endpapers are often excluded or altered in paperback and library editions of picturebooks; therefore, when teachers have a choice of which edition to present to their students, they should consider selecting the trade edition, which is the fullest expression of the intentions of the book's designer, editor and illustrator. When children make their own books, if they know about the significance of endpapers they will want to include them as part of their own creations. The teacher's interest in and knowledge and excitement about endpapers are key, and can unlock the great meaning-making potential that endpapers present.

References

Derrida, J. (1981). *Dissemination*, trans. B. Johnson. Chicago: University of Chicago Press

Genette, G. (1987/1997) *Paratexts: Thresholds of Interpretation*, trans. J. E. Lewin. Cambridge: Cambridge University Press

Higonnet, M. R. (1990) 'The playground of the peritext'. *Children's Literature Association Quarterly* 15: 47–9

Kiefer, B. (1995). *The Potential of Picturebooks: From Visual Literacy to Aesthetic Understanding*. Englewood Cliffs, New Jersey: Prentice-Hall

Lewis, D. (2001). *Reading Contemporary Picturebooks: Picturing Text*. London: RoutledgeFalmer

Nikolajeva, M. & Scott, C. (2001). *How Picturebooks Work*. New York: Garland

Nodelman, P. (1988). *Words About Pictures: The Narrative Art of Children's Picture Books*. Athens, Georgia: University of Georgia Press

Pantaleo, S. (2003). '"Godzilla lives in New York": Grade 1 students and the peritextual features of picture books'. *Journal of Children's Literature* 29(2): 66–77

Raschka, C. (2006). Personal communication

Roberts, M. & Etherington, D. (1982). *Bookbinding and the Conservation of Books: A Dictionary of Descriptive Terminology*. Washington: Library of Congress

Silvey, A. (2001). 'Pigs in space'. *School Library Journal* 47(11): 48–50

Sipe, L. R. (1998). 'Learning the language of picturebooks'. *Journal of Children's Literature* 24(2): 66–75

Sipe, L. R. (2000). 'The construction of literary understanding by first and second graders in oral response to picture storybook read-alouds'. *Reading Research Quarterly* 35: 252–75

Sipe, L. R. (2008). *Storytime: Young Children's Literary Understanding in the Classroom*. New York: Teachers College Press

Sipe, L. R. & Bauer, J. (2001). 'Urban kindergartners' literary understanding of picture storybooks'. *The New Advocate* 14: 329–42

Sipe, L. R. & Pantaleo, S. (2008). *Postmodern Picturebooks: Play, Parody, and Self-Referentiality*. New York: Routledge

Stewig, J. W. (1995). *Looking at Picture Books*. Fort Atkinson, Wisconsin: Highsmith Press

Turner, V. (1969). *The Ritual Process: Structure and Anti-Structure*. Chicago: Aldine

Wolfe, R. J. (1990). *Marbled Paper: Its History, Techniques, and Patterns*. Philadelphia: University of Pennsylvania Press

Children's literature

Ahlberg, A. & Ingman, B. (2007). *Previously*. London: Walker Books

Bloom, B. (1999). *A Cultivated Wolf!* Hampshire: Siphano Picture Books

Browne, A. (1989). *The Tunnel*. New York: Alfred A. Knopf

Browne, A. (1990). *Changes*. New York: Alfred A. Knopf

Browne, A. (1992). *Zoo*. New York: Alfred A. Knopf

Bunting, E. (1994). *Smoky Night*. San Diego, California: Harcourt Brace

Carle, E. (1969). *The Very Hungry Caterpillar*. New York: World Publishing Company

Coady, C. (1991). *Red Riding Hood*. New York: Dutton Children's Books

Cronin, D. (2003). *Diary of a Worm*. New York: Joanna Cotler Books

Cronin, D. (2004). *Duck for President*. New York: Simon & Schuster

Falconer, I. (2003). *Olivia ... and the Missing Toy*. New York: Atheneum

Gravett, E. (2005). *Wolves*. London: Macmillan

Gravett, E. (2006). *Meerkat Mail*. London: Macmillan

Gutiérrez, E. (2005). *Picturescape*. Vancouver: Simply Read Books

Hathorn, L. (1994). *Way Home*. New York: Crown

Henkes, K. (1993). *Owen*. New York: Greenwillow

Henkes, K. (2004). *Kitten's First Full Moon*. New York: Greenwillow

Hesse, K. (1999). *Come On, Rain!* New York: Scholastic

Hodges, M. (1984). *Saint George and the Dragon*. Boston: Little, Brown
Juster, N. (2005). *The Hello, Goodbye Window*. New York: Michael Di Capua Books
Kalman, M. (1999). *Next Stop Grand Central*. New York: Putnam
Kellogg, S. (1991). *Jack and the Beanstalk*. New York: Morrow Junior Books
Kushner, T. & Sendak, M. (2003). *Brundibar*. New York: Hyperion
Lehman, B. (2007). *Rainstorm*. Boston: Houghton Mifflin
Macaulay, D. (1990). *Black and White*. Boston: Houghton Mifflin
Marshall, J. (1989). *The Three Little Pigs*. New York: Dial
Martin, Jr., B. (1967). *Brown Bear, Brown Bear, What Do You See?* New York: Holt, Rinehart & Winston
McCloskey, R. (1941). *Make Way for Ducklings*. New York: Viking Press
Myers, C. (2000). *Wings*. New York: Scholastic
Myers, C. (2007). *Jabberwocky*. New York: Hyperion
Olaleye, I. O. (2000). *In the Rainfield: Who Is the Greatest?* New York: Blue Sky Press
Pinkney, J. (2002). *Noah's Ark*. New York: SeaStar Books
Reid, B. (2003). *The Subway Mouse*. Markham, Ontario, Canada: North Winds Press
Scieszka, J. (1992). *The Stinky Cheese Man and Other Fairly Stupid Tales*. New York: Viking.
Scieszka, J. (1994). *The Book that Jack Wrote*. New York: Viking
Sendak, M. (1963). *Where the Wild Things Are*. New York: HarperCollins
Sendak, M. (1993). *We Are All in the Dumps with Jack and Guy*. New York: HarperCollins
Sís, P. (2000). *Madlenka*. New York: Farrar, Straus and Giroux
Spier, P. (1977). *Noah's Ark*. New York: Dell
Tsuchiya, Y. (1988). *Faithful Elephants: A True Story of Animals, People and War*. Boston: Houghton Mifflin
Van Allsburg, C. (1995). *Bad Day at Riverbend*. Boston: Houghton Mifflin
Waddell, M. (1992). *Owl Babies*. London: Walker Books
Wild, M. (2000). *Fox*. St Leonards, Australia: Allen & Unwin
Wiesner, D. (1999). *Sector 7*. New York: Clarion
Wiesner, D. (2001). *The Three Pigs*. New York: Clarion
Wiesner, D. (2006). *Flotsam*. New York: Clarion
Willems, M. (2003). *Don't Let the Pigeon Drive the Bus*. New York: Hyperion
Willems, M. (2004). *Knuffle Bunny*. New York: Hyperion
Willems, M. (2007). *Knuffle Bunny Too*. New York: Hyperion
Wood, A. (1984). *The Napping House*. San Diego, California: Harcourt Brace
Yorinks, A. (1990). *Ugh*. New York: Farrar, Straus and Giroux
Zelinsky, P. O. (1997). *Rapunzel*. New York: Dutton

5   Making and breaking frames

Crossing the borders of expectation in picturebooks

Vivienne Smith

Casual readers are inclined to take frames for granted, but any serious examination of how picturebooks work is bound to identify the important job framing does in focusing and directing the reader's attention on both what is seen and how this is understood by the reader. This chapter looks at some of the deliberate framing choices made by the author-illustrators in two recent prize-winning picture-books: *Flotsam* by David Wiesner and *Little Mouse's Big Book of Fears* by Emily Gravett. Analysis of framing shows clearly how sophisticated these texts are, and how flexible the reader must be to make them mean. Can we expect so much from children? This chapter considers the responses of two boys, aged 9 and 11, to these books, and argues that changes in pedagogy are needed if children are to meet the challenge of reading them.

Frames and framing

We tend to take looking for granted, because – for most of us, most of the time – seeing is a natural thing to do. It is only when something happens to disrupt the ordinariness of our everyday seeing that we take time to really look at and think about looking.

Such a disruption happened for me a couple of weeks ago, when I went to the optician to get new glasses. After the appointment, I stood in the shop and surveyed the rows of new frames. I knew I had to choose, and I knew how hard the choice would be: not so much because of the dazzling choice in front of me, but rather because, when I took off my old glasses to fit new frames, my face would be reduced to a blob in the mirror, and I would have very little idea of what anything looked like. And it mattered that I got it right. The frames I chose would sit on my face for, probably, about a year. Would they make me look too serious, too silly, too old, too zany, too boring?

The experience reminded me of how important frames are. Most practically, in glasses, they hold the lenses in place that make the world come in to focus: that is, they help *me*, the looker, the originator, see out. Secondly, they affect what *others* see when they look at me: they influence the way people interpret the persona I present. In other words, frames serve a two-way, intermediary function: they focus an image for the one who sees out, and they select and present that image to whoever looks in. Frames assume, perhaps even demand, a relationship between seer and spectator.

This is obviously true for glasses, but it is true for other sorts of frame too. Think of how the frame around a painting in an art gallery is chosen by the artist or the curator to complement and enhance the picture, or to draw attention to colours or to particular features in the painting. The framer uses the frame to direct the viewer's gaze: to help the viewer see the image as the framer, or artist wants it to be seen.

It is, of course the same in picturebooks, although the word 'frame' is used more precisely here. Doonan (1992) makes clear that in picturebooks, what we call a frame in everyday speech – the line that separates the image from the rest of the page – is actually a *border*. The *frame* itself is harder to define. It can be the space that surrounds the image, the space between the image and the border, the space between the image and the edge of the page or, sometimes, the space between the image and the rest of the text. This ambiguity makes 'the frame' a difficult concept to pin down, but, in all instances, one thing remains constant. Picturebook makers and illustrators have had to make conscious decisions about how and where to use frames in their work and what effect that usage will have on the readership.

Frames are important. If you doubt this, think of Sendak's *Where The Wild Things Are* (1963). You will probably have noticed the way Sendak uses frames there to draw the reader into Max's fantasy. At the beginning of the book, Max is depicted – contained, almost – in a small tight picture of his room in the centre of the page, framed by wide, creamy white space. As Max's wildness grows, so too does the size of the image, until the frame has disappeared entirely and the picture has bled, first to the edges of the page, and then across the gutter, and further, until there is no space even for words to be given to describe the action. The rumpus that ensues shows Max at his wildest. And now the reader too is unconstrained: the adult lens of rationality and realism that the frames and the language provide no longer focus particular attention, and the reader is free to revel with Max at will. But Max tires and the rumpus recedes. So too, then, do the pictures. Words reappear and the frame is reinstated and strengthened, until Max is secure again in the controlled world of his bedroom and supper is waiting.

Other uses of frames are common in picturebooks. In wordless picturebooks, such as Hughes's *Up and Up* (1979) and Ormerod's *Sunshine* (1981), they provide narrative structure, presenting closely sequenced snapshots of action that carry the plot forward as surely as temporal connectives. They can establish pace. Contrast Oxenbury's leisurely, unframed double-page spreads in the main part of *We're Going on a Bear Hunt* (Rosen & Oxenbury, 1989), where the reader's imagination is encouraged to meander through meadows and squelch through mud, with the family's mad, headlong rush home, pursued by the bear. Now a series of thin, horizontal frames carries the action and the reader's eye urgently across the page and on to the frames below. The movement is linear. Frames, just as much as words, persuade the reader that there is no time to linger. In other picturebooks, frames reinforce character. Think of Jez Alborough's Duck. In *Fix it Duck* (2001), the eponymous hero attempts a little DIY. Duck is stupid, clumsy and incompetent, but gloriously self-unaware and enthusiastic. Keen to begin work, he bursts out of his frame, tools in hand, breaking the constraints of reasoned behaviour and forcing himself on to the reader's attention. The sheer physicality of Duck, awkwardly bursting through a frame that ought to hold him shows the size of his ego and is a measure of his incompetence. He is too self-important and too clumsy to obey convention.

We see then, that framing – just as much as the interplay of words and pictures – affects what Scott and Nikolajeva (2000) call the *dynamics* of picturebook interaction. Frames direct what the reader sees and influence how the reader thinks and feels about what he or she sees. They play a major role in helping readers make pictures mean. Because of this, it is not surprising that artists and illustrators of picturebooks have long experimented with what frames can do and with what they can do with frames. What is surprising is that there has been little critical attention paid to this framing. It is as if, like the glasses on my nose, readers get so used to frames that they no longer notice them. This chapter argues that frames are worth noticing!

Bringing framing to the fore: postmodernism

Lewis (2001), Thacker & Webb (2002), Smith (2001) and Anstey (2002) have all noted the influence of postmodernism in contemporary picturebook making. Postmodernism, in its various manifestations, attempts to 'problematize' cultural assumptions and so prompt readers and onlookers to reconsider what they take for granted. Why should the plumbing of a building be hidden inside the walls? Why should a painting have a recognizable subject? Why should a story have a beginning, a middle and a nice, tidy end? In terms of literature, this has meant that writers of postmodern fiction have experimented with narrative and form, overturning readers' expectations of strong, single narrative; linear construction and determinate endings. Italo Calvino, for example, wrote a novel that consists mostly of beginnings (Calvino, 1979) and Martin Amis, one where the plot actually runs backwards (Amis, 1992). In these and many other postmodern novels, writers show that they are interested in the constructedness of text. They want to explore not just the story they have to tell, but how the form achieves that story. Writers play with words and with structures, and readers, in turn, find themselves teased or, sometimes, frustrated, by the disruption of their expectations. Those readers who are prepared to put up with the game and play along find that they are jolted into a new awareness of the act of reading itself, just as those who struggle to choose new glasses find themselves thinking afresh about seeing.

The picturebook has proved to be a wonderful medium for postmodernism.

Author-illustrators have used it to experiment with multiple narratives (*The Jolly Postman or Other People's Letters* by Janet and Alan Ahlberg, 1986; *Black and White* by David Macaulay, 1990), to subvert traditional storytelling (*The Stinky Cheese Man and Other Fairly Stupid Tales* by Jon Scieszka and Lane Smith, 1993), to blur the differences between fiction and non-fiction (*Wolves*, by Emily Gravett, 2006) and to exploit the affordances of juxtaposing genre in unexpected ways (*The Adventures of the Dish and the Spoon* by Mini Grey, 2006). In recent texts, innovative illustrators have pushed postmodernism away from these literary concerns towards matters more visual. Lauren Child, for example, confronts the reader with the fractured complexity of twenty-first century family life through her quirky use of drawing, collage and photography: a glance at any double-page spread in a Clarice Bean book (e.g. *Clarice Bean, That's Me*, 1999) shows us that Clarice does not live the tidy, ordered life of Sophie, the girl who so long ago, in reassuringly regular, block-coloured images, entertained a tiger to tea (*The Tiger who came to tea*, Judith Kerr, 1968).

An interest in framing is a natural development of the postmodern experiment in picturebooks. Author-illustrators, already aware of the potential of framing, see it as a way of highlighting the constructedness of text, and exploring its affordances for readers. Emily Gravett, in the UK, and David Wiesner, in the US, are two contemporary, prize-winning author-illustrators who have both, in very different ways and in more than one book, begun to push at the boundaries of what readers expect frames to do. They forefront framing in their texts and so challenge the reader to notice and respond.

In this chapter I will look at recent texts by both of them: *Flotsam*, by Wiesner (2006), and *Little Mouse's Big Book of Fears*, by Gravett (2007). First, by presenting my own reading of these texts, I will explain what it is about the framing in each that interests me. Then I will report on conversations about these books with two young readers: Josh, aged ten and Harry, aged nine. Finally, I will tackle the question: What sense do children make of the framing games these author-illustrators play, and what, if anything, are the implications of this for us?

Looking through frames into frames with *Flotsam*

Flotsam (see Figure 28) is a wordless picturebook that shows the story of a boy's day on the beach. Like Shirley (*Come Away From The Water, Shirley* by John Burningham, 1977), this boy is left to his own devices while his parents read. He might have been building sandcastles earlier, for an ornate citadel can be seen in the background, but now his interest is scientific. His buckets are full of marine specimens, and he has with him binoculars, a hand lens and a microscope. After peering through his lens at a small crustacean, the boy wanders off to the water's edge. He crouches down to examine a crab, and, as he does so, a large wave sweeps over him. When the wave recedes, the boy finds that an old Box Brownie has been washed up beside him: a Melville Underwater Camera. The boy opens the camera and looks inside. There is a film (see Figure 29).

Figure 28 Flotsam by David Wiesner

He gets the film developed and rushes back to the beach, where he looks at the results. What he sees astonishes him. A clockwork fish swims in the ocean with a shoal of real fish. A family of octopuses sit down to read on sofas in their underwater sitting room. Two giant starfish, with islands on their backs, rear up to fight. Aliens have landed and families of little green tourists pose for underwater holiday snaps. The final print is of a child holding a photograph of another child who is also holding a photograph. Using first the lens and then the microscope, the boy discovers a sequence of ten embedded photographs of the children who found the camera before him, going back to about 1900. As they all must have done, he takes a photograph of himself holding the last photograph, and throws the camera back into the sea. The final pages of the book show how the camera journeys back through the sea, until it is washed up on a beach for another child to find.

Framing is perhaps not the first thing the reader notices in this book. More immediately apparent is the factual style of illustration. The tone and colour are natural, suited to a summer's day on the beach. Full-bodied people are shown with accurately represented scientific equipment and carefully drawn wildlife. So lifelike are these images that this could almost be a natural-history text. Other images show similar attention to detail: the Box Brownie that opens up, just like the one I had as a child, to reveal a convincing mechanism

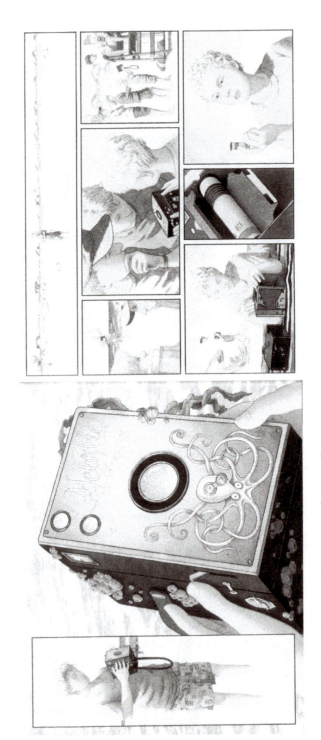

Figure 29 The boy discovers the Melville Underwater Camera

and a 120 mm film; the journalistic attention to fashion and hairstyle in the pictures of the children who had found the camera in the past; the banality of the photo-shop interior. Wiesner uses realistic image, I suggest, to accentuate the real world of his base story. By doing this, he sets up a *conceptual* framework in which he positions the underwater fantasy. Because the surreal is framed and embedded so firmly in real life, it seems both more plausible and more shocking. What if, Wiesner seems to ask the reader, the world is not so solidly ordinary as we imagine?

Structural framing techniques, when they are introduced a few pages into the book, look conventional at first glance: small, inset frames tell the story of the boy wandering off along the beach, or show him waiting for the film to be ready. On one level the reader is presented with a simple strip narrative that conveys the sequence of events and carries the story. But the way these episodes are punctuated by the unframed single- and double-spreads that bleed to edges of the page and, typically, demand a different, more thoughtful attention, moves us beyond comic-strip narrative. A rhythm is set up: quick bursts of plot that represent action are framed and modified by lengthy stills, many of which are what Kress and van Leeuwen (1996) call 'demand images'. These pages, where characters look out of frames directly at the reader and demand attention, are common in picturebooks, but they are complicated here because frequently there is a *double layer* of demand. Characters, or eyes, look out to the reader towards, or through, something else, and challenge us to notice not just what is depicted, but the very notion of seeing itself. A crustacean stares out, framed by a human eye. Later, a human eye, framed and magnified by a hand lens, looks at the crustacean. The demand here is clear: Reader! Slow down. Step aside from the daily action. Look!

Looking is seminal to this text. In almost every image, the boy is shown actively looking at something. He stares out at the horizon; he concentrates on creatures, or cameras or photographs; he looks out at the reader. In contrast to the adults in the book – his parents and the woman in the photo shop – he is engaged in looking. They are disengaged. They gaze, unfocused at the near distance, too busy to look at the boy, or they focus rigidly on the reality of the moment. To use a common metaphor literally, they cannot see out of the frames they are in. The boy, more connected with the imaginative play of sandcastles and the wonder of the natural world, can. That, presumably, is why he is the one privileged with the camera.

Instances of framing explored in *Flotsam* so far here have been implicit. I have shown how frames structure the text, position the reader and delineate characters. Wiesner, as a postmodern author-illustrator, uses frames explicitly too, running them like a trope through the book to embellish his theme. Cameras, hand lenses and microscopes frame, capture and focus images. Photographs are shown though the ring of a hand lens and framed by the eyepiece of the microscope. The boy is seen framed and reflected in the lens of the camera. Frames and images are layered in the embedded photographs of children that need to be unpicked by the boy and the reader, hinting at the march of time and the universality of childhood. The point, surely, is to notice; to look at frames actual, conceptual and metaphorical; and consider how we, as readers, frame the world ourselves.

Breaking into and out of frames with *Little Mouse's Big Book of Fears*

Little Mouse's Big Book of Fears (see Figure 30) is in many ways a simpler book, but it too sets challenges for the reader. The immediate difficulty is to know what to call the text in the first place, for it is clear from the title that this is not Little Mouse's book at all, but Emily Gravett's. Little Mouse, it seems, has come along, crossed out Ms Gravett's name on the front cover, and substituted

Figure 30 Little Mouse's Big Book of Fears by Emily Gravett

his own. He sits, on the title page, holding his pencil and surveying his hand-iwork, framed by and looking through the hole he has chewed in the cover. Instructions to the reader on the right-hand front endpaper suggest that this is not altogether inappropriate behaviour: readers are supposed to deface this text. For this is a book especially designed to scaffold readers in overcoming their fears by artwork.

Each page presents the reader with a blank space for drawing and a posh scientific word that acts as a title to focus the fear. Little Mouse, wracked by fears of all sorts, seizes the opportunity. He creeps through the pages of the book, interpreting fears in mousey terms. He draws, sticks and writes, all the time nervously chewing at his pencil and nibbling the pages, frightening himself more and more surely, until he eventually gets to the musophobia page, and learns that people are scared of him.

The book is playful and funny, and some of the humour is derived from the source of Little Mouse's fears. His fear of sharp knives (aichmophobia), for example, is illustrated by a poster for the amazing mousecrobatic circus act (cancelled), a photograph of the three blind stars, now tailless and unable to perform, and a newspaper cutting: the story of Mrs Sabatier's success in slashing mouse numbers at her farm. On the back of this cutting are plumbing advertisements, and these lead Little Mouse to his next fear: ablutophobia (fear of bathing). He might, of course, get sucked down the plughole or, worse still, flushed down the loo. This reminds him that toilets are built big, for humans, and that mice are notoriously incontinent (dystychiphobia – fear of accidents). Red-faced, he picks his way carefully out of his own puddle and poo, and, not at all safely, crawls on to the next page (see Figure 31).

More humour comes from the illustration: feathers (perhaps stuck in by a former reader) on the ornithophobia page are given eyes and teeth and so turn into scary monsters. But, when an owl swoops down towards Little Mouse on the next page (phagophobia – fear of being eaten), he has found a much smaller white feather to tie to the end of his pencil. Is this a sign of cowardice, or non-aggression under the Geneva convention?

Framing in this text is complex. There are, of course, the explicit frames that make the conventional, blank book that Little Mouse walks through. His progress breaks those frames, physically, by chewing away at the edges, and conceptually, by disrupting their integrity as he appears simultaneously inside them and out. How can he be both the subject of the book, shown on every page with his pencil, *and* the maker of the images that scare him? We see him caught up in a spider's web and hunted by an owl. How can he interact with the images he has drawn? The frames in which the fiction exists are constantly shifting.

This is clear too in the way the covers and endpapers work. Readers use book covers as frames, as transitional devices that separate the story within the book from their everyday lives without, and to help them to focus their minds on the possibilities of story. When Little Mouse breaks out of the pages and damages the cover itself, he disrupts these framing assumptions. Is he in the

Figure 31 Dystychiphobia and rupophobia in *Little Mouse's Big Book of Fears*

book or out of it? Does he exist in the grown-up world, where real mice actually do damage second-hand books, or is he part of the story? This book teases the reader, challenging the conventional expectations of how stories in books work and what covers are for.

Frames of reference and expectation shift too in various ways throughout the text. The reader constantly has to adapt to new modes of thinking as Gravett introduces the diverse texts that need to be tackled. In quick succession, there are nursery rhymes, newspaper small ads, tourist maps and natural-history texts to be assimilated and related playfully to Little Mouse's plight. The reader needs to be as prepared to be flexible in his or her thinking as the mousecrobats were in their performing days. Frames and trapezes do not stay still.

The framing of reading habits made by the pattern of the page is another joke. Each page is headed by a plausible, but unusual, scientific term. Just as the reader has become trained into accepting the validity of words such as teratophobia and chronomentrophobia, the game is altered and whereamiophobia is thrown in. It seems to be there just to jolt the reader into noticing. Similarly, at one point, the sequence of drawing and collage prompted by the words is disrupted by that stalwart device of postmodern texts since *Tristram Shandy* (Sterne, 1768), the blank page. Little Mouse is afraid of the dark, but how is the reader supposed to respond to a page of black nothingness, broken only by the end of a small mouse's tail?

Framing in *Little Mouse's Big Book of Fears* is playful and lighthearted. It does not share the didactic intensity of Wiesner's *Flotsam*. Gravett seems more intent on helping her readers enjoy the fun that framing affords than in making any serious point. But this does not mean that reading the book is easy. As discussed, considerable demands are made of the reader, who needs, at least, to be observant, open to surprise and flexible in approach. In short, the reader of both these books needs to be prepared to cross another sort of frame: the frame of his or her own expectation. To what extent, I wondered, were children to whom the books are marketed able to do this?

The children's responses

Studies of children and their responses to picturebooks have typically been conducted in classrooms where teachers were already interested in what picturebooks have to offer, for example, Arizpe and Styles (2003). Some children, perhaps ones who had already worked with picturebooks more than others, did more of this work and saw it valued by their teachers and by researchers from universities. No wonder they did it well – no wonder they worked hard to show these interested people how much they could do with picturebooks. Children know that being good at high-status activity is always worth the effort.

But what about the others? How do children whose teachers do not celebrate picturebooks, and who have nothing extrinsic to gain from working with them, respond? Because I wanted to know this, I chose to read *Flotsam* and *Little Mouse's Big Book of Fears* with two boys: Josh, nearly eleven, and Harry, who was nine. I knew that both Josh and Harry were competent readers, and that both came from highly literate, professional families. I guessed correctly that picturebooks were no longer part of their normal literary diet, either at home or school, but that both boys had read picture-books with their parents extensively when they were younger. This, I thought, would make their responses to these challenging, more grown-up books particularly interesting.

The readings were done *out* of school. I wanted to free the boys from the constraints of classroom expectations of texts and reading, and wanted them to see me as an independent and curious adult rather than as a limb of the school system. I told them that I was interested in these books, but needed to know what children of their age thought of them. I asked them to read the books in my presence and to 'think out loud' as they did so, so that I could tell what was going on in their heads. I told them that if they wanted to talk to me about what they saw, that was fine; I would answer. But I wouldn't ask them anything. I didn't want to prompt their thinking.

Harry

Harry set to reading the books with enthusiasm. He spent ages with *Flotsam*, carefully following the story, laughing at the underwater photographs and saying 'it's really cool'. He particularly liked the fantasy details: the inven-tiveness of the puffer-fish hot-air balloon and the intricate barnacle civiliza-tions. It was these bizarre worlds that held his attention, not the story of the boy or the record of the other children that the camera contained. When I talked to him afterwards, a number of points emerged. He had found the story hard to fit together, but this 'puzzling' had not marred his enjoyment. He had never seen a camera with a film before, but he could make sense of the plot once he knew what it was. I asked him if he had noticed that there were eyes and lenses on so many pages and he told me he had not; he didn't know why they had been included and said 'perhaps he just likes drawing eyes'. What Harry liked best were the fantasy pages. They were 'funny and cool' and, for him, the point of the book. He hardly noticed the postmodern games, the play with structure and multiple layers of framing. He saw through the frames without thinking to look at them and went straight to the core of the book, where he responded to the fantasy worlds of Wiesner's imagination.

With *Little Mouse's Big Book of Fears*, Harry's engagement was more animated still. He spent time exploring the holes and fingering the drawn fixings that hold the images of postcards and cuttings in place to see if they were real. 'Because of the first bit with holes, you think it's real sellotape and paperclips and things,' he said. He giggled at the toilet page and Little Mouse's accident, and laughed and sighed with contentment at the last image, where Little Mouse at last finds someone who is scared of him. 'He's scared of an *awful* lot,' he said at the end.

Harry spent less time than I expected on the pages where there were other things to read. He barely looked at the posters and newspaper advertisements and looked only briefly at the map of the Isle of Fright. He did not notice, until I showed him, that the map was mouse shaped, and even then he did not see the place-name jokes. The black page stumped him entirely, and he needed to look up to me for reassurance before he could move on. Books, in his experience, did not blank the reader like this, or expect him to gather resources from his infancy and play intertextual games.

With this book too it seemed to me that Harry was concentrating on what was inside the frames rather than engaging with framing itself. He found the record of Little Mouse's fears and enjoyed it immensely, but he didn't know he could look beyond that to see how those fears were presented. The intertextuality and the word games were it seemed, a distraction too far: they held up the business of finding out what was happening to Little Mouse. Despite the hints to do otherwise, Harry wanted to read this as a linear text.

Josh

Josh's approach to both books was more languid. He took both books to a sofa, and there, half reclining, he flicked though them, fairly quickly, one after the other. He spoke very little, looking up only as he came to the end of each book, and sometimes allowing a faint smile to play about his lips. He read *Flotsam* first, and he too was most interested in the fantasy pages. He spent most time looking at the mechanical fish and the octopus's sitting room, and least time on the photographs of the children who had found the camera before. He didn't seem at all interested in the passage of time or in the degrees of magnification needed to see them. When I asked him afterwards what he thought, he said he thought the book was 'really weird'. That, I think, was not necessarily a criticism. He was responding to the surrealism of the central images and, like Harry, was intrigued by them.

Josh had more time for *Little Mouse* and, although again he flicked through the pages quickly, he seemed to spend more time noticing the structure. 'I like the long words,' he said, 'I could use them to show off to my friends.' He was better than Harry at recognising intertexuality. He could explain the link with the three blind mice, but he didn't take the time to explore the joke through the cards, posters and newspaper cuttings that Gravett provides. He gave the map only a cursory glance, and didn't look at the endpapers. It was not surprising therefore that he had nothing to say about Little Mouse's intrusion or journey through the frames. He had not allowed Gravett to set him up to see them.

My feeling was that Josh's interaction with these books was half-hearted at best. One reason for this became apparent when I spoke to him afterwards: he really believed he was too old for books such as these. Despite the complexity of the texts, the craftsmanship of their making and the sheer intellectual energy needed to make sense of them fully, Josh clung on to his belief that picturebooks were for babies. 'Would you recommend these books?' I asked. 'Yes,' he said, 'to little children. Ones who can't read much yet.'

What are we to make of this?

Four main points arise from the children's responses to these books.

Picturebooks as rich and complex as these need time

It would be easy to be disheartened by the fact that the boys found relatively little in these books in one reading. This would be a mistake. Books as rich and complex as these need time. They need to be pored over and revisited. As Arizpe and Styles (2003) discovered in their study of younger children reading picturebooks, much of the understanding of what to make of books like this goes on in the thinking *between* readings. Harry, especially, I thought, would have gained much, and learned more, from looking at these books again, when he was sure of the story and felt free to explore details. A more comprehensive study of these boys and their reading of these books would have given time for this, and perhaps helped Josh overcome his initial reluctance to take picturebooks seriously.

Picturebooks challenge children's expectations of reading and their understanding of progression in reading

Even though we need not be disheartened, we *do* need to listen to these children and take account of the social and cognitive implications of what they say. We need to notice how resistant both were to books that challenged so thoroughly their expectations of reading. Josh really didn't want to read books that he thought were too young for him. His need to see himself as a competent reader made him reluctant to engage with books that might suggest he could not yet manage continuous print and chapters. Harry, on the other hand, could not quite cope with a book that demanded intertextual engagement rather than linear plot realization. These are separate problems, but both are founded in the way we value books and reading in school and society. The boys had learned too well the lessons that picturebooks are for babies, and that story is linear. In the multimodal world in which we now live this is clearly nonsense, but if we want children to think differently we need to raise the profile of good-quality picturebooks in school for children of all ages and all abilities.

Reading picturebooks is a learned skill

We sometimes assume that reading pictures is a skill people are born with. As Harry and Josh show, this is not so. Children and adults need to learn what to do to make sense of complex pictorial texts, and they need to keep learning throughout their lives, because, as with written texts, the best picturebooks always offer new and interesting challenges. We need, therefore, to give children material to practise on. That means lots of good picturebooks in schools and in homes and libraries for children of all ages, and the pedagogy and the encouragement to help children read them. Only then will children develop the acuity to identify the games that postmodern author-illustrators play, and be able to enter into the discourse of constructedness.

Being able to make sophisticated readings of picturebooks matters

Some people will argue that none of this matters. They will say that it is enough that children like Harry simply enjoy texts such as *Flotsam* and *Little Mouse's Big Book of Fears*. I disagree. I think it does matter. I want them to enjoy these books, but I also want them to be able to see through the texts and notice how they are achieved. In this increasingly image-dominated world, young people need to be able to deconstruct the images that confront and manipulate them. They need to be able to ask, with Margaret Meek (1996), 'Who sees?' and 'How do I see?' as well as 'What do I see?' An understanding of framing devices in text will help children develop the facility to do this. They need books that play with frames to stop them from taking the world as it is presented to them for granted.

References

Amis, M. (1992). *Time's Arrow.* London: Penguin

Anstey, M. (2002). 'It's not all black and white: Postmodern picturebooks and new literacies'. *Journal of Adolescent & Adult Literacy* 45(6): 444–57

Arizpe, E. & Styles, S. (2003). *Children Reading Pictures: Interpreting Visual Texts.* London: RoutledgeFalmer

Calvino, I. (1979). *If on a Winter's Night a Traveller.* Everyman Edition

Doonan, J. (1992). *Looking at Pictures in Picturebooks.* Stroud: Thimble Press

Kress, G. & van Leeuwen, T. (1996). *Reading Images: Grammar of Visual Design.* London: Routledge

Lewis, D. (2001). *Picturing Text: The Contemporary Children's Picturebook.* London: RoutledgeFalmer

Meek, M. (1996). *Information and Book Learning.* Stroud: Thimble Press

Scott, C. & Nikolajeva, M. (2000). 'The Dynamics of Picturebook Communication'. *Children's Literature in Education* 31(4): 225–39

Smith, V. (2001). 'All in a flap about reading: Catherine Morland, Spot and Mister Wolf'. *Children's Literature in Education* 32(3): 225–36

Sterne, L. (1768). *Tristram Shandy.* Penguin Classics

Thacker, D. & Webb, J. (2002). *Introducing Children's Literature: From Romanticism to Postmodernism.* London: Routledge

Children's literature

Ahlberg, J. & Ahlberg, A. (1986). *The Jolly Postman or Other People's Letters.* London: Puffin

Alborough, J. (2001). *Fix it Duck.* London: Picture Lions

Burningham, J. (1977). *Come Away From The Water, Shirley.* London: Harper Collins

Child, L. (1999). *Clarice Bean, That's Me.* London: Orchard Books

Gravett, E. (2006). *Wolves.* London: Macmillan Children's Books

Gravett, E. (2007). *Little Mouse's Big Book of Fears.* London: Macmillan Children's Books

Grey, M. (2006). *The Adventures of the Dish and the Spoon.* London: Jonathan Cape

Hughes, S. (1979). *Up and Up.* Oxford: The Bodley Head

Kerr, J. (1968). *The Tiger Who Came to Tea.* London: Collins and Sons

Macaulay, D. (1990). *Black and White.* New York: Houghton Mifflin Juvenile Books

Ormerod, J. (1981). *Sunshine.* London: Penguin

Rosen, M. & Oxenbury, H. (1989). *We're Going on a Bear Hunt.* London: Walker

Scieszka, J. (1993). *The Stinky Cheese Man and Other Fairly Stupid Tales.* London: Puffin

Sendak, M. (1963). *Where the Wild Things Are.* New York: Harper and Row

Wiesner, D. (2006). *Flotsam.* New York: Clarion Books

Part Two

Different texts, different responses

6 Reading the visual

Creative and aesthetic responses to picturebooks and fine art

Janet Evans

It has long been accepted that one can respond to fine art in a variety of different ways. However, it is only in the last decade or so that picturebooks have been attracting the kind of recognition that they have long deserved, as art forms to be considered and responded to both creatively and aesthetically. There is a growing body of research focusing on how we can respond creatively to the illustrations in picturebooks in addition to the picturebooks themselves as art objects. There is also a growing number of author-illustrators who use famous works of art as an integral part of the storyline in their picuturebooks. This chapter describes how one such book, *Katie's Picture Show*, was initially used as the stimulus for some reader-response work, which quickly led on to more in-depth, detailed responses to fine art, in particular Fernando Botero's art. It goes on to share the oral, written and illustrative responses of some ten-year-old children, demonstrating the creative and aesthetic links between picturebooks and fine art.

Picturebooks as works of art

— literally from cover to cover — the picture book is an art object, an aesthetic whole; that is, every one of its parts contributes to the total effect, and therefore every part is worthy of study and interpretation.

Sipe (2006: 135)

Sipe's statement, that we should attend to all parts of picturebooks, quite simply celebrates them as a total art form. He argues that picturebooks are worthy of serious recognition and should be credited as such. Stephens and Watkins (2003) emphasize the pleasure and intrigue that picturebooks can cause when they note that one of the strengths of the contemporary picture book is its power to delight, challenge and even mystify its readers. Arizpe and Styles (2003: 22) note that picturebooks are most certainly not just 'books with illustrations, but books in which the story depends on the interaction between written text and image and where both have been created with a conscious aesthetic intention.'

For centuries, books have been celebrated as works of art. One need only to visit museums famous throughout the world to see books displayed as treasured art works. Handmade books such as *The Book of Kells*, old precious versions of the *Koran* and other religious tomes written and illustrated by monks and religious scribes have covers encrusted with precious and semi-precious jewels, pages written with real gold, and illustrations of such beauty and intricacy that they almost defy belief. Artists would spend many months and even years on just one book. Every page was an individual work of art and so was the book as a whole. It was not just what the book was about that was important but how it was presented; these books were revered. Possession of such books confirmed the owners as high-status individuals who could afford and appreciate them. Even during these early times it was recognized that 'the book unifies art and language, for both forms exist one inside the other. One sees the art through the writing and the writing through the art.' (Johnson, 1990: 8).

In our contemporary society, scholars are once again considering books as art forms. Marantz (1977) considered the picturebook as an art object, and it is now accepted that the fusion of art and text results in more than the two separate parts: it forms one cohesive, often beautifully crafted whole. In 1988 the book artist Robert Sabuda began recreating pop-up book works of art to which readers could respond. Paul Johnson in 1987 started *The Book Art Project*, funded by the Crafts Council of Great Britain and the Gulbenkian Foundation, which aimed to encourage and advance writing and visual communication skills through the book arts. Johnson (1993, 1997) promoted the teaching of literacy through book making, and his work with children clearly makes the links between art and literacy. More recently, Wasserman (2007) curated 'the book as art' and her book, itself a work of art, provokes unexpected and surprising conclusions about what actually constitutes a book.

The importance of creativity and art education

Art is for all! Increasingly, however it is being squeezed out of the curriculum. Despite research projects that have produced detailed reports arguing for the inclusion of the arts and creativity for all children, such as the influential *All our Futures* (National Advisory Committee on Creative and Cultural Education, 1999), *Creativity: Find it, Promote it* (Qualifications and Curriculum Authority, 2005) and the significant study *Creativity and Literacy: Many Routes to Meaning* by Safford and Barrs (2005), which looks at how a range of creative art projects influenced children's language and literacy learning, art education is still not seen as an important area of the curriculum. So should it be considered as important, and what links can be made between art and literacy?

The National Art Education Association of America (2007) poses the question 'Why Art Education? What does art education do for the individual and society?' One of its three responses to this question (the other two being 'art means work' and 'art means values') is that 'art means language'. It states that:

Art is a language of visual images that everyone must learn to read ... the individual who cannot understand, or read images is incompletely educated. Complete literacy includes the ability to understand, respond to, and talk about visual images. Therefore, to carry out its total mission, art education stimulates language – spoken and written – about visual images.

This notion of reading and responding to visual images has been studied academically (Anstey & Bull, 2000; Bearne, 2005; Kress, 2003; Kress & van Leeuwen, 2006; Nikolajeva & Scott, 2001; Nodelman,1988), while Molly Bang, in her seminal picturebook *Picture This* (1991), shows the reader how to respond to visual images using the book itself as the exemplar in terms of colour, shape, texture, size, positioning, and so on.

During a one-year project, Visual Learning in the Community School, Brice Heath and Wolf (2004) looked at how children's language and cognitive abilities developed when they learned how to look carefully at, talk about and draw the works of art they were considering. They found that by talking about works of art children were better able to understand the art, and that the closer they looked the more able they were to understand what they saw. Olsen (1992: 33) noted that 'children can be taught to appreciate the great works of art by talking about them ... When young children are permitted to become personally involved by talking about the narrative content of a work of art, their attention span is amazingly long.' In their research into how children think and talk about art, Safford and Barrs (2005) found that when children were involved in creative arts projects, they used talk while *doing* art as well as when *responding* to art. The researchers noted a difference between the creative 'free' talk that comes when children create art and the creative 'response' talk that comes when they talk about art. Carger (2004) noted similar results: while working with some eight-year-old bilingual children to investigate how the visual arts could support language and literacy learning, she found that children developed as art critics when they were given opportunities to talk about picturebooks and record their responses in different ways, including creating their own personal art. Similarly, in looking at the impact that early art experiences have on literacy development, Danko-McGhee and Slutsky (2007) found that early meaningful art experiences can really inspire children in the field of literacy, and that when children are encouraged to appreciate art and to talk about their artistic creations both their oral and written language is enhanced.

Creative responses to picturebooks and fine art

Many children's first exposure to fine art is through picturebooks, and as such these books can be used as an important part of the art education curriculum. As previously noted, contemporary picturebooks can certainly be works of art in their own right, stimulating and demanding responses to their very existence in the form of their shape, form, feel, smell and overall presentation. This is in addition to their narrative, which is often presented in words (except in wordless picturebooks) and which is usually what the reader responds to when he or she interacts with a text. Our changing concept of the nature of text is continually widening our awareness of how we can use visual and multimodal texts to promote children's aesthetic, oral and literate responses. Louise Rosenblatt developed the 'reader response' field of literacy criticism. She emphasized the important relationship between the reader and the text, stating that 'The text is merely an object of paper and ink until some reader responds to the marks on the page as verbal symbols.' (Rosenblatt, 1978: 23). It is the reader who brings background information, previous experience and a whole range of sociocultural issues to the text, and these interact with the words and images to make them come alive (Evans, 1998).

In considering young children's responses to narrative, Wolfenbarger and Sipe (2007) identified three main 'impulses' that they felt guide children's responses to picturebooks: '1. the hermeneutic impulse or the desire to know; 2. the personal impulse or the need to connect stories to one's own life; and, 3. the aesthetic impulse.' It is this aesthetic impulse that 'pushes readers' creative potential to shape the story and make it their own' Sipe (2007). It is also this aesthetic response to texts in their broadest sense that is of prime concern when we provide young readers with opportunities to respond creatively to picturebooks as art forms, then to fine art; both being viewed as aesthetic art objects.

Fine art is there to be responded to, and over the centuries many art histo-rians have looked at, talked about and passed judgment on the great works of art. However, it has been said that most people when walking around an art gallery spend on average approximately 30 seconds in front of each work of art – certainly not enough time for any kind of considered response! When responding to picturebooks the reader-responder 'must find routes through the text that connect words and images' (Lewis, 2001: 32). In a similar vein, when responding to works of art the viewer-responder needs to find compa-rable routes, that is, routes that allow us to view, 'read' and respond to all aspects of the art work as a whole. It seems that maybe we can view and respond to works of art in the same way that we can read and respond to picturebooks; however, one important difference is that when responding to picturebooks the story is made explicit from the words in combination with the illustrations, while with works of art there are no words, so the viewer-responder needs to have an expectation that the art will 'tell a story' in the same way that a picturebook does, even if the 'story' is hidden behind symbols and isn't always easy to detect at first glance. Viewers need be shown and taught how to look at and respond to great works of art in just the same way that they need showing how to respond to books.

Author and artist-illustrator Anthony Browne was placed in this kind of tutorial position during his artist residency at the Tate Britain gallery in London. Some of his previous picturebooks, *Willy the Dreamer* (1997) and

Willy's Pictures (2000), had famous works of art as the focus for the narrative, but this one-year residency enabled him to personally encourage and show children how to appreciate fine art. As a result of the residency he wrote *The Shape Game* (2003), in which there is a real fusion between the picturebook narrative and fine art. *The Shape Game,* while a work of art in its own right, can be also be used to 'teach' readers how to respond to and appreciate works of art: at one point Browne shows how to interpret a nineteenth-century painting, *Past and Present 1: The Infidelity Discovered* by Augustus Leopold Egg (1858). At a personal level Browne saw the whole project as 'an opportunity to advance what I'd been trying to do for years: encourage children to appreciate fine art.' (see Chapter 10 for more of Anthony Browne's views).

Quentin Blake, another great author and artist-illustrator, did something similar when he created *Tell Me A Picture* (2001). This book was published to accompany an exhibition with the same title at the National Gallery. In it Blake chose 26 works of art for children to respond to. He realized that, just as there is a story in books, there is also a story in art; we expect a book to tell a story, so why not expect a piece of art to tell a story as well? We can use open statements and questions to elicit a story from art, and this is just what Blake attempted to do: with help from a diverse group of children he encouraged the viewer-responder to interact with the paintings and tell a story from looking at and talking about them.

Picturebooks focusing on fine art

Along with Anthony Browne's *The Shape Game* there are many other picture-books that feature works of art as part of their storyline whilst also being works of art in their own right. Author-illustrators are increasingly using famous works of art as a central part of their narrative. Although these picture-books are fiction books first and foremost, they serve a dual function, in also exposing the reader to fine art and thereby encourage him or her to begin to appreciate and respond to it. A range of different story plots are used, but a recurring plot is where the reader is drawn into the paintings with the help of a story character: little girls and boys, angels, dogs, flying babies and detec-tives are all depicted stepping into and out of famous paintings, having adven-tures and interacting with the characters from the paintings. *Katie's Picture Show* by James Mayhew (1989) is one such picturebook, but others include *Smudge* by Mike Dickenson (1987); *Lulu and the Flying Babies* by Posy Simmonds (1988); *Dogs' Night Out,* written by Meredith Hooper and illus-trated by Allan Curless (2000); *Dan's Angel,* written by Alexander Sturges and illustrated by Lauren Child (2002); *Art Fraud Detective* by Anna Nilsen (2000); and *Picturescape* by Elisa Gutiérrez (2005). In these kinds of picturebooks there is a further fusion between the art and the words. The reader is invited to look at, think about and respond to the words and illustrations within the picturebook as an art form, as well as thinking about and responding to the famous works of fine art that are featured as part of the story.

Jumping into the painting with Katie

Katie's Picture Show (see Figure 32) is the first of nine *Katie* books, most of which feature Katie interacting with works of art. Mayhew's latest, *Katie and the British Artists* (2008a), particularly focuses on the great works of British art. In these books Katie doesn't just talk about the works of art, she interacts with them by jumping into each painting and meeting the characters themselves. Mayhew (2008b:3) states, 'the idea of art coming alive goes back at least to Ovid, and in children's fiction it's not an uncommon fantasy. But I think *Katie's Picture Show* was the first time real paintings were used in a picture book story for young children.'

Katie is a cheeky little girl whose first visit to an art gallery finds her touching, then disrespectfully clambering into, a series of famous paintings and having adventures with the characters in each of them.

Her first encounter is with *The Haywain* by John Constable (see Figure 33). Once inside the painting she tramps through the mud and eats her way through the whole of an apple pie cooling on a window ledge of the cottage. Workmen start to shout and a dog begins to bark. Katie realizes that it is time to leave. She climbs back over the picture frame, only to find her next adventure is with *Madame Moitessier Seated* by Jean-Auguste-Dominique Ingres. In each of the

Figure 32 Katie's Picture Show by James Mayhew

There were lots of pictures in the room. Katie
didn't know which one to look at first. She stopped
in front of a painting of a horse-drawn cart.

The Hay Wain by *John Constable*, she read.
PLEASE DO NOT TOUCH.

"Why not?" said Katie, poking a rather dirty
finger at the picture. To her surprise, it went right
past the frame and into the painting.

"This isn't a picture at all," cried Katie,
astonished. "It's real!" Then, looking carefully
around her, *she climbed right into the painting!*

Figure 33 Katie looking at Constable's *The Haywain*

other paintings she climbs into – *Les Parapluies* by Pierre Auguste Renoir, *Tropical Storm with a Tiger* by Henri Rousseau and *Dynamic Suprematism* by Kasimir Malevich – Katie causes some kind of commotion simply by interacting with the characters. The principal storyline has Katie as the central character, but there are stories within stories and each has a series of mini-adventures that also feature Katie interacting with characters from the different paintings.

Thinking and talking about art: making a start

I was totally enamoured with *Katie's Picture Show*. What a wonderful stimulus the book would provide in enabling children to look at and respond to fine art as a focus for their own literacy activities! I decided to share it with the class of 30 ten-year-old children with whom I had been working. Initially we used just the five paintings from the book; however, we soon started to consider the work of other artists. Lucy Micklethwait's book *I Spy: An Alphabet in Art* (1991) proved to be a good starting point as it contains 26 very different and varied works of art.

When I initially began to share paintings with children of differing ages I wanted their responses to be open and personal. Closed questions would result in very narrow answers. However, 'getting into' the paintings wasn't always easy, so I started by sharing a series of 'speculative ponderings' with the children and by letting them know that I didn't have answers, quite simply because there were no right or wrong answers – we were simply sharing our thoughts and ideas.

Some of the speculative ponderings included:

- I wonder what this painting is about. What do you think?
- What can you see in the painting? I wonder what is happening.
- Who do you think that is? Do you think s/he is the main character?
- I wonder what s/he is doing. Maybe s/he is talking/running/thinking, etc.
- What are the other characters doing/thinking?
- I would quite like to be there, it looks really calm, exciting, cosy, etc.
- I would like to have this painting! Would you?
- I wonder what sort of person painted it.
- How much would you pay for this painting?
- If you could give this painting a title what might it be?
- Would you like to add or would you take anything away?

Chambers (1993) suggested that children should be asked what they liked and/or disliked about a text and also whether there were any things that puzzled them or made them think about other, similar texts. Open questions and a sharing of uncertainties proved to be good starting points for responding to works of art. The children with whom I worked responded to statements such as:

- I wonder what the artist is trying to depict. What do you think? I wonder if he is trying to convey a particular ambience, emotion, feeling, time or place?

- The artist has managed to create a particular atmosphere. How do you think she has created this? Let's consider: the subject matter; her use of colours and the style and technique she uses. Look at how she paints perspective with characters both close up and in the distance; also the position of main focal point. Do you think that position make a difference?
- Do you think these points make a difference to the finished painting?
- Do you have a favourite painting? Why do you like it?

Initially these guidance points, questions and speculative ponderings were used to home in on the art at a descriptive, literal level – What can you see? How does it look? Who is in it? As the discussions evolved the children became more speculative and their oral contributions became much more adventurous and creative. It was now that they began to use the painting as a stimulus for their story recounts, followed by using the painting in the book as a springboard into their text innovations – their own adventures that sprang from the initial painting.

What does the painting 'say'? Responding to Fernando Botero's *Family*

The next stage was to see if the work that the children had done previously, responding to paintings within picturebook narratives, would help them to respond to works of art when viewed independently from picturebooks. Would the children be able to respond to and see the story in a work of art if it was introduced away from the context of a picturebook?

The paintings from *Katie's Picture Show* had elicited many varied responses; however, it was when the children responded to Fernando Botero's painting *Family* (see Figure 34) that some really interesting work emerged. Botero is a Columbian artist born in 1932. I chose to use Botero's work with the children because of his often-familiar subject matter and yet strangely unsettling situations. His oeuvre is diverse and wide-ranging. It contains many paintings and sculptures of human characters positioned individually and together in recognizable and sometimes unusual settings. Botero's work is often controversial and always thought-provoking, and because of this I felt it would be ideal to use with the children. His painting *Family* depicts four characters, two adults and two children, presumably family members, sitting and standing under a tree with a dog.

The children were aware of Fernando Botero's work in general but had not previously seen this painting in particular. The response work, which spread over a period of six full days and culminated in some very creative, written text innovations, involved them working in a variety of different organizational styles, including the whole class, small groups, talk partners and individuals. The children were told the title of the painting and that the artist was called Fernando Botero. Initially they were asked where they thought Botero might be from and what they thought the painting might be about. They also

Figure 34 Family by Fernando Botero

considered what they could see in the painting and what was happening. They responded in a whole-class format, paying attention to each other's viewpoints and using them to move their own viewpoints further on. It was heartening to see how they listened to each other respectfully even if they didn't agree. They took turns to give their views; shouting out was not acceptable – they showed respect for their peers.

The children's initial thoughts and responses were mainly descriptive, although even at this early stage in the work some of them were beginning to speculate on whether there were deeper meanings in the painting:

- He has painted everybody fat.
- They are wearing fancy clothes, there is a dog (or a cat), they look a bit posh.
- The picture is not very good because they have managed to drag an armchair outside – it isn't very realistic.
- There are apples flying in the air, like floating apples.
- They could be falling.

- How come they look like gold, the sun might be shining on them?
- There's a snake falling on top of the woman's head.
- How come they would take a picture with a snake?
- (aside) I think there is some hidden meaning here.
- The boy has a stick in his hand – maybe he is throwing it for the dog.

After this initial whole-class discussion the children were asked to write about the picture, anything they could see in the painting or any questions that the painting made them want to ask and to talk about later. The children were used to doing a daily writer's workshop, which typically lasted about ten minutes; they knew that their ideas were crucial to later discussions.

Back in the whole-class discussion with their written notes to draw upon, they were asked to consider who the people in the painting might be and to think about them as characters in a story. What might have happened to bring these characters together? Why are they under a tree? What feelings and/or emotions have they got – for example, are they happy/sad/annoyed? The children started to talk about the painting, drawing on their written notes to inform their ideas. The focus questions enabled them to talk about the painting from a different perspective and elicited some unique responses:

Chelsea: They look as if they are all in a mood – they are all pulled up like this [she sits up straight].

Imran: I know this sounds a bit far-fetched but maybe they have been thrown out of their house for not paying their rent, that's why they have the armchair under the tree.

Adam: They all look angry apart from the dog.

Bryn: Oh I see what you mean, the dog doesn't know why they are upset. The people have feelings but the dog's feelings are different. Something is going on in their lives.

Janet: I want to ask why do you think the artist has put apples on the ground and falling from the tree and a snake coming from the tree above?

Oliver: Maybe they are magic apples and they will take a bite and die.

Bryn: Maybe they aren't real.

Janet: But why has the artist put things in the painting if they aren't real?

Imran: I have two points. Firstly maybe they are there as a space filler so the picture is not blank. Secondly everyone [in the painting] looks sad so the tree is reflecting their mood … because everyone is sad the tree makes the apples fall to reflect their mood!

Matthew: I know this might not be right but this story reminds me of Adam and Eve because there is a snake in it and they are told to eat the forbidden fruit and there is a snake in that story as well.

It was at the end of this part of the discussion that Matthew made the Adam-and-Eve suggestion. I was delighted that the children, working together and drawing on their own personal knowledge base, noted the symbolism used by Botero to determine that the painting might represent the Biblical story of Adam and Eve. Their shared responses had helped to move their ideas on in terms of complexity. The children were invited to think about what each of the characters might be thinking and feeling, after which they were asked to choose one character and to place themselves in the position of that character, that is, to empathize with that character. Focus questions helped them with this:

- What does the character think is happening?
- What are the character's feelings and/or emotions?
- Why might the character be feeling this way?
- What might the character do next?

The children then wrote an account of the events from that character's point of view. Matt's account, empathizing with the child in the painting's point of view was highly imaginative:

> *Once my dad and my mum were having a walk in the park. My mum got tired so they sat down on a chair under the shade of a tree.*
> *'Funny this chair should be here,' said my dad, rather confused.*
> *My dad picked up a golden apple and examined it, then ate it. 'Mmmm!' my dad said, 'You should try these dear!'*
> *So my mum picked up an apple as well and also ate it. 'Yes they are very tasty!'*
> *Seconds later my mum and dad were huge.*
> *'I warned you!' came the big booming voice of God. 'You shall leave my garden!' 'Now!'*
> *So my mum and dad, screaming and shouting, ran for home.*
> *Several years later my mum and dad and me and little Dolly came back to the garden and asked God forgiveness. Whilst we were waiting I got bored. Not surprising really. Also I was hungry so I looked around for a snack. The closest snack was a golden apple. Was it edible, I wondered.*
> *'Go on try one, they are soooooo tassssty!'*
> *I turned to see a long red snake hanging from a tree just shy of my mother's head.*
> *'Huh, a talking snake, in London??!!'*
> *So I picked up an apple and bit into it. 'Mmmm,' I said as I took another bite. Soon there was nothing but a core on the ground.*
> *'What are you eating?' commanded my father. Then he saw the apple core on the ground. 'Stupid – bad word – boy!' yelled my dad.*
> *God's voice boomed again, 'Leave now!' and as the heavens opened and lightning streaked down from the sky we fled, never to return.*

Botero's painting stimulated much discussion and debate, with the children being more than willing to share their ideas and viewpoints. The final part of the work took place in small response discussion groups. The groups were asked to discuss Botero's work in much more detail, prior to writing about it in draft form with a view to publishing their responses at a later stage. Imran quickly turned the general conversation back to the subject of Adam and Eve:

Imran: Personally I sort of disagree with the Adam-and-Eve theory as I don't think that Adam and Eve would drag an armchair up a hill in the Garden of Eden. Secondly they wouldn't have their clothes on, and thirdly, they have been thrown out of their home – that's why they are all looking sad, but the dog looks happy as it doesn't know and he likes being outside.

Hannah: I think the man is going away on a job – a business job because he is all dressed up in a suit and hat.

Matthew: You know what Imran said earlier about the armchair – well, maybe the clothes and the armchair is the painter's style. Some people, when they draw things connected to stories – well, it's not always what you expect – it's to get the observer to look closer.

Imran: I think I have an idea. They look very rich so maybe there is a moral to the story. They are a rich family. Money is the root of all evil. The snake is tempting them, the apples represent greed.

Hannah: In the Garden of Eden, the good-and-evil tree is how God keeps track of who is being good or evil.

Libby: The apples represent choices, the family could enter the garden to eat the apple (and disobey God), or leave the apple on the tree (and obey God). This family has disobeyed God because they have eaten the apples.

Matthew: Despite everything that is done evil will not go away. There is always a dark side to everyone. The devil has come back to earth as many different creatures to do bad things, it came back as a serpent, a small snake to tempt people. Jesus was tempted once. The devil is red so the snake is red – like the devil.

Bryn: But look, the devil was an angel first.

Nicole: What was the point of the tree if God didn't want people to eat from it?

Imran: I'm not being funny here but it is so easy to be bad, to be a criminal. Look at the drug trade, it is worth millions.

Matthew: That reminds me of what Dumbledore says in Harry Potter, 'Soon we will have to make the choice between what is good and what is bad.'

Bryn and
Libby: [together] Choices ... again!

Matthew: Some people don't know what being good is and you can't base everyone's behaviour on one test, there are lots of different people.

Libby: What if there is no such thing as hell?

Bryn: The Bible says God always forgives so what is the point of hell if God always forgives and sends everyone to heaven?

Imran: In the *Koran* it says everyone goes to hell but just for a period of
            time and then they go to heaven, so Adolf Hitler and Saddam
            Hussein might go for 200 years then go to heaven.
Libby: Jesus Christ died to save us all.
Hannah: If God made the world – why did he need to make evil?
Matthew: To test us.
Bryn: Some religions say God is the only thing that is perfect so why not
            make us perfect as well to get rid of evil?
Hannah: Jesus died on the cross. If Jesus is God's son he can't just give special
            treatment to one person.
Nicole: God is in everyone but He is different in everyone.
Libby: God and Jesus is a belief.

Lunch time bell goes

Imran: We have learned something from all this ... we have learned a lot
            from this session. Botero did this painting to make us think and he
            has made us think. He has made us think a lot.
Hannah: Also, we have talked about talking.

The conversation ranged over complex and philosophical topics. These ten-year-old children had started talking about *Katie's Picture Show* and ended by talking about the representation of Adam and Eve in Botero's painting, which led to a wide-ranging discussion about the existence of God, the nature of good and evil and the reasons for having Jesus and God. All of the group members had contributed, to a greater or lesser extent, and I had stayed virtually silent for most of the time.

The six sessions culminated in the children writing about why they thought Botero had painted *Family* (see Figure 35). They also produced their own versions of Botero's painting (see Figure 36).

Conclusion

The children's own words sum up in part some of the reasons for responding to art as well as to picturebooks. They were asked what they felt they had learned from talking about Botero's work and the project in general. They were succinct and to the point, stating that they had learned:

- Art isn't always what it seems.
- Paintings don't always have to be obvious or straightforward; they can have hidden meanings.
- A painting can represent other things.
- Adults in general do not know everything.
- Maybe Botero was trying to tell us about important things in life.
- Botero could have been a Christian.

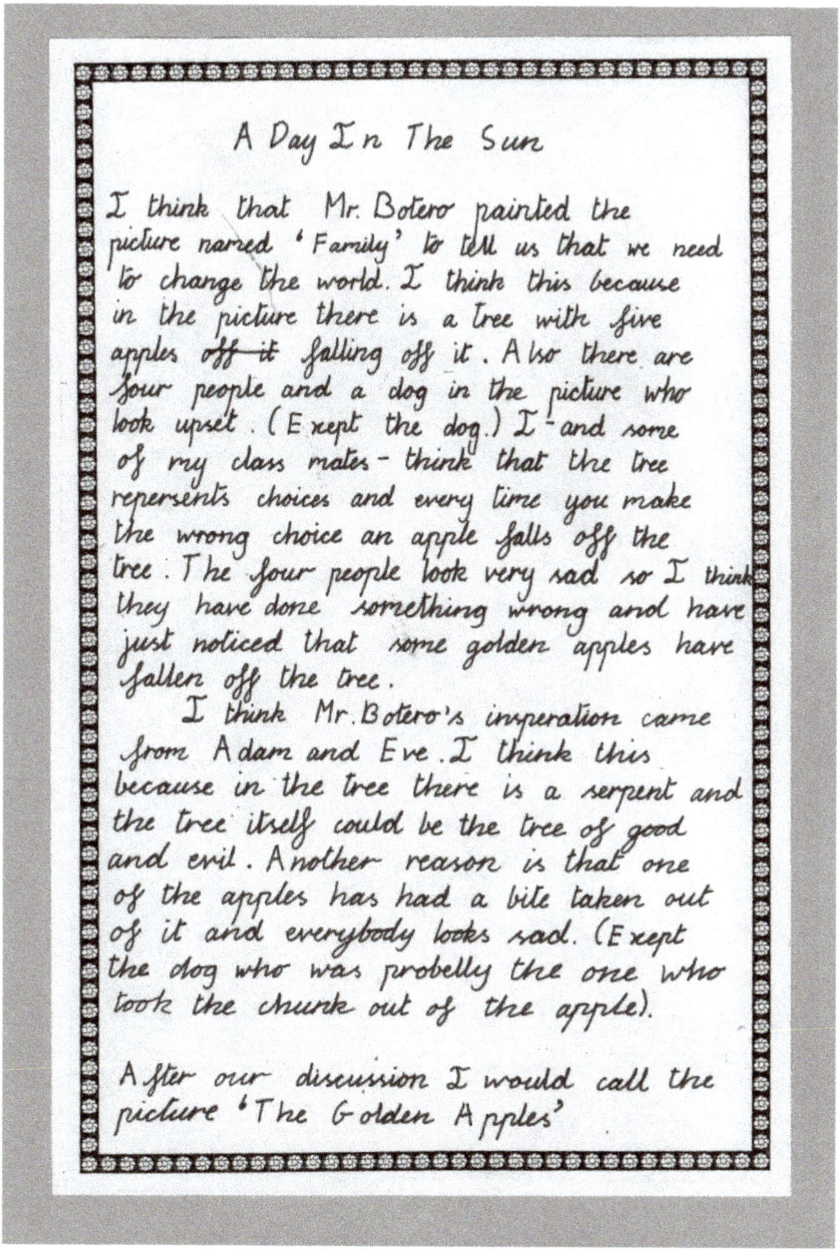

A Day In The Sun

I think that Mr. Botero painted the picture named 'Family' to tell us that we need to change the world. I think this because in the picture there is a tree with five apples ~~off it~~ falling off it. Also there are four people and a dog in the picture who look upset. (Exept the dog.) I - and some of my class mates - think that the tree repersents choices and every time you make the wrong choice an apple falls off the tree. The four people look very sad so I think they have done something wrong and have just noticed that some golden apples have fallen off the tree.

I think Mr. Botero's imperation came from Adam and Eve. I think this because in the tree there is a serpent and the tree itself could be the tree of good and evil. Another reason is that one of the apples has had a bite taken out of it and everybody looks sad. (Exept the dog who was probelly the one who took the chunk out of the apple).

After our discussion I would call the picture 'The Golden Apples'

Figure 35 Imran's writing

Figure 36 Matthew's illustration

- To use my imagination to discover new things.
- You can make a chain of ideas that link on to each other.
- To listen to other people's point of view.
- Teamwork is important.
- A painting is worth a thousand words.

This last comment is a well-known phrase but nevertheless makes an interesting point. We can create opportunities for extremely creative oral language interactions if we provide stimulating reasons to talk and if we give children opportunities to feel at ease and the chance to offer viewpoints without feeling threatened. The children's comments show that studying a work of art can fulfil these conditions. In fact, one could argue that responding to works of art is very similar to responding to picturebooks, because both are art forms and both tell a story; the acts are complementary and support each other in enhancing children's deepening understanding.

I have tried to illustrate how spending time looking closely at pictures, whether in picturebooks or as individual works of art, can help children understand more about the story within the picture. Imran was right when he stated that 'A painting is worth a thousand words.'

Acknowledgements

Thanks go to Michèle Anstey and Geoff Bull for permission to use part of their book title, *Reading the Visual: Written and Illustrated Children's Literature*, in the title of this chapter.

References

Anstey, M. & Bull, G. (2000). *Reading the Visual: Written and Illustrated Children's Literature*. London: Harcourt Publishers

Arizpe, E. & Styles, M. (2003). *Children Reading Pictures: Interpreting Visual Texts*. London: RoutledgeFalmer

Bang, M. (1991). *Picture This: How Pictures Work*. New York: SeaStar Books

Bearne, E. (2005). 'Multimodal texts: What they are and how to use them' in Evans, J. (ed) *Literacy Moves On: Using Popular Culture, New Technologies and Critical Literacy in the Primary Classroom*. London: David Fulton, pp.16–30

Brice Heath, S. & Wolf, S. (2004). *Art is all about Looking: Drawing and Detail*. London: Creative Partnerships

Carger, C. L. (2004). 'Art and literacy with bilingual children'. *Language Arts* 81: 283–92

Chambers, A. (1993). *Tell Me: Children, Reading and Talk*. Stroud: Thimble Press

Danko-McGhee, K. & Slutsky, R. (2007). *Impact of Early Art Experiences on Literacy Development*. Reston, Virginia: National Art Education Association

Evans, J. (ed.) (1998). *What's in the Picture?: Responding to Illustrations in Picture Books*. London: Paul Chapman Publishing

Johnson, P. (1990). *A Book of One's Own: Developing Literacy Through Making Books*. London: Hodder & Stoughton

Johnson, P. (1993). *Literacy Through the Book Arts*. Portsmouth, New Hampshire: Heinemann

Johnson, P. (1997). *Pictures and Words Together: Children Illustrating and Writing Their Own Books*. Portsmouth, New Hampshire: Heinemann

Kress, G. (2003). *Literacy in the New Media Age*. London: Routledge

Kress, G. & van Leeuwen, T. (2006). *Reading Images: The Grammar of Visual Design*. London: RoutledgeFalmer

Lewis, D. (2001). *Reading Contemporary Picturebooks: Picturing Text*. London: RoutledgeFalmer

Marantz, K. (1977). 'The picture book as an art object: A call for balanced reviewing'. *Wilson Library Bulletin* October 1977: 148–51

Mayhew, J. (2008b). 'Katie's Picture Show'. *Books for Keeps* 171, July 2008: 3–5

National Advisory Committee on Creative and Cultural Education (NACCCE) (1999). *All Our Futures: Creativity, Culture and Education*. London: Department for Education and Employment

National Art Education Association of America (2007). 'Why Art Education?' http://www.naea-reston.org/whyart.html

Nikolajeva, M. & Scott, C. (2001). *How Picturebooks Work*. New York: Garland

Nodelman, P. (1988). *Words about Pictures: The Narrative Art of Children's Picture Books*. Athens, Georgia: University of Georgia Press

Olsen, J. L. (1992). *Envisioning Writing: Toward an Integration of Drawing and Writing*. Portsmouth, New Hampshire: Heinemann

Rosenblatt, L. (1978). *The Reader, the Text, the Poem: The Transactional Theory of the Literary Work*. Carbondale: Southern Illinois University Press

Qualifications and Curriculum Authority (QCA) (2005). *Creativity: Find it, Promote it*. London: QCA

Safford, K. & Barrs, M. (2005). *Creativity and Literacy: Many Routes to Meaning*. London: Centre for Literacy in Primary Education

Sipe, L. (2006). 'Learning from illustrations in picturebooks' in Fisher, D. & Frey, N. (eds) *Picture This! The Role Visual Information Plays in Literacy Learning*. Thousand Oaks, California: Corwin Press; SAGE Publications

Stephens, J. & Watkins, K. (eds) (2003). *From Picture Book to Literary Theory*. Sydney: St Clair Press

Wasserman, K. (2007). *The Book as Art: Artists' Books from the National Museum of Women in the Arts*. New York: Princeton Architectural Press

Wolfenbarger, C. D. & Sipe, L. (2007). 'A unique visual and literary art form: Recent research on picturebooks'. *Language Arts* 84: 273–80

Children's literature

Blake, Q. (2001). *Tell Me A Picture*. London: Frances Lincoln

Browne, A. (1997). *Willy the Dreamer*. London: Walker Books

Browne, A. (2000). *Willy's Pictures*. London: Walker Books

Browne, A. (2003). *The Shape Game*. London: Doubleday

Dickenson, M. (1987). *Smudge*. London: Andre Deutsch Limited

Gutiérrez, E. (2005). *Picturescape*. Vancouver, British Columbia: Simply Read Books

Hooper, M. (2000). *Dogs' Night Out* (illustrated by A. Curless). London: Frances Lincoln

Mayhew, J. (1989). *Katie's Picture Show.* London: Orchard Books
Mayhew, J. (2008a). *Katie and the British Artists.* London: Orchard Books
Micklethwait, L. (1991). *I Spy: An Alphabet in Art.* London: Collins
Nilsen, A. (2000). *Art Fraud Detective.* London: Kingfisher
Simmonds, P. (1988). *Lulu and the Flying Babies.* London: Picture Puffin
Sturges, A. (2002) *Dan's Angel* (illustrated by L. Child). London: Frances Lincoln

7 Thinking in action

Analysing children's multimodal responses to multimodal picturebooks

Morag Styles and Kate Noble

In this chapter we consider how children aged five to nine responded orally, physically and visually to different versions of *The Frog Prince*. We examine the evidence from an in-depth study of the different ways children reveal their cognitive understanding, aesthetic awareness and affective responses to picturebooks, with particular reference to their drawing. Although we were interested in the finished products, our key focus was what was learned during the process of drawing, and the talk and actions that surrounded it. We believe the data will offer new insights on how children develop visual literacy.

> Children act multimodally, both in the things they use, the objects they make, and in the engagement of their bodies: there is no separation of body and mind. The differing modes and materials which they employ offer differing potentials for the making of meaning; and therefore offer different affective, cognitive and conceptual possibilities.
>
> Kress (1997: 97)

Many researchers have demonstrated how communication and learning in the young child is multimodal (Paley, 1981; Barrs, 1988; Jewitt & van Leeuwan, 2000; Pahl, 2000, 2001; Anning, 2003; Bearne, 2003). Young children switch with great ease between the different modes of word and image. Through play and experimentation they move from talking to making and to drawing, according to the different purposes of their activity. For many years, research into picturebooks focused on the form itself or concentrated on children's reading and writing in relation to visual literacy. Recently, scholars and educators have taken a greater interest in the value of children's oral responses to visual texts (Wells, 1986; Meek, 1988; Kiefer, 1993; Madura, 1998; Harris & McKenzie, 2005; Sharpe, 2005). As the concept of multimodality has taken a more central place in thinking about picturebooks, so too has the interest in children's responses to visual texts expanded to include body language and gesture (Mackey, 2002) as well as children's drawings (Dyson, 1986; Arizpe & Styles, 2003).

Researching children's responses to picturebooks

This chapter is based on the findings of a study that examined the development of visual literacy in 24 children aged five, seven and nine years. The children, from two different schools in England, were interviewed five times in mixed-ability, mixed-gender pairs, responding to three different picturebook retellings of the same fairy tale. The three picturebooks were: *The Frog Prince* (1990), written and illustrated by Jan Ormerod; *The Princess and the Frog* (1994), written by Molly Perham and illustrated by Sue King; and *The Frog Prince Continued* (1991), written by Jon Scieszka and illustrated by Steve Johnson. We looked at the strategies that young children used to make sense of complex multimodal texts, considering both interpretation and production through talk, gesture and drawing.

In the first interview, the children were asked what they knew about the fairy tale *The Frog Prince*, which is, of course, a story about keeping promises, however unpleasant they turn out to be. In the event, the princess reluctantly kisses the frog who has helped her and he miraculously turns into a handsome prince! The story was discussed from memory, with details of the narrative, which were unknown or forgotten by the children, supplied from a simple prompt sheet summarizing the main points of the story. The children were then asked to draw a scene from the story using their imagination. The first interview was the most open-ended of the five and allowed the children to get to know the researcher and to talk generally about drawing and reading. The next three interviews all took the same form. They began with an initial read-through of the book, followed by an in-depth discussion of the text and pictures using a semi-structured interview schedule developed after pilot studies and an in-depth analysis of the three chosen picturebooks. The children were then asked to draw a scene from the book and to 'make their drawing like the ones in the book'. In the fifth and final interview, the children were asked to compare the three books they had studied and the four drawings they had made so far, and to talk about their experiences during the course of the research. They were then asked to make a final drawing of the story from their imagination.

The five interviews were planned in order to collect detailed data on change and development within the individual child, as well as to provide a comparison between the different ages. The use of the three versions of the same story provided data on the role played by different styles of illustration, examining both children's understanding of the three picturebooks and the effects of these multimodal texts on the children's own visual narratives. The interviews were videotaped throughout in order to capture the children's talk and non-verbal communication such as gesture, expression and other physical responses whilst reading and making their own drawings. The use of video allowed for the simultaneous recording of the 'full repertoire of modes' described by Kress and others (Barrs, 1988; Kress, 1997; Pahl, 2000; Bearne, 2003). The video footage of the children making their drawings was then analysed alongside the final drawings and the children's comments made whilst reading the books. Reading picturebooks was found to be an active, interactive and creative process consisting of a multimodal dialogue between child, picturebook and the child's personal and textual experience up to that point.

Multimodality

The natural disposition of young readers towards multimodality makes picturebooks the ideal primary texts of childhood, owing to the way in which these books communicate through the dual modes of word and image. The different properties of the two modes afford many different possibilities of interpretation and response. Lewis (2001) locates picturebooks within current scholarly debates on postmodernism to celebrate their inherently playful nature. Children and picturebook makers have been described as powerful allies (Meek *et al.*, 1977), and parallels can be drawn between the characteristics of postmodern picturebooks and the anarchy of childhood such as boundary testing, excess, indeterminacy, parody and performance (Lewis, 2001). Lewis (2001: 137) concludes that 'The picturebook is thus ideally suited to the task of absorbing, reinterpreting and re-presenting the world to an audience for whom negotiating newness is a daily task.'

The dialogue between child and picturebook is fluid, dynamic and subject to change. Within this dialogue the text undergoes a series of transformations as the child talks, acts and draws his or her own personal responses. As Kress (1997: 58) suggests, 'Reading is a transformative action, in which the reader makes sense of the signs provided to her or to him within a frame of reference of their own experience.'

The process of reading can be seen to be the co-construction of meaning culturally mediated within the specific context in which the reader is acting. As the children in Noble's (2007) study responded to the various picturebook versions of *The Frog Prince*, they could be seen to draw upon extensive knowledge taken both from personal experience and from the wide and varied range of multimodal texts within their world. Golden (1990) describes the potential of picturebooks to generate multiple meanings that are based on the imagination of the individual doing the meaning-making. Prior knowledge and experience are recognized as being key to the reading process. As Watson (1993: 15) argues, 'every reader reads a different story'. There is a complex network of relations within and between texts and readers. Indeed, many commentators have argued for the need to listen carefully and seriously to the voice of the child in relation to these complex texts (Watson, 1993; Watson & Styles, 1996; Meek, 1998; Lewis, 2001; Bearne, 2003; Arizpe & Styles, 2003).

Another important implication of a multimodal approach to understanding children's responses to visual texts is the need to examine the physical interaction between the reader and the picturebook. Mackey (2002) looked at the ecology of literacy through different media to explore the relationship between young people and the texts they read. She highlighted the two-way interaction between body and text and described reading as a playful process of negotiation, imagination, orchestration, interpretation and experimentation. This process was seen to be both physical and cognitive: hands, eyes and bodies are all active. After dividing responses to multimodal texts into the two categories of word and image, Mackey noted particular visual strategies of noticing, searching, exploring, experimenting, hypothesizing, comparing, consolidating, labelling and strategizing.

Mackey's findings were corroborated by Arizpe and Styles (2003) during their two-year study of visual literacy and picturebooks. After analysing the responses of 84 children, aged between four and eleven years, talking and drawing in response to three carefully chosen picturebooks, they found evidence of sophisticated readings at all ages. The children demonstrated that they were able to make sense of complex images on literal, moral, aesthetic, visual and metaphorical levels. The researchers also found many examples of the children talking about the metacognitive process involved in reading and drawing in response to picturebooks. This was particularly true of the older children they worked with. Their comments revealed some of the strategies the children used for making sense of what they saw through selective scanning, comparison, deduction, questioning and hypothesis. The children revealed a mature understanding of the different communicative functions of word and image, as discussed above and described here by ten-year-old Lara.

> The writing doesn't explain everything what they think. The writing only explains what the book is about and what is happening, but it doesn't explain what you feel and what they feel. So I like the pictures better because you can think about more stuff.
>
> Arizpe & Styles (2003: 196)

Arizpe and Styles also found evidence of the children's understanding of the processes involved in making pictures, both in the way they talked about the illustrations and in their own drawings. The highest levels of response were recorded within classrooms where the children were provided with time, space and opportunities to explore and produce their own visual texts. Indeed, in many cases the production of children's own visual texts was found to be key to the process of interpretation.

The case studies in this chapter are taken from the fourth interview from Noble's (2007) study with two of the five- and nine-year-olds after examining *The Frog Prince Continued* by John Scieszka and Steve Johnson. The interview questions focused in particular on the role of the pictures and how they communicated meaning in relation to the main narrative. Before we consider the children's responses we begin with a brief analysis of the picturebook itself, as this was what shaped the research questions and stimulated the children's responses.

The Frog Prince Continued

The Frog Prince Continued (see Figure 37) can be described as a 'counter-pointing' picturebook, where the words and pictures contain two mutually dependent narratives (Nikolajeva & Scott, 2001). The writer/illustrator team plays with this counterpoint in a variety of different ways. The main narrative is dependent on intertextual references to other fairy tales and the discovery of these allusions, which reveal many jokes hidden in both the words and the pictures. The reader is invited to fill these textual gaps him- or herself. Within these pages, Bahktin's theory of 'heteroglossia' – the many voices in the text – is taken to its extreme.

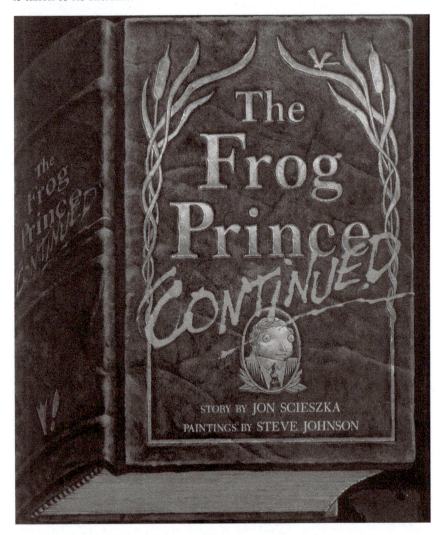

Figure 37 The Frog Prince Continued by Jon Scieszka

Languages of heteroglossia, like mirrors that face each other, each reflecting in its own way a piece, a tiny corner of the world, force us to guess at and grasp for a world behind their mutually reflecting aspects that is broader, more multileveled, containing more and varied horizons than would be available to a single language or multiple mirror.

> Bahktin (1981: 414)

The story itself provides a clever postmodern subversion of the original fairy tale and uses metafictive devices to 'undermine expectations' and expose 'the fictional nature of fictions' (Lewis, 2001: 94). This playfulness encourages the young reader to feel confident and to adventure further with his or her own meaning-making, as outlined by Bahktin.

Laughter demolishes fear and piety before an object, before a world, making of it an object for familiar contact and thus clearing the ground for an absolutely free investigation of it. Laughter is a vital factor in lying down that prerequisite for fearlessness, without which it would be impossible to approach the world realistically.

> Bahktin (1981: 23)

The humorous nature of the situations encountered by the prince encourages the reader to take risks and have the confidence to play with the text. The possibilities of meaning-making are extended and expanded to allow for infinite creative possibilities and transformations. It was interesting to see how the children responded to the many voices within the text, and to examine their own transformations through talk and drawings.

Throughout the book, word and image are separated with pictures contained in what appear to be pages torn from a book. The design and style of the illustrations is central to the narrative. The artist uses a dark green, pond-like palette, creating rich and slippery opaque painted surfaces in contrast to the luminescent transparency of the watercolours employed in the other two *Frog Prince* books. In the opening pages, dark colours echo the depression of the prince and the state of his marriage. Relief from this gloom is provided only on the penultimate page, when the unhappy couple are reunited. The characters themselves seem awkward and uncomfortable in their fairy-tale world, and they poke out of the picture boxes with arms, legs and magic wands. In this version, traditional stereotypes are turned upside down. The central character of the frog prince is portrayed as ungainly and ineffectual, blundering from one witch to another, his big head and bulging eyes seeming progressively frog-like. The princess wears the obligatory pink dress but is portrayed as the archetypal nagging wife, bossing her inadequate husband to get out of the castle and do something useful.

The first double-page spread of the book (see Figure 38) demonstrates how disaffected the prince and princess have become since the happy conclusion of the previous episode. The verbal text describing their unhappiness and how

ell, let's just say they lived sort of
happily for a long time.

Okay, so they weren't so happy.

In fact, they were miserable.

"Stop sticking your tongue out like that,"
nagged the Princess.

"How come you never want to go down to
the pond anymore?" whined the Prince.

The Prince and Princess were so unhappy.
They didn't know what to do.

Figure 38 First spread of *The Frog Prince Continued*

they have grown apart is echoed in the picture. Their position relative to each other and body language demonstrate their emotional distance and failure to relate to and engage with one another. The prince is turned away, head resting nonchalantly on his hand whilst he plays at catching the printed dragonflies, dreaming of the pond referred to in the words. The princess is depicted as angular and bossy, her angry eyes directed away from the prince and focused instead on a newspaper. On the table between them sits a vase of dead flowers, also depicted underneath the writing on the facing page. The flowers provide a powerful metaphor for their own dying relationship. The style of the illustrations is determined by the narrative. The artist's use of greens and dark tertiary colours creates a pond-like murkiness that hints at the eventual outcome. This double-page spread of the princess and the frog prince elicited some of the most interesting responses in the interviews with the children.

Multimodal responses to multimodal texts

Gestures and pointing

After we had read the book all the way through for the first time we returned to the beginning and the children were asked if there was anything in the first double spread, described above, that made them think that the prince and the princess were unhappy. The following extracts demonstrate how five-year-old Timothy and Imogen, and nine-year-old Christina and Brian, drew upon a wide range of knowledge and experience to make sense of what they saw. The transcripts also demonstrate some of the multimodal and performative aspects of their responses through the use of gesture and pointing.

Five-year-old Timothy and Imogen

Kate:	Can you tell they are unhappy by looking at the picture?
Timothy:	Yeah.
Kate:	It says it in the words but can you tell from the picture?
Timothy:	His eyes ...
Kate:	His eyes. What about his eyes are unhappy?
Timothy:	Well he's bored and unhappy.
Kate:	How can you tell he is bored and unhappy?
Imogen:	[mimes what Frog Prince is doing]
Timothy:	Well his eyes and hand. His hand [mimes hand on chin] like that.
Kate:	What about the rest of his body?
Timothy:	No he's just [mimes with hands] like that.
Kate:	Like that. Yeah. Is there anything about the rest of his body ... that tells you that he is unhappy?
Timothy:	No.
Kate:	Ok, tell me about the princess and how she is feeling. How can you tell how she is feeling from the picture?

Imogen:	Because her face looks unhappy.
Kate:	She does look unhappy doesn't she? What is it that makes her look unhappy?
Imogen:	Because she's frowning.
Kate:	What about her body? Is there anything about her body and what she is doing?

[…]

[both lean over the picture]

Imogen:	The flowers are unhappy!
Kate:	How do you know the flowers are unhappy? That's a good answer.
Timothy:	Because they're drooping.
Kate:	They're drooping. Why are the flowers drooping?
Timothy:	Because they haven't got any water.
Kate:	They haven't got any water.
Imogen:	And no sunlight.
Kate:	And no sunlight. So it's not very nice in there then?
Imogen:	No.
Timothy:	They have got sunlight. It is light in there. [points]
Kate:	But not enough.
Imogen:	Yeah that's what I mean. Not enough.
Kate:	OK. Why do you think the artist has put the flowers drooping?

[…]

Imogen:	Because he thought that 'cos they were unhappy they'd forgotten about the flowers.

Nine-year-old Ben and Christina

Kate:	So looking at this picture again, is there anything in this picture that shows you that the prince and princess are unhappy?
Christina:	He's got these [mimes with fingers rubbing under eyes] under his eyes.
Kate:	Bags under his eyes?
Christina:	Yeah, and his eyes are sort of squinting and he keeps licking the wall.
Ben:	That could just be tired though with bags under his eyes 'cos I've got bags like that.
Christina:	[speaking at the same time as Ben] And her eyes are really bright [mimes open eyes with fingers] and her eyebrows go down. My mum always crosses her legs like that sometimes, stiffly, when she's annoyed … and you can see that the paper's sort of creased. She's like [mimes the tension with which she is holding the newspaper].
Kate:	What about the way they are sitting?
Christina:	Well he's sort of [mimes turning head away and resting it on hand].

Ben: He is drunk.
Kate: He looks a bit drunk; he's kind of all floppy.
Christina: Yes and he's sticking his tongue out on the wall really like irritated, [whining voice] 'Why can't I do this?' 'Why can't I go down to the pond anymore?'
Kate: And she's kind of …
Christina: She's like [miming princess's pose].
Kate: … sitting upright.
Christina: She's like [mimes sitting up straight grasping newspaper tightly and looking sideways with gritted teeth] … She's reading the paper and going [makes face again].
Ben: She's like, 'Touch me and I'll kill you.'
Christina: Yeah!

In both extracts the children's use of gesture supports their readings and through the role play they go on to create their own mini-text based on the story. Five-year-old Imogen is mimicking the poses of the characters with her body language and gestures. Her final comment about the flowers reveals she has also accurately interpreted this visual symbol despite her partner's literal understanding (they haven't got any water). At both five and nine years old the children's use of gesture reinforces the point that communication is multi-modal and underlines the importance of allowing personal and individual responses to be acknowledged in whatever form they take, be that word, image or gesture. Had the interviews not been videotaped, the important points that the children were making through gesture would have been lost within the later analysis. This also restates the point that opportunities must be provided to allow a response that is true to the original form (Dewey, 1934; Benson, 1986). When describing non-verbal interaction such as facial expression and body language it is not surprising that mime provided the most direct way of communicating what the children saw.

The children's comments demonstrated that they could recognize and interpret non-verbal signs through body language and gesture and indicate empathy with others. Five-year-old Timothy identified boredom and unhappiness in the eyes of the prince, a sophisticated reading for a child of his age in light of theories of the egocentricity of the young child (Piaget, 1929; Athey, 1990). Christina and Brian are drawing on knowledge from both personal (bags under my eyes) and family experience (My mum always crosses her legs …). There are also distant echoes of popular culture, such as television and film knowledge, for example, 'Touch me and I'll kill you.' Throughout the course of the study, the children demonstrated an impressive knowledge of other multi-modal texts and drew on this knowledge repeatedly to make sense of what they saw, drawing in particular on the visual medium of film. In the following extract, where they are describing the role of the fairy-tale witches in the story, they can be seen to jump from the traditional fairy story to Shakespeare and to film. They move from genre to genre, medium to medium, with confidence and fluency – their comments serving as a reminder of how complex and multi-layered children's contemporary intertextual scenery can be.

Christina: You would expect like them to be standing around a cauldron going 'eye of newt, tail of toad'.
Kate: Which they are not doing at all!
Christina: Which they are not doing!
Ben: No. There is usually [gesture with right hand] a group of witches in one film making a poison bottle or something.
Christina: [speaking at the same time as Ben] A potion to kill everyone in town.

Drawing and transformation

The preceding extracts reveal some of the many creative and imaginative ways in which the children interpreted and transformed the texts by entertaining different imaginative possibilities whilst reading. The video data of the children drawing also provided insight into the transformative processes of drawing. The finished drawing told only a small part of the full story in terms of the motivation and narrative intention of the young artist. As they drew, the children made many alterations to the original narrative offered by the picturebook they had examined. The different reasons for implementing changes included avoiding difficulty, repositioning the narrative, and making improvements to add realism or increase the drawing's aesthetic beauty. The motivations behind these transformations were personal and, therefore, individual to each child.

Five-year-old Timothy encountered problems with planning and scale when he started drawing the frog prince's head. He eventually resolved this problem by starting again on a clean sheet of paper. His finished drawing in Figure 39 shows that although he moved on successfully from the original problem with the head and was able to plan and control this element of the design, he stumbled on the same difficulties with size and scale when he was drawing the hands.

Although Timothy has carefully controlled the head, body and neck in his drawing, the arms and legs of the frog prince and the brick path have taken on a life of their own as their heavy forms stretch uncomfortably towards the edges of the paper. This time Timothy was unable to resolve the problem to achieve a realistic portrayal. His solution was to add as many fingers as he could, which eventually numbered 61 in total!

Timothy: [counts slowly as he adds fingers] 1, 2, 3, 4, 5, 6, 7, 8, 9, 10, 11, 12.
Imogen: [stops and looks over at Timothy]
Kate: What are those bits Timothy?
Timothy: They're fingers … 13, 14, 15, 16, 17, 18, 19, 20, 21. [counting continues as he draws]
Timothy: There are 61 fingers on that.

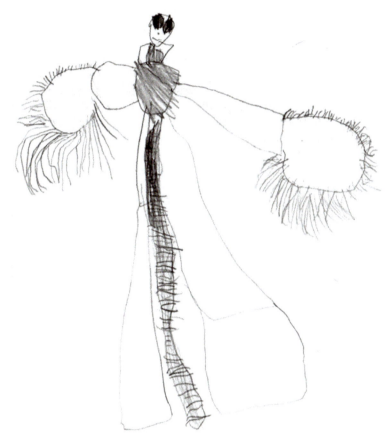

Figure 39 Five-year-old Timothy's drawing in response to *The Frog Prince Continued*

Kate: Why have you given him 61 fingers?
Timothy: Oh 'cos he's got a big hand.

Timothy carefully counted the fingers one by one as he added them to his drawing. His explanation for the large number of fingers shows that the resolution was primarily concerned with balancing salient features of the object. Fingers are placed around the hand and so this continues until the space is filled. This example shows a young artist working hard to develop new conventional equivalents for the depiction of the figure but still bound by old routines and schema (Goodnow, 1977; Whitebread & Leader, 2003; Willats, 2005). Despite a concern with the representative function of his drawing (as seen in his continued attempts to master the drawing of the head), for Timothy the process and pleasure of realizing his creation is all-consuming. The task of adding the fingers became a mesmerising and enjoyable repeating pattern of action and mark-making (Kellog, 1969; Matthews, 2003).

This example demonstrates the problem-solving aspect of the drawing process for young children and how they experiment with the media they use to test their properties. When Timothy made this drawing, the process of experimentation was clearly more important to him then the realism of his drawing. This ties in with Bronson's (2000) description of the exploratory nature of early childhood thinking. Timothy has only a passing interest in the use of conventional equivalents to depict reality. Instead, drawing is a process of experimentation experienced through the sensory pleasure derived from the activity of mark-making and through the movement of arms and body together. This was a common feature of many of the drawings by the other five-year-olds in the study, and highlights how drawing has many functions outside the representational (Atkinson, 1991; Cox, 2005).

In contrast to Timothy, nine-year-old Christina is preoccupied with the representational qualities of her drawings. Throughout the interviews, she and Brian state repeatedly 'I am not very good at drawing', and Christina goes on to say 'because now I am much better at writing ... now I want to be a poet or a writer.' After reading the *The Frog Prince Continued,* she used the character of the fairy godmother from the picturebooks but then added her own imaginary characters, creating new narratives as she drew. She added captions to her drawing to explain these changes (see Figure 40).

Christina: [has finished colouring the fairy godmother and sits back to look at drawing with hand on forehead as if thinking] Some extras in now.

Kate: Are you going to put some extras in?

Figure 40 Nine-year-old Christina's drawing in response to *The Frog Prince Continued*

Christina: I always do. Um … I like doing it …

[…]

Kate: I like that bit! [pointing to the owl] What's that say? Hansel and
          Gretel?
Christina: Hansel or Gretel, it used to be them but …
Kate: She's turned them into an owl!
Christina: Yeah.
Kate: That's good! … What's that? [pointing to the side of the owl]
Christina: The wheels. She turns everything into a carriage!

[…]

Christina: If we were finished by lunch I'd put in my story if we were going to
          write a story and, I think I'd write that the evil witch thingy
          turned herself into a cat and turned her cat into her, so and then she
          got narked with them and as they went off she turned them into an
          owl …

Christina's desire to write demonstrates her recognition of the different role of
words and pictures and their different communicative functions. Whilst the
picture 'shows' the reader the characters, the labels gave them a context whilst
providing explanations. Her plan for a verbal text would have exploited the
'telling' function of words and demonstrated her confidence in another
expressive mode. Her comments also reveal the pull towards realism and
verbal forms of representation in middle childhood, as documented by
Gardner (1980), Benson (1986) and others.

Conclusions

When young children engage with picturebooks they respond physically,
intellectually and emotionally. The action of engagement is multisensory and
multimodal, and is intricately linked to the child's burgeoning cognitive
powers. The dual modes of word and image within the picturebook offer
distinct but complementary possibilities for this action. In this study the joint
emphasis on talk, drawing and gesture revealed much about how children read
picturebooks but also offered a glimpse into their rich and multilayered
visual-textual worlds. The analysis of different modes of response can be
particularly relevant for the very young and those who are less articulate or
confident with the verbal mode. However, this research has shown that it is
just as important to allow older, more confident children the opportunity to
express themselves through these different modes in order to exploit the
different communicative functions of word, image and gesture. Observing and
listening to children as they talk and draw allows precious opportunities to
witness at first hand this multimodal thinking in action.

References

Anning, A. (2003). 'Pathways to the graphicacy club: The crossroad of home and school'. *Early Childhood Literacy* 3(1): 5–35

Arizpe, E. & Styles, M. (2003). *Children Reading Pictures: Interpreting Visual Texts.* London: RoutledgeFalmer

Athey, C. (1990). *Extending Thought in Young Children.* London: Paul Chapman Publishing

Atkinson, D. (1991). 'How children use drawing'. *International Journal of Art and Design Education* 10(1): 57–72

Bakhtin, M. (1981). *The Dialogic Imagination.* Austin: University of Texas Press

Barrs, M. (1988). 'Maps of play' in Meek, M. & Mills, C. *Language and Literacy in the Primary School.* London: Falmer Press

Bearne, E. (2003). 'Rethinking literacy: Communication, representation and text'. *Reading* 37(3), November 2003: 98–103

Benson, C. (1986). 'Art and language in middle childhood: A question of translation'. *Word and Image* 2(2): 123–39

Bronson, M. (2000). *Self-Regulation in Early Childhood.* New York: City Press

Cox, S. (2005). 'Intention and meaning in young children's drawing'. *International Journal of Art and Design Education* 24(2): 115–25

Dewey, J. (1934). *Art as Experience.* New York: Perigee Books

Dyson, A. (1986). 'The three card trick: the reading of images by young children'. *International Journal of Art and Design Education* 5(1–2): 69–80

Gardner, H. (1980). *Artful Scribbles.* New York: Basic Books

Golden, J. (1990). *The Narrative Symbol in Childhood Literature.* Berlin: Mouton de Gruyter

Goodnow, J. (1977). *Children's Drawings: the Developing Child.* London: Fontana

Harris, P. & McKenzie, B. (2005). 'Networking around the Waterhole and other tales: the importance of relationships among texts for reading and related instruction'. *Literacy* 39(1), April 2005: 31–7

Jewitt, C. & van Leeuwan, T. (2000). *Handbook of visual analysis.* London: SAGE Publications

Kellogg, R. (1969). *Analyzing Children's Art.* California: Mayfield

Kiefer, B. (1993). 'Children's responses to picture books: A developmental perspective' in Holland, K., Hungerford, R. & Ernst, S. *Journeying: Children Responding to Literature.* Portsmouth, New Hampshire: Heinemann, pp.267–83

Kress, G. (1997). *Before Writing: Rethinking Paths to Literacy.* London: Routledge

Lewis, D. (2001). *Reading Contemporary Picturebooks.* London: Routledge

Mackey, M. (2002). 'The most thinking book: Attention, performance and the picturebook' in Styles, M. and Bearne, E. (eds) *Art, Narrative and Childhood.* London: Trentham Books, pp.101–13

Madura, S. (1998). 'An artistic element: Four transitional readers and writers respond to the picture books of Patricia Polacco and Gerald McDermott'. *National Reading Conference Yearbook* 47: 366–76

Matthews, J. (2003). *Drawing and Painting: Children and Visual Representation.* London: SAGE Publications

Meek, M. (1988). *How Texts Teach What Readers Learn.* Stroud: Thimble Press

Meek, M., Warlow, A. & Barton, G. (1977). *The Cool Web: Pattern of Children's Reading.* London: The Bodley Head

Nikolajeva, M. & Scott, C. (2001). *How Picturebooks Work*. New York: Garland

Noble, K. (2007). *Picture Thinking: The Development of Visual Thinking in Young Children*. Cambridge: Faculty of Education, University of Cambridge (unpublished PhD thesis)

Pahl, K. (2000). *Transformations: Meaning Making in Nursery Education*. London: Trentham Books

Pahl, K. (2001). Texts as artefacts crossing sites: Map making at home and at school. *Reading: Literacy and Language* 35(3): 120–5

Paley, V. G. (1981). *Wally's Stories*. Massachusetts: Harvard University Press

Piaget, J. (1929). *The Child's Conception of the World*. New York: Harcourt, Brace and World

Sharpe, T. (2005). 'Scaffolding students' response to picturebooks'. *Literacy Learning: The Middle Years* 13(1): i–xii

Watson, V. (1993). 'Multi-layered texts and multi-layered readers' in Styles, M. & Drummond, M. J. *The Politics of Reading*. Cambridge: University of Cambridge

Watson, V. & Styles, M. (1996). *Talking Pictures: Pictorial Texts and Young Readers*. London: Hodder & Stoughton

Wells, G. (1986). *The Meaning Makers: Children Learning Language and Using Language to Learn*. London: Hodder & Stoughton

Whitebread, D. & Leader, L. (2003). 'Sequencing and Differentiation in Young Children's Drawings'. *Early Years Journal* 23(2): 155–76

Willats, J. (2005). *Making Sense of Children's Drawings*. New Jersey: Erlbaum

Children's literature

Ormerod, J. (1990). *The Frog Prince*. London: Walker Books

Perham, M. (1994). *The Princess and the Frog* (illustrated by S. King). London: Ladybird

Scieszka, J. (1991). *The Frog Prince Continued* (illustrated by S. Johnson). New York: Penguin

8   Sharing visual experiences of a new culture

Immigrant children's responses to picturebooks and other visual texts

Evelyn Arizpe

This chapter brings together the findings of two research projects with a group of immigrant pupils from primary schools in Glasgow, Scotland, which examined the ways in which children from immigrant and ethnic minority backgrounds made sense of their new culture and identity through texts and images. Although some of the children's comments about different types of image will be described, at the centre of this chapter are their responses to picturebooks. The results confirm that shared reading and looking allows a deeper engagement with the texts and access to more layers of meaning, and leads to a more critical understanding. The findings suggest that creating the opportunities for immigrant children to build on their visual experiences and knowledge could help them to more fully understand the new cultural images and the relationship of these to written text.

For those children who arrive in a new country with little or no knowledge of its language and culture, the visual image becomes a powerful source of information. Their responses to the array of images before them will be based on their experiences of the visual and on their cognitive skills. In turn, these experiences and skills will depend on their home culture (and how image is regarded in this context), personal experiences and previous encounters with text and pictures. However, as Kathy Coulthard reminds us, 'Although children's knowledge, understanding and values are culturally saturated, the extent to which this affects literary interpretation will always be mediated by each child's unique personality as well as the influence of peers.' (Coulthard, 2003: 184.) In other words, the sharing of experiences and skills can have a strong impact on the ways in which children think about and accept new ideas. The work summarized below provides insights into the ways in which immigrant children's interpretation and evaluation of visual images reflects both their cultural experiences and their shared conversations with their peers and, in some cases, with the researchers as well.

Shirley Brice Heath (2000: 124) highlights one of the more important findings of research on contexts of learning by linguists and psychologists: 'Having to make decisions collaboratively engages beliefs, experience, abstractions, argument and application – a combination of mental and linguistic processes that enable essential practice in developing theories about how the world works.'

The aim of this chapter is to show how a group of immigrant children from different backgrounds developed theories about how their 'new' world works. It will describe their responses to a sample of visual images, the sharing of experiences and beliefs, and the collaboration between them. The theories they constructed include not only an understanding of general customs, values or beliefs, but also an understanding of how images work – often in conjunction with written text – to portray, advance or question these customs, values and beliefs.

In a more recent essay, 'The Deeper Game: Intuition, imagination, and embodiment' (2009), Heath refers to the work of neurologists, particularly Semir Zeki, to argue that visual aesthetic reactions involve similar processes to the selection, connection and projection demanded by art: 'We view a visual item, select those properties or features that further mental work, connect what we see with memory, and cast ahead from the visual artifact into our own ability to create narrative and analogy.' This process of sorting, selecting and linking, Heath adds, allows us to 'navigate the world', and it is precisely this process that children entering a new culture must follow in order to 'navigate' new meanings.

This chapter brings together the findings of two research projects with a group of immigrant pupils from four Glasgow primary schools. One project was based on their reading of a sample of Scottish literature for children (i.e. written by Scottish authors) and included texts written in Scots (Scots is a language of Scotland, distinct from Scottish Gaelic). At one point during the interviews for this project, the opportunity arose of having a conversation around Anthony Browne's *Zoo* (1992). Highlights of this conversation are also described below, and it provides a bridge between the Scottish project and the second project, which involved the same immigrant children but this time explored their responses to multilayered, non-Scottish picturebooks. Together, the findings from these projects form part of my continuing research, which examines the ways in which children from immigrant and ethnic minority backgrounds make sense of their new culture and identity through texts and images. Although some of the children's comments about different types of image will be described, at the centre of this chapter are their responses to picturebooks, which provide some of the most stimulating and challenging images for children, including those in the later years of primary school.

Studies on response to picturebooks have revealed their potential not only for 'teaching' the reading of both words and pictures but also for providing a space for reflection, dialogue and creativity (e.g. Kiefer, 1995; Arizpe & Styles, 2003, Arizpe & Styles *et al.*, 2008; Pantaleo, 2006; and various essays in Watson & Styles, 1996, and Evans, 1998). They have shown how older pupils, as well as younger ones, can engage with apparently simple picturebooks and also how pupils whose language skills do not match the average level for their age, can develop their literacy skills and their visual literacy skills through careful looking and interactive discussion (Coulthard *et al.*, 2003). This chapter extends the body of research carried out with bilingual or ethnic minority pupils (e.g. Mines, 2000; Coulthard, 2003; Walsh, 2003; Colledge, 2005; and various essays in Enever & Schmid-Schönbein, 2006) by taking into account their findings on the ways in which cultural resources are transformed and linked, through emotional and aesthetic engagement with picturebooks and through interaction with other readers.

Visual clues of 'Scottishness'

In terms of immigration, Glasgow is the fastest-growing city in the UK after London, with 3,000 foreign national children from more than 100 countries enrolling in schools since 2005. In an attempt to find out how different groups of immigrant children have coped with learning not only English but also Scots, and understanding Scottish accents and dialects, James McGonigal and I obtained a grant from the Scottish Government in 2005 to carry out research in this neglected area (McGonigal & Arizpe, 2007; Arizpe & McGonigal, 2008), using texts by Scottish authors and artists. Among our general findings was that the pictures in these texts were not only immensely attractive to the group of refugee and asylum-seeking children but also helped them to engage with, and to deepen, their understanding of the written words.

We initially worked in three Glasgow primary schools, all of which had a multiethnic population, although two of them in particular had a high percentage of refugee and asylum-seeking pupils. Altogether, we interviewed 14 children (aged between 10 and 11) in depth, among them (all names are pseudonyms): Datse (Latvia), Rasha (Iran), Precious (Rwanda), Gabriel (Congo), Abdul (Algeria), Sirwa (Iraq), Neylan and Umay (Turkey), and Usman and Hashid (Pakistan). With the exception of Hashid, who was second-generation Pakistani, all these children had arrived in Scotland within the last four to five years before the interviews took place. The group was told that we were doing a study about Scottish books for children, looking for 'clues' that make these particular books Scottish, and were asked to be 'detectives' in this search (a similar strategy was successfully carried out in Canada by Sylvia Pantaleo, 2000). A variety of creative approaches was used to help the children to begin to think about aspects of their new culture, such as keeping a notebook of Scottish words and places, filling in the blanks in a comic book and drawing in response to the texts.

With two exceptions, the texts used in this study contained images of some kind. The extracts discussed below are from *Janet Reachfar and the Kelpie* (2002), by Jane Duncan and illustrated by Mairi Hedderwick; *The Mean Team from Mars* (2003), written and illustrated by Scoular Anderson, and 'Blethertoun Rovers' (2004), a poem by Matthew Fitt from a Scots poetry anthology, *Blethertoun Braes* (Fitt & Robertson, 2004), illustrated by Bob Dewar. *Janet Reachfar and the Kelpie* is a traditional picturebook in that there is a clear graphic separation between words and pictures, and the illustrations generally represent what the words have to say. *The Mean Team from Mars* combines text and image in a comic-book style, which is presumably meant to help beginner readers.

Although the visual image was not the main focus of the original research, the interview included a question about the images and about the Scottish 'clues' within them. In general, comments from the children showed a keen interest in the illustrations. The pictures not only helped them understand the unfamiliar words (particularly Scots words), follow the story and make predictions but also provided them with knowledge about Scottish culture. The pictures also provided an opportunity to discuss the meaning of the text and 'Scottishness', and to make comparisons with stories and images from the children's home cultures and from Western popular culture. Finally, the discussion led to comments about the children's own creative attempts at drawing, and they began to look more closely at style and how the illustrator had helped to create the atmosphere through the pictures. In the following example, Precious recognized Mairi Hedderwick's style, linking Janet Reachfar with the character Katie Morag from Hedderwick's famous series of picturebooks (it may be that Precious also recognized that grandmothers are an important presence in both stories).

Evelyn: Does this book [*Janet Reachfar and the Kelpie*] remind you of any
            other Scottish book you've seen?
Precious: ... reminds me once, girl called Janet as well, she looks like that
            and she had a dog as well but she had to get a red letter to her
            granny [she is referring to *Katie Morag Delivers the Mail*
            (Hedderwick, 1984)].
James: Is that Katie Morag? Did she live on an island and have one granny
            on the island and one on the mainland?
Precious: Yes, the granny lived on the island and [the girl] had to deliver the
            mail but she dropped the letters in water so she didn't know where
            to go and the mail got mixed up.

The discussion about the illustrations in *Janet Reachfar and the Kelpie* continued and, although the group did not go into the illustrations in depth, their observations suggest that they were looking at the details and bringing their feelings and their own artistic abilities to bear on their observations.

Evelyn: How does this [picture] make you feel?
Hashid: This one is scary and spooky [referring to a picture of the
            Whigmaleerie, a monster that sucks people into the bog].

[...]

Datse: This picture, where is it? See the people from the farm? They look
            like real things, like the grass [is] made of shapes

Precious: [speaking at the same time as Datse] like shiny water
Datse: When some people draw in books they look like real persons, sometimes, they look like real.

[…]

Datse: I like this one, I like to draw things that are outside, make up
things, you know, sky and woods [referring to the picture of Janet
walking with her dog with the Scottish highland landscape in the
background (see Figure 41)].

Figure 41 From *Janet Reachfar and the Kelpie* by Mairi Hedderwick

Because the sectarian divide around football is (unfortunately) a feature of Glaswegian culture, we chose both *The Mean Team from Mars* and the poem 'Blethertoun Rovers' to find out whether the children had views on this issue. Supporters of Glasgow's two football teams, Celtic and Rangers, have been traditionally divided along the lines of Catholics and Protestants. Green is the colour for Celtic; blue is the colour for Rangers. The colours of the team depicted by Anderson are both green and blue. Interestingly, the pupils did not refer to the sectarian issues; only two of the Pakistani boys, when asked directly, said they tended to keep their preferences to themselves. The images for both teams were closely scrutinized by the children, but they were particularly gripped by the image of the hopeless players in the fictional Blethertoun Rovers team (see Figure 42).

Blethertoun Rovers

Blethertoun Rovers play in blue
But they havenae got a clue.
Jist last Sunday oot they ran
And got banjaxed fifteen-wan.

Their striker's name is Magnus Shore,
Couldnae hit a coo shed door.
Last week, he got the baw and spooned it –
Even noo, they havenae foond it.

The left-back has them aw in fits
When he forgets his fitbaw bitts.
If he cannae get the skipper's,
He plays in the groondsman's slippers.

Jooglie the goalie lowps and rolls,
Bields the Blethertouners' goals.
Where the baw is he jist guesses
Through his muckle jam-jar glesses.

The Rovers fans are never singin,
The coach's heid is ayewis hingin.
His team are sic a bunch o duddies –
He should hae signed eleeven cuddies.

Matthew Fitt

Figure 42 Illustration by Bob Dewar accompanying the poem 'Blethertoun Rovers' by Matthew Fitt

The group spontaneously began to point out the different football players and comment on their appearance:

Datse: [This is] very bad, look at this yellow guy.
Rasha: Look at him!
Datse: They look unhealthy!
Usman: He's the funniest, see.
Rasha: He's got the chicken pox.
Hashid: This guy's face is like a ghost.

Hashid also made a connection between a player's description from the text ('Their striker's name is Magnus Shore,/Couldnae hit a coo shed door.') and one of the footballers portrayed: 'I think it's him who can't hit the door.' Datse and Rasha were more concerned with the unhealthy aspect and eating habits of the players (one is eating potato chips), probably as a result of the healthy eating campaign which was going on in schools in Scotland at the time of this study.

In a final class session we linked the theme of monsters in *Janet Reachfar and the Kelpie* to poems that mentioned other Scottish legendary creatures, and then asked the pupils to draw their own 'Scottish monster'. The visual responses were revealing of what some children felt were salient aspects of Scottish culture. Within the group we had been working with, Neylan created an 'Irn Bru Bottle Monster', with a 'big mouth' and 'long nails' (see Figure 43).

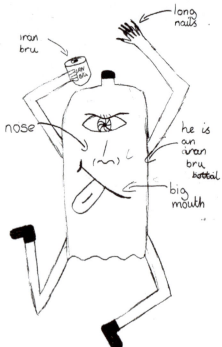

Figure 43 'Irn Bru Bottle Monster' by Neylan

Irn Bru is a popular carbonated soft drink produced in Scotland, and it is suggestive that this icon of Scottish culture is portrayed by Neylan as a rather aggressive cartoon-style character, especially when we consider some of his comments about the manners and habits of the Scots: 'Mostly the Scottish people when they talk they always swear [and] tell bad words.' This is consistent with references made by the other children to the violence and aggression of young Scottish people (some of it directed towards them). During one of the classroom readings, we discussed the subject of the thistle as the national flower of Scotland and several children chose to draw 'thistle monsters'. None, however, was as stylized as the one drawn by Sirwa, which has 'creasy' eyes that are reminiscent of Middle-Eastern ornamental patterns (see Figure 44).

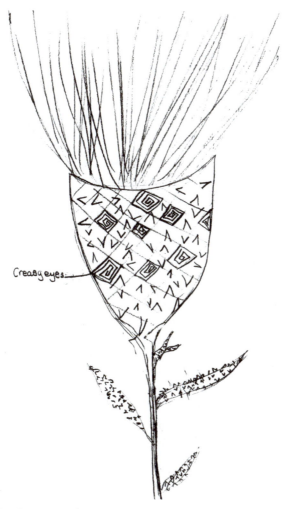

Figure 44 'Thistle Monster' by Sirwa

These two contrasting drawings are examples of the way in which old and new cultural icons (the thistle and the Irn Bru bottle) were mediated through experiences of the visual (cartoons, traditional patterns) and expressed the emotional and aesthetic reactions of their creators to the culture in which they now lived.

Deeper understandings through shared interpretation

During the Scottish project, as a follow-up to reading *Tigger* by Anne Donovan (2002) (a short story about a pet cat who must be given away because of a sibling's allergy), we showed the pupils the image of the tiger that appears in one of Anthony Browne's picturebooks, *Zoo* (1992). After we had discussed *Tigger* and just as I was about to leave, the group of three girls with whom I'd been talking noticed that I had *Zoo* in my bag and asked to read it. Given their enthusiasm (although this picturebook was not meant to be part of the Scottish project), I took advantage of this opportunity to talk about the picturebook in an informal manner but along the lines of a previous study in which we had discussed this same book (Arizpe & Styles, 2003). In her chapter about bilingual children reading *Zoo*, Coulthard speculates that cultural differences may mean that the theme of animal rights in this picturebook (both in terms of captivity in zoos and domestic pets) 'does not provide the same reference points for those whose cultural experience does not encompass this issue' (Coulthard, 2003: 184). Although this may be true in some contexts, I would argue that the connections between human and animal behaviour, particularly in relation to the father, do have the potential to become a common reference point for readers from different cultural backgrounds. The discussion that followed showed how the three girls accessed deeper understandings of the picturebook through a shared process of working towards making meaning, which involved engaging beliefs and experiences, making abstractions and arriving at a common explanation that, in Heath's words, contributed to 'developing theories about how the world works' (Heath, 2009).

The girls in this session were Datse, Precious and Rasha, and, although they were coming together from very different countries and cultures, they had a shared experience of migration and of trauma (some of these details were provided by the girls; others by their teacher). Datse was from Latvia, but her Roma culture meant that she had spent most of her childhood travelling, moving back and forth between Latvia, Belgium, England and Scotland. From the comments she made, it appeared that her family situation was difficult: her mother was working long hours and her father did not perceive any value in Datse's education. Precious had come to Scotland from Rwanda as a refugee with her single mother. Precious and her brother were sometimes looked after by Scottish carers owing to their mother's mental health problems. Rasha had also come as a refugee, with both her parents (who were, from what we gathered, highly educated), from Iran, leaving behind the bookshop that was the family's livelihood.

As the girls struggled to read *Zoo*, taking turns by page (they asked to read it themselves), all three became engrossed in the story and the pictures, frequently exclaiming 'Look!' 'Look!' They began by linking the image of the hamster in the cage with the discussion we had had previously as a whole class on the subject of pets. The theme of 'Tigger' was recalled and also the fact that several pupils had had to leave their pets behind when they emigrated. During the whole-class discussion, we had also raised the question of whether it is cruel to keep animals in cages, why people keep pets and whether it was right to spend so much money on them, as some pet owners do in Britain. Therefore, by the time we came to the reading of *Zoo*, the girls had been reminiscing about their own pets and expressing their negative views on keeping animals in captivity. While I talked to the girls, Jim McGonigal was talking to the boys and a different view of pets and captivity was put forth by Usman (an asylum seeker from Pakistan) and Hashid (whose family regularly travelled back and forth to Pakistan).

Usman: In my country, people keep them as pets – lions and tigers – it's not cruel.

James: When they are young?

Usman: Even when they grow up, they train them.

[…]

Hashid: … in our country you get massive big houses {describes courtyards} and they keep them in there.

The boys did not read *Zoo* with Jim but, given these comments, it would have been interesting to find out how their cultural perspective would have affected their reading of this particular picturebook.

In the case of the girls, little by little and together they worked out the main irony of Browne's book, from the discussion about pets and cages to the humans having animal features and acting like them. Datse, for example, described the father as being 'like a bull' after Precious pointed out that the clouds over his head look like 'cow horns'. Datse then brought her own experience to bear on this point: 'He looks kind of nasty but the mum looks kind, this is what always happens, my mum's kind, my dad's nasty.' She criticized the boy narrator when he says that the polar bear 'looks stupid', again bringing in her experience of the 'healthy eating' message: 'It doesn't look stupid and all the food they [the boys] were eating was unhealthy!' Shortly afterwards, Rasha also added her criticism of the boys: 'They fight too, they too look like monkeys.'

In response to the father and sons' attitudes to the animals, Precious remarked that 'some people make fun of animals and the animals get mad and start to roar'. As the girls reached the images of the orang-utan and the gorilla, their comments related more and more to the moral relationship between humans and animals:

Precious: Animals are more scared of you than [you are] of them.
Evelyn: Why does [the orang-utan] feel scared?
Rasha: … because they think we want to kill them.
Datse: I know! It's like they want to kill him.

Their comments about the gorilla were very similar to those made by some of the children in Arizpe and Styles' (2003) study where the gorilla was 'humanized'. In this case Datse supports her case about this similarity by using scientific knowledge acquired in a visit to the museum:

Precious: The eyes look like the eyes of a man.
Datse: I know! I wonder what kind of pencils he used?
Evelyn: Maybe very thin ones.
Datse: Look at the eyes, they look like real eyes, they look like my eyes, look at them!
Precious: Yes!
Datse: You see monkeys or gorillas or whatever they are, they have the same skeleton bones as people, 'cause I saw them in the museum.

The last image brought them back to the discussion of pets and cages:

Datse: Yeah, it's not good to keep animals in cages.
Precious: Some people like they take animals to the zoo and the circus.
Evelyn: Why are those birds there, do you think?
Datse: They're bats.
Rasha: No! They are birds flying for … they are flying free!

These final comments reveal their grasp of Browne's point about captivity, and Rasha's observation and excitement suggest that she has also arrived at an awareness of how Browne has made use of the contrasting motifs of freedom and captivity. These extracts from the girls' discussion reveal the potential of children's sharing and building on each other's interpretations of visual images in picturebooks, not only as an strategy for developing literacy skills but also, perhaps, for approaching and understanding the differences in personal experiences, leading the way to sharing values as future citizens of the same country.

Developing a critical eye

After concluding the Scottish project, I decided to invite some of the children to participate in another project based on two 'postmodern', or multilayered, non-Scottish picturebooks: *Traction Man is Here* (2005) by Mini Grey and *The Incredible Book Eating Boy* by Oliver Jeffers (2006). Some pupils from one of the schools previously visited were involved, as well as pupils from a new school, among them Nabila and Eshan (Pakistan), Soraya (Malaysia) and Andzej

(Slovakia) (again, these names are pseudonyms). I held two hour-long sessions, one for each book, with either two or three children. Of particular interest here was their response to the metafictive elements in these books, and the connections they made that would help them make sense of these elements. In this section the focus will be on their comments about the visual image itself, some of which reveal an ability to step back from personal involvement in the narrative and use a more critical 'eye' to describe and explain the text. In order to encourage this critical perspective, I asked the children to think about whether younger children would enjoy these books and what, if any, aspects they might find difficult to understand.

'Traction Man' is a toy figure that comes with outfits for carrying out missions in different locations: under the water, in the jungle or in space. His adventures with other toys and various household objects are narrated in the book through both words and images, including comic-book sequences and speech bubbles. The twist in the superhero narrative comes when Granny presents him with a new outfit, 'an all-in-one knitted green romper suit and matching bonnet', which undermines his male ego and superman image. The children in the study did not find it difficult to relate Traction Man to superheroes from popular culture, and they came close to understanding the author's aim in subverting this image.

Comments from two of the girls, Nabila and Soraya, revealed their eye for detail and their awareness of different artistic styles. Here they note pattern, shadow and line and link these features to the theme of the picturebook, which plays with the distinction between the boy's 'reality' and the imaginary play involving Traction Man (see Figure 45).

Nabila: It kind of looks real but then it looks like a cartoon at the same time because it's got lots of detail in it.
Evelyn: What sort of detail?
Nabila: Like in the parcels [the wrapped Christmas presents], they've got flowery patterns and things like that, they show the shading.
Soraya: They show the shades [shadows].
Evelyn: So the details make it look real?
Both: Yeah.
Evelyn: And what makes it look like a cartoon?
Nabila: Because of the way they're drawn [pointing to Traction Man's face], because like a real person wouldn't really have a square kind of chin.

Abdul was fascinated by the way in which the images entirely covered the pages, 'bleeding' to the edges, so that there were hardly any 'white spaces' or margins of any kind:

> ... in this book it's really good because like you can see what your eyes can see. Like, there's not little white spaces like over here [points to margin], like you can just see the whole thing ... I think this book should be quite

Figure 45 From *Traction Man* by Mini Grey

expensive. I think so it should be like £6 so that's the right price for it because like there's lots of colourful pictures in it [and] it's a really, really interesting story.

When Abdul says 'you can see what your eyes can see', he seems to mean that you see the whole picture, as you do in real life, as opposed to an image on a page that contains 'white spaces', because he then pointed out that in most books he had seen, there was usually a bit of writing in the 'white space' or bottom margin, under the pictures. In this picturebook the design integrates the writing into the images through scraps of paper that seem to be stuck on to the pictures. For Abdul, this total, colourful visual experience means that it must be an expensive book and, in his own judgement, rightly so.

The Incredible Book Eating Boy proved more visually puzzling and challenging than *Traction Man*. The story, told in a straightforward manner, is about Henry, a boy who discovers he likes eating books and that they make him smarter. However, eating too many too quickly has the opposite effect and he gets ill and confused. In the end, Henry realizes that reading books is more rewarding (although he is not averse to the occasional bite). Jeffers adds a metafictive layer to the picturebook through his use of discarded bits of books and different types of paper as canvases for the illustrations. At first, the children were too absorbed in the plot to speculate about these backgrounds; however, towards the end of each of the sessions they began to notice and relate the background papers to the story, such as when Andzej associated the background map with Henry's travels (Figure 46). It was Eshan, however, who excitedly summed up Jeffers' merging of the theme and the artistic materials into words: 'All this book is about books!'

Comparisons between the two picturebooks also encouraged the children to step back and take an objective view of the artistic features. It made Abdul come back to his remark about the image covering the whole page in *Traction Man*: 'There's something they've got in common because they've got like [a] full page of paint, like the whole page is coloured in.' This led Gabriel to notice that both books also use bits of 'real' paper in their pictures, and he and Abdul speculated that this was because both artists wanted to 'try and make it real'. Abdul and Gabriel were interviewed together, and parts of their discussion show how their mental and linguistic processes were at work as they shared their beliefs about books and reading, and moved in collaboration towards creating arguments and reaching insights about the art in these picturebooks.

Navigating within a new world

Although the first part in this chapter was particularly concerned with a Scottish context, if the results are taken together with the findings about response to visual images from the other research, they have implications beyond this context – both for research on visual literacy and for teaching

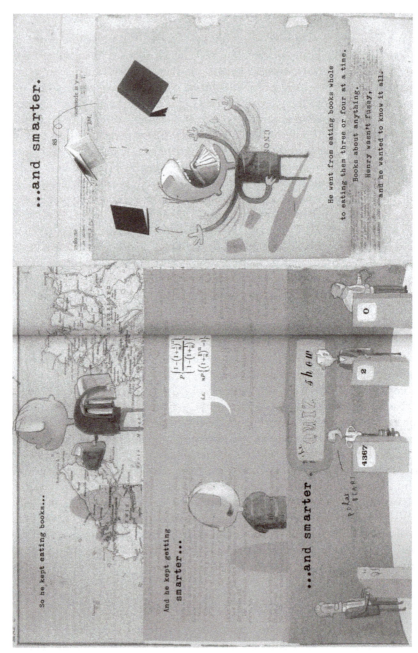

Figure 46 From *The Incredible Book Eating Boy* by Oliver Jeffers

children from diverse cultural backgrounds in other countries. All the findings support Heath's arguments for the way in which visual art encourages connections between knowledge and experience and leads to creating meaningful narratives. This was evident in the inclusion of the 'healthy eating' messages in the interpretation of the texts and in the references to books the children had read before, both in the UK and in, or from, their countries of origin. Explanation and analogy helped the children build 'theories' together, despite their diverse backgrounds and pasts, about moral issues such as the consequences of disobedience or the treatment of animals. Complex texts, with features such as metafiction and intertextuality, made the readers stand back and move towards a more critical examination of genre and popular culture, of the relationship between books and knowledge, and implied audiences.

All these findings also suggest a preoccupation with what is 'real' about an image or a written text. For some of the children, the ability to portray things realistically seemed to be a sign of a good artist, and they were interested in the techniques employed by the artist to achieve this. This may have to do with the stage they are going through as artists themselves. Writing about children's drawings, Benson (1986) and Davis (1993) describe the period of middle childhood (8–11 years) as a time when children become preoccupied with the rules of graphic representation and attempt to draw reality as they see it. However, given the immigrant identity of the children in this study, this might also have to do with a need to know 'the facts' about their new context and the desire to become 'knowledgeable insiders' rather than 'ignorant outsiders' (McGonigal & Arizpe, 2007).

Finally, the results provide some insights into how children perceive visual images and how they begin to grasp the ways in which they work. This includes what strikes the children as significant or unusual and what they find hard to comprehend. These insights suggest it is important to understand how children 'see' because this tells us about their meaning-making processes. The results also suggest that bringing experiences, and knowledge of life and texts, together enriches the child's interaction with the image. Finally, they confirm that shared reading and looking allows a deeper engagement with the texts and access to more layers of meaning, and leads to a more critical understanding.

Creating the opportunities for immigrant children to build on their visual experiences and knowledge could help them to more fully understand the new cultural images that surround them (and the relationship of images to written text). However, these types of practice do involve allowing plenty of time for looking, reading and talking, as well as inviting references to home-culture texts and images. Needless to say, they also require a sensitivity when dealing with themes that may affect refugee or asylum-seeking pupils in particular. Interactive dialogue around visual images can further oral, reading and writing skills and also encourage children's own creative expressions. It is an important resource not only for adapting to the children's new circumstances but also for transfiguring their new environments.

Acknowledgements

I would like to acknowledge the help of the Scottish Government, who provided the grant for the first research project mentioned in this chapter. The data presented and the views expressed are solely the responsibility of the author.

References

Arizpe, E. & McGonigal, J. (2008). 'Global citizens, local linguists: How migrant children explore cultural identity through vernacular texts' in Peters, M., Britton, A. & Blee, H. (eds) *Global Citizenship in Education*. Rotterdam: Sense, 459–76

Arizpe, E. & Styles, M. (2003). *Children Reading Pictures: Interpreting Visual Texts*. London: RoutledgeFalmer

Arizpe, E. & Styles, M., with Cowan, K., Mallouri, L. & Wolpert, M. A. (2008). 'The voices behind the pictures: Children responding to postmodern picturebooks' in Sipe, L. & Pantaleo, S. (eds) *Postmodern Picturebooks: Play, Parody, and Self-Referentiality*. London: Routledge, pp.207–22

Benson, C. (1986). 'Art and language in middle childhood: A question of translation'. *Word and Image* 2: 123–40

Colledge, M. (2005). 'Baby Bear or Mrs Bear? Young English Bengali-speaking children's responses to narrative picture books at school'. *Literacy* 39: 24–30

Coulthard, K. (2003). 'The words to say it: Young bilingual learners responding to visual texts' in Arizpe, E. & Styles, M. *Children Reading Pictures*. London: RoutledgeFalmer, pp.164–89

Coulthard, K., Arizpe, E. & Styles, M. (2003). 'Getting inside Anthony Browne's head: Pupils and teachers asking questions and reading pictures' in Bearne, E., Dombey, H. & Grainger, T. (eds) *Interactions in Language, Literacy and the Classroom*. Milton Keynes: Open University Press, pp.77–89

Davis, J. (1993) 'Why Sally can draw. An aesthetic perspective'. *Educational Horizons* 71: 86–93

Enever, J. & Schmid-Schönbein, G. (eds) (2006). *Picturebooks and Primary EFL Learners*. Munich: Langenscheidt

Evans, J. (ed) (1998). *What's in the Picture?: Responding to Illustrations in Picture Books*. London: SAGE Publications

Heath, S. B. (2000). 'Seeing our way into learning'. *Cambridge Journal of Education* 30(1): 121–32

Heath, S. B. (2009). 'The deeper game: Intuition, imagination and embodiment' in Styles, M. & Arizpe, E. (eds) *Acts of Reading: Teachers, Texts and Childhood*. London: Trentham Books

Kiefer, B. (1995). *The Potential of Picture Books: From Visual Literacy to Aesthetic Understanding*. Englewood Cliff, New Jersey: Merrill

McGonigal, J. & Arizpe, E. (2007). *Learning to Read a New Culture: How Immigrant and Asylum-Seeking Children Experience Scottish Identity Through Classroom Books*. Final Report. Edinburgh: Scottish Government. http: //www.scotland.gov.uk/ Publications/2007/10/31125406/0

Mines, H. (2000). *The Relationship Between Children's Cultural Literacies and their Readings of Literary Texts*. University of Brighton (unpublished PhD thesis)

Pantaleo, S. (2000). 'Grade 3 Students Explore the Question "What's Canadian about Canadian Children's Literature?"'. *English Quarterly* 32: 3–4

Pantaleo, S. (2006). 'Pickles, pastiche and parody: Exploring humour in an undone fairytale'. *The Journal of Reading, Writing and Literacy* 1(3): 43–62

Walsh, M. (2003). '"Reading" pictures: What do they reveal? Young children's reading of visual texts'. *Reading* 37: 123–30

Watson, V. & Styles, M. (eds) (1996). *Talking Pictures*. London: Hodder & Stoughton

Children's literature

Anderson, S. (2003). *The Mean Team from Mars*. London: A&C Black

Browne, A. (1992). *Zoo*. London: Red Fox

Donovan, A. (2002). 'Tigger' in Breslin, T., McGonigal, J. & Whyte, H. (eds) *My Mum's a Punk*. Dalkeith: Scottish Children's Press

Duncan, J. (2002). *Janet Reachfar and the Kelpie* (illustrated by M. Hedderwick). Edinburgh: Birlinn

Fitt, M. (2004). 'Blethertoun Rovers' in Fitt, M. & Robertson, J. (eds) *Blethertoun Braes*. Edinburgh: Itchy Coo

Fitt, M. & Robertson, J. (eds) (2004). *Blethertoun Braes* (illustrated by B. Dewar). Edinburgh: Itchy Coo

Grey, M. (2005). *Traction Man is Here*. London: Red Fox

Hedderwick, M. (1984). *Katie Morag Delivers the Mail*. London: The Bodley Head

Jeffers, O. (2006). *The Incredible Book Eating Boy*. London: HarperCollins

9 Developing understanding of narrative, empathy and inference through picturebooks

Prue Goodwin

As a genre of literature in its own right, the picturebook provides some of the most powerful reading experiences available to young readers. This chapter considers three outstanding picturebooks that stimulate readers to:

- empathize with the characters and with the life-changing situations in which they find themselves
- read beyond the literal to infer deeper meanings from the text through exploration of words and images
- relate to complex narratives – plots and subplots – that are woven through the pages of each book
- share their responses to the book with other readers.

Whilst recognizing that the purpose of these texts is first and foremost the pleasure of their readers, this chapter demonstrates the potential learning that can accompany the sharing of great picturebooks with children as they become confident young readers.

'I love this book because it is like real life.'

Eleanor's comment was one among many by the group of nine-year-olds who had pored over the book *Archie's War* by Marcia Williams (2007) (see Figure 47). Other children gathered round to share the delight of spotting the comic-strip characters, reading the letters and lifting a flap to discover a picture of an outside privy.

On a different occasion, Hannah, a teenager, was equally absorbed by the same book and, as an experienced reader, she commented thoughtfully on the impact of Williams' creation:

> It led me to believe I was really connecting with Archie – the 'privacy' in which he was writing allowed him to write with real honesty, and some humour. I was moved by the innocence of such a young boy, who at the same time was able to write so intelligently about such a massive war. The factual basis of the book is very good but, for me, this isn't what makes it

Figure 47 Children enjoy sharing *Archie's War*

such a success. It is the story of a young boy that is really moving – to the point of being inspiring, as it encourages a childlike way of thinking. Archie is clearly a boy with a positive outlook on life and I feel that this gives the book a lot to teach – a lot more than just facts and figures.

Hannah, aged 16

Hannah's father also read *Archie's War* (independently of his children) and was moved to comment that 'Archie Albright's scrapbook is a tender insight into a working family through the years of the First World War seen by a boy of ten. It is beautifully presented and asks to be read again and again.' He went on to describe his second reading and predicted a need to return to the book as there were still aspects of the story that, for him, were unresolved.

Catriona Nicholson, a lecturer in children's literature, confirmed the appeal of *Archie's War* to readers of vastly differing ages and experience when she commented:

From Archie's touching frontispiece dedication, 'For all other children touched by war', to his pasted newspaper cuttings on the final cover declaring that WW1 was over, I was immersed in the multiple delights and sorrows of his five scrapbooked years. However, the pleasures offered by each teeming page posed a challenge for me: my instinctive urge to read Archie's ongoing narrative was countered always by an equally insistent need to linger on each sheet or double spread in order to absorb fully the finely worked detail of word and image.

Catriona Nicholson (2008)

The three books cited in this chapter – *Archie's War* by Marcia Williams, *Going West* by Martin Waddell and Philippe Dupasquier (1985) and *The Arrival* by Shaun Tan (2006) – are examples of picturebooks that offer complex narratives that make sophisticated demands on readers. To fully appreciate the intricacies of the story, each book requires readers to infer meanings that go a long way beyond the literal and to bring a level of empathy to the situations in which the characters find themselves. Brief descriptions of *Archie's War* and *The Arrival* give a flavour of the texts, whilst a deeper look at *Going West* will consider in more detail how the book develops literary elements through narrative structure, character and setting.

Reading beyond the literal

It is clear that as children develop as readers they learn to appreciate that important information can lie beyond the literal. Becoming a reader means reading closely and learning to detect the possible layers of meaning embedded in a text. It is important that, in their role as meaning makers, pupils learn to value their prior knowledge and to recognize the potency of an emotional connection with a narrative, whether presented in words or images. The inter-action between reader and text is central to the process of becoming a reader and, inspired by such educationalists as Aidan Chambers (1993) and Margaret Meek (1987), it is now common practice in many schools for teachers to engage learners in purposeful discussions about their reading. In addition to obtaining deeper understanding, and consequently greater enjoyment, of a text, such discussions enable inexperienced readers to acquire the knowledge of how an author or artist makes choices. Meek (1987) points out that as children become more experienced with a variety of writing styles and different text types, the books themselves teach them to be aware of how an author has selected particular literary features: examples of how this learning process comes about are an awareness of settings and characters, changes in the pace of the narrative or well-placed intertextual references. Accomplished teachers know that picturebooks will engender meaningful discussion and enable readers to make connections between the different multimodal texts they meet. It follows, therefore, that picturebooks should play a central role in enabling young readers to empathize with characters, to infer deeper meanings from the infor-mation gleaned from both the written and the visual texts, and to engage in the meaning-making processes that construct a narrative.

For decades, teachers and librarians who have valued high-quality picture-books have incorporated them into their work with young people (Moss, 1986; Nicholson 2005). However, this is still not the norm. In the past, many picture-books were given labels announcing them as 'easy to read' or intended for 'less able and reluctant readers'. In the twenty-first century, however, it is becoming more common in schools to see age-appropriate picturebooks for pupils of 9 years and above. Happily, such texts are beginning to take their place on bookshelves beside more traditional forms of literature such as novels, poetry and short stories. Much anecdotal evidence, increasingly being confirmed by more measured research, informs us that youngsters, in their study of pictorial images, construct thoughtful, sophisticated levels of meaning and express abstract concepts about what they observe (Arizpe & Styles, 2003). An example of this maturity of perception is described by a school advisor who spent time with a group of nine-year-old bilingual pupils from a primary school in London:

> ... we were continually impressed by the children's 'in depth' readings of complex picture books. It was also a joy to see their collaboration in sharing their understandings, reflections and questions to the text ... their ability to unpick the layers of meanings led us to not be surprised but very delighted when they used powerful figurative language in their poems.
>
> Bednall & Bearne (2008: 19)

Young readers respond to challenging picturebook texts; they appreciate images, engage with the ideas and allow their imaginations to work in ways that support a thorough understanding of the work. The potential for learning is enormous – too significant to be ignored by teachers who wish to help their students to become competent and lifelong readers.

Discussion about visual texts encourages awareness of literary conventions and vocabulary in young readers. This primary interaction through word and image will, in turn, significantly increase critical readings of other texts. Most school curriculum documents outlining the teaching of literacy – whether from individual schools or government departments – agree on the content of literary study. In general, it is recognized that, among other things, learners need to be able to understand: the creation of character and setting; how narrative structure is developed; and the differences between author, narrator and character. Close reading of high-quality picturebooks promotes such understandings as well as providing thought-provoking 'ideas and themes that broaden perspectives and extend thinking' (DfEE, 1999).

Looking closely

In any text, the starting point for exploring meanings beyond the literal is to look closely at how meanings are constructed. With writing this may mean looking at aspects of style, such as vocabulary choices and sentence structure. With two-dimensional images we apply the same level of consideration to the lines, colours, shapes and spaces created by the artist. As with the written word, images may have subtexts that are conveyed through symbolism, iconography and visual cultural significance. But whether meanings are created through words or images, or a combination of both, it is the ideas, the imaginative possibilities and the values carried by the text and images that contribute to overall understanding.

Adults who support children as they become readers need to familiarize themselves with books that offer opportunities for youngsters to evaluate the ideas generated by texts. There are plenty of picturebooks that will help learners achieve those ends, because 'the best picture books can and do portray the intangible and invisible, ideas and concepts such as love, responsibility, a truth beyond the individual, ideas that escape easy definition in pictures or words.' (Moebius, 1990.)

Archie's War

Archie's War (see Figure 48) is a non-fiction narrative. Set at a particularly disturbing time, it inspires reflection and invites analysis. It is also a

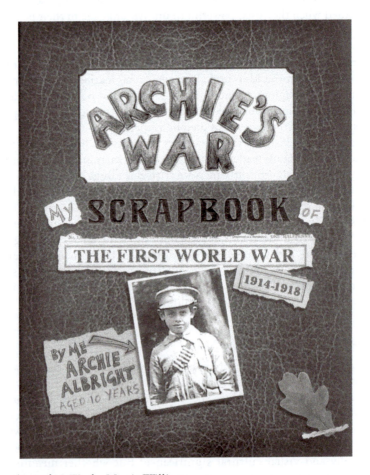

Figure 48 Archie's War by Marcia Williams

picturebook. Perhaps not the sort of text commonly associated with school classrooms, this distinctively different book provides artistic and literary experiences that can support inexperienced readers in their understanding of how full comprehension of narrative requires the ability to read beyond the literal. Readers' comments show not only enriched comprehension of the information communicated through the book but also refer, more tellingly, to their feelings of empathy for the young narrator.

Marcia Williams has been creating picturebooks for 20 years. Her first non-fiction book, *Three Cheers for Inventors* (2005), was so successful that she was invited to create a book, using her individual technique, to describe and explain the First World War to children. Williams' work always involves detailed cartoon-style pictures, with the main narrative presented in a comic-strip format. However, in this unusual text, each page offers the reader more in terms of narrative than that of Archie's immediate experience: margins and gutters are peopled with additional characters whose comments, judgments and observations about local and national wartime happenings serve to extend and unfold the central story. Alongside the cartoons, *Archie's War* incorporates lift-the-flap pages, letters tucked into envelopes and items of everyday ephemera – tickets, postcards, bits of newspaper, etc. (see Figure 49). The whole book is presented as a scrapbook that Archie starts to fill in 1914 when, as a way to amuse himself, he records his daily life by 'publishing' a comic accompanied by his collection of 'interesting' items.

In an interview in October 2007, Marcia Williams explained how she decided to use the scrapbook format. 'When I was trying to find a "way in" to the book, I started Archie's box, which was a collection of First World War memorabilia. I then had to work out how this would translate into a book that might have been written by Archie himself. I thought of the diary/scrapbooks that my son used to keep as a child and felt this would be a way he would have kept a record of the war. It would be both intensely personal and also maintain a sense of history.' Williams describes 'being Archie' for the best part of a year: 'I sat at his table with his pencils and crayons and let his story unfold. It made me cry quite a lot, but there were also lots of laughs along the way.' The decision to dedicate this book to 'all other children touched by war' came about, as Williams explained, 'partly because it is what I thought Archie might have put and partly because Archie is just one amongst millions, both in the past and in the present.' Such a close identification with the child narrator and the engagement with his world may account for the impact that the book can have on readers. There are no over-sentimental responses to the distressing situations that Archie finds himself in. The way that Archie carries on despite his growing unhappiness makes it easy for a reader to empathize with a boy who is living through the painful experiences suffered by many children between the years 1914 and 1918.

Archie is an ordinary lad living at a time when families were separated as fathers, brothers and uncles marched away to the battlefields of northern Europe. The opening endpaper of the book contains a note from Archie

Figure 49 Archie's War incorporates items of ephemera

explaining how he felt in June 1919 when the war was over. It explains that, having survived the emotional, psychological and physical turmoils of war, Archie wants to put it behind him. His notes say 'I want to forget the war and start again.' As we start to read his scrapbook, we already know the effect war has had on Archie's world. So true to reality is this fiction that a consideration of it is included in a notable academic text on children and war, *Children: Invisible Victims of War* (Parsons, 2008), from which the following description is adapted.

Archie Albright is 11 in 1914 when he decides to keep a scrapbook of his drawings and collected 'souvenirs' from family life. The first pages introduce us to Dad, Mum, brothers Ron and Baby Billy, sister Ethel, grumpy Grandma Albright, best friend Tom and Old Georgie, the family's much-loved pet dog. Dad's brothers, Teddy and Colin, are also mentioned. The next few pages are covered with comments, jokes and cartoons about home and school, accompanied by cigarette cards, cat's teeth and other trivia so dear to boys of Archie's age. Family life is pretty uncomplicated until rumours of war create different feelings in the family, causing arguments to break out between pacifist Ethel and resolutely patriotic Dad and Grandma. Despite family disagreements, and the real threat of imminent war, the children find this an exciting time. Archie tells us 'The summer has been spiffing. We have spent nearly all our time playing war games.'

However, small but significant aspects of Archie's life begin to change. He is warned not to play with Peter Schoenfeld (a German neighbour), he takes precautions at night to avoid being 'grabbed' by any lurking enemy soldiers, and then his Uncle Teddy is sent to the front. Within a year the real consequences of war begin to dawn on Archie when zeppelins bomb London, and troops returning from the front describe trenches and poisoned gas. When a telegram arrives announcing that Uncle Teddy has been killed in action Archie's eyes are opened to the anguish of the situation: 'Lord Kitchener sent his sympathy. So don't that make it better.' Things really become worrying when Dad signs up and Mum starts work at a munitions factory. Over the next few months, Archie encounters conscription, shell shock and the social inequalities that leave his family miserable and hungry while the officer classes are well fed: 'The government keeps telling us to eat less food. A lot they know – any less and we'll all be skeletons.' An explosion at the factory followed by the bombing of the next street eventually drives Mum to seek refuge with Uncle Colin in Dorset. The escape to the country allows Archie's scrapbook to have an optimistic ending, although there is no pretence that he is the same happy-go-lucky child we met at the beginning of the book. Despite living in the midst of a loving family, he knows about the hunger, the exhaustion and the depression that affected all working-class Londoners during the war years and, although his father and brother return alive, he has also come into contact with the fear, grief and hopelessness of war.

Archie knows that compared with his contemporaries he is 'lucky' and, in a 'very private' note towards the end of the book, he expresses the sense of guilt that many war survivors experience when he writes 'Uncle Teddy will never come home, Uncle Derek might never get well and hundreds of children who lived in homes now live in orphanages. If my dad comes home safe, I'll be the luckiest boy in the whole world and I don't know if I deserve to be that lucky.'

The clarity and integrity of Williams' book enables young readers to share Archie's feelings and to gain an understanding of how it felt to live in an insecure world. *Archie's War* provides a thoughtful read for youngsters, especially for those who are beginning to read between the lines and to see beyond the literal.

Going West

Going West (see Figure 50) is the story of a pioneer family in America who join a wagon train in order to travel west in search of a place to settle. The story

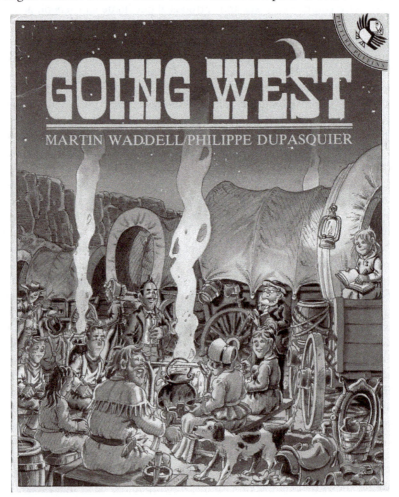

Figure 50 Going West by Martin Waddell

involves a dangerous journey, sickness and death; there are unexpected issues subtly conveyed in the text involving stereotypes, different cultures and political rights to territory. Despite the rather 'wholesome' family atmosphere portrayed on the opening pages, this is by no means a comfortable story to read.

Waddell's text is written in the first person in the form of journal entries by Kate, the youngest member of the family. The images enable readers to become aware of events that the narrator cannot possibly see or know about. A child reader may identify with Kate and, being in a similarly inexperienced position, may not be fully awake to the impact of each image. More experienced readers, especially those who are familiar with the Wild West film genre, will constantly be some steps ahead of the narrator in their understanding of circumstances endured by the characters as the tale unfolds.

Dupasquier, the illustrator, has chosen to place the reader in the position of an imagined camera lens, taking in whole landscapes and dramatic action. The advent of the moving image in film and television produced a new vocabulary for discussing and describing picture. People who are familiar with film techniques develop a set of conventional understandings about how stories work in visual sequences and, literally, from different points of view. They learn that camera angles and the distances between the characters and the camera are important. A film director chooses a set of visual images to build plot or character, or to create feelings of tension or calm, in the same way that a writer makes linguistic choices. Throughout *Going West*, Dupasquier uses filmic devices (see Figure 51) that not only make visual demands on the reader but may also challenge and disturb them.

Going West was first published in 1983. Readers who were growing up between the 1950s and 1970s would be very familiar with classic Westerns TV shows such as *The Lone Ranger*, *Hopalong Cassidy*, *Wagon Train* and *Rawhide*. Children of the 1980s and 1990s would be less familiar with this era but would still have enjoyed a diet of repeated later series such as *Bonanza*, *The Virginian* and *High Chaparral*. To many adult readers the stereotypical characters presented at the beginning of *Going West* may seem like old friends; in fact, the true fan of 'Westerns' may even be able to name the Hollywood actors likely to be playing the parts in a film. For youngsters of the twenty-first century, however, the characters, settings and other intertextual visual devices may mask the developing narrative unless close looking and focused discussion are encouraged. Once their eyes and minds are opened to the potential meanings of the images, young readers often 'see' beyond the imaginative range of an adult's vision. And you do have to 'see' the meanings because little essential aspects of the visual narrative are not revealed in the written text.

Going West is so rich in the conventions of a variety of multimodal texts that it offers a wealth of ideas for any reader to explore. There follows a brief consideration of the structure of Waddell's work and its possible impact on thoughtful readers.

Figure 51 Going West: the Indians attacked us

Narrative structure

The 'story map' for *Going West* consists of a journey from A to B – from the east to the west of North America. The series of events follows a straightforward chronological pattern but the reader views these in differently paced time sequences. The images are used to indicate time and space. Double-page spreads expressing the fragility of human life in the midst of the natural world appear to make time stand still, whilst pages with as many as nine frames depict the urgency of battle or the progress of building a home.

Setting

The setting for *Going West* is a vast canvas. Tiny, flimsy wagons that serve as both transport and homes for the characters move across three thousand miles of uncharted terrain. The landscape, the climate and the native peoples of America are backdrop characters in the epic narrative. Deserts, mountains, rivers and forests have to be navigated under baking sun, rain storms and blizzards. At the journey's end, though, for these pioneer travellers, the land is inviting and the weather temperate.

Character

As the narrative opens, it is easy to accept the stereotypes presented in the story, but as the tale unfolds the characters develop more individual personas. Taking one character, Mr Sullivan, it is possible to trace how a reader's initial view of his personality might change through the book. Although he is pictured in the early plates, he is not named until well into the narrative when we learn that his wife is sick. Clearly he cares deeply for her – despite his 'rough diamond' appearance – and later in the story he shows great courage, risking his life to rescue Kate's brother from a swollen river. His fondness for drink, however, leads to his death when he is ambushed by a hostile Indian. Reviewing our reading of the book enables us to see that Mr Sullivan has always been a flawed character. He is a loving husband and a noble friend, but his weakness for the bottle can be traced from the opening spread until his demise.

Author, narrator, character?

Any story has at least three potential points of view, for example, author, narrator and character. These are sometimes the same – for example, if the author just tells the story from a narrator's point of view. In the case of *Going West* the narrator is not aware of much of the narrative because her character within the story could not actually know it all. For many young readers, the concept of a creator behind the ideas in a book can be difficult. In *Going West* there are two added difficulties: first, the limited number of words printed on each page makes the written element of the work seem very slight; second, the narrator, Kate, is unaware of everything that is going on. She is also too young to fully appreciate the impact of events on the other characters. Rather than telling us the whole story, Kate comments on it from her point of view and keeps it in the domain of childhood experience. The innocence of Kate's character is balanced by the brutality of the story offered to the reader by the author and artist. Although written in the first person, it is not possible for this narrator to construct a full version of the narrative.

Going West is a sensitive book, dealing in a straightforward way with the fragility of life, people's struggle against a hostile environment and the drive to achieve security. It is one of a wealth of picturebooks that offers unexpected depths of meaning in accessible and unthreatening forms.

The Arrival

Another book that is exceptional in its power to inspire empathy is Shaun Tan's award-winning *The Arrival* (see Figure 52), which was first published in

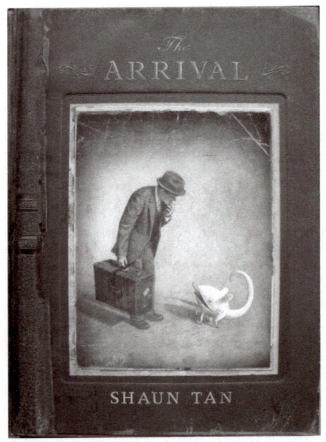

Figure 52 The Arrival by Shaun Tan

2006. This text calls on the reader to apply inference, deduction, intertextual reference and personal response to the powerful narrative, which is constructed entirely through pictorial images. Tan is an Australian artist who has been involved in the creation of picturebooks since the mid-1990s. His work is uncompromising in its portrayal of emotive themes. Examples of this are the depiction of depression in *The Red Tree* (2001), and his illustrations of the effects of war in Gary Crew's *Memorial* (1999) and the abuse of indigenous peoples through colonization in *The Rabbits* (1998) by John Marsden.

The Arrival tells what appears at first to be a straightforward tale of immigration, but every page reveals the raw reality of being an immigrant. A man leaves his wife and child in a country that is dominated by a nameless dread that is illustrated only as a jagged tail-like shadow: it could be plague, politics or poverty. It seems that the man has not been forced to leave, but seeks a better life for his family. Tan's drawings meticulously pull the reader into the world of confusion, anxiety and hope that is the immigrant experience.

From page to page, our understanding is more deeply informed by the personal aspects of the pictures – details of hands, facial expressions and gestures express the true feelings of a man disoriented within extraordinary cityscapes, bizarre methods of transport and dehumanizing systems. Although the visual invention of a 'new world' is fascinating, it is the familiar queues of drab, passive folk waiting for permission to stay that touch the heart. For the immigrant everything is different, nothing is easy, time is relentless and loneliness dominates. *The Arrival* captures the true sense of utter isolation – of being an alien, a stranger, a foreigner. And yet the indomitable spirit of humanity ultimately prevails: our immigrant is befriended by others and his perseverance and determination to find a new life for his family are rewarded.

No matter what the age and experience of the reader, *The Arrival* is a work that requires concentrated application of all aspects of meaning making. It is a book with no written text, but it is packed with language – an ironic twist, since a central theme of the story is the loss of one's native tongue. On his website, Shaun Tan expresses his views on the potency of making meaning from image. He quotes from an article he wrote for *Viewpoint Magazine* in Australia:

> In *The Arrival*, the absence of any written description plants the reader more firmly in the shoes of an immigrant character. There is no guidance as to how the images might be interpreted, and we must ourselves search for meaning and seek familiarity in a world where such things are either scarce or concealed. Words have a remarkable magnetic pull on our attention, and how we interpret attendant images: in their absence, an image can often have more conceptual space around it, and invite more lingering attention from a reader who might otherwise reach for the nearest convenient caption, and let that rule their imagination.
>
> Tan (2008)

Shaun Tan brings an artist's eye to his work and, in doing so, not only reinforces the power of image to enhance readers' meaning-making processes but reminds us that, first and foremost, images exist in their own right. This text demands time and thought. Readers of the powerful images in *The Arrival* will be rewarded with a rich 'fictional' experience on a par with reading the works of a great poet or novelist. (see Figure 53)

Conclusion

As has always been the case, encounters with good books provide the most effective and pleasurable means of creating readers. Engaging with books such as *Archie's War, Going West* and *The Arrival* cannot help but increase a young

Figure 53 A young reader is absorbed by the detailed drawings in *The Arrival*

reader's facility to comprehend verbal and visual texts. However, adults must resist the urge to see picturebooks purely as light-hearted reads or resources to support a literacy curriculum. Whilst high-quality picturebooks will always enhance a growing proficiency at making meaning, develop the ability to infer and to empathize, such powerful texts need no didactic purpose. Sharing picturebooks with young readers is principally about enjoyment, the engagement of the imagination and the excitement of being totally absorbed in a wonderful work of art.

Acknowledgements

Many thanks to the children of St Joseph's RC Primary School, Guildford, and to Hannah and Jonathan Perkins for allowing me to use their comments about *Archie's War*. Special thanks to my friend and colleague Catriona Nicholson for her wise words and support.

References

Arizpe, E. & Styles, M. (2003). *Children Reading Pictures: Interpreting Visual Texts.* London: RoutledgeFalmer

Bednell, J. & Bearne, E. (2008). 'The most wonderful adventure … Going beyond the literal'. *English 4–11* 32, Spring 2008: 19–25

Chambers, A. (1993). *Tell Me: Children, Reading and Talk.* Stroud: Thimble Press

Department for Education and Employment (DfEE) (1999). *The National Curriculum: Handbook for Primary Teachers.* Norwich: HMSO

Meek, M. (1987). *How Texts Teach What Readers Learn.* Stroud: Thimble Press

Moebius, W. (1990). 'Introduction to picturebook codes' in Hunt, P. (ed) *Children's Literature: The Development of Criticism.* London: Routledge, pp.131–47

Moss, E. (1986). *Part of the Pattern.* London: The Bodley Head

Nicholson, C. (2005). 'Reading the pictures: Children's responses to *Rose Blanche*' in Goodwin, P. (ed.) *The Literate Classroom.* London: David Fulton, pp.66–75

Nicholson, C. (2008). Personal communication

Parsons, M. (ed.) (2008). *Children: Invisible Victims of War.* Peterborough: DSM

Tan, S. (2008). 'The Arrival'. http: //www.shauntan.net/books/the-arrival.html

Children's literature

Crew, G. (1999). *Memorial.* London: Lothian Children's Books

Marsden, J. (1998). *The Rabbits.* Andover: Ragged Bears

Tan, S. (2006). *The Arrival.* Melbourne: Lothian Children's Books

Tan, S. (2001). *The Red Tree.* London: Orchard Books

Waddell, M. & Dupasquier, P. (1983). *Going West.* London: Puffin

Williams, M. (2007). *Archie's War.* London: Walker Books

Williams, M. (2005). *Three Cheers for Inventors!* London: Walker Books

Part Three

Thoughts from an author-illustrator

10 A master in his time

Anthony Browne shares thoughts about his work

Anthony Browne with Janet Evans

Anthony Browne is an outstandingly talented author/illustrator, in addition to which he is also a fast worker! In 32 years he has written and illustrated 30 picturebooks, as well as illustrating over 9 for other writers. His first book was *Through the Magic Mirror.* His latest, *Little Beauty*, will soon be followed by another, *You and Me*, which he is currently working on.

Browne's books have received many distinctions, including the Kate Greenaway Medal in 1983 for *Gorilla* and again in 1992 for *Zoo*. Three of his books, *Gorilla* (1983), *Alice's Adventure in Wonderland* (1988) and *Voices in the Park* (1998) all won the Kurt Maschler Emil Award, and in 2000 Browne received the highest international honour for illustration, the Hans Christian Andersen Award, for his services to children's literature. He was the first British illustrator ever to win the prize.

I first interviewed Anthony Browne in 1998 for my book *What's in the Picture?: Responding to Illustrations in Picture Books.* It is patently obvious that since that time his thoughts, ideas and ingenuity have moved on, changed and reached new levels of intensity and inventiveness. Now, over ten years later, I wanted to ask how he perceives his own progress and how some of his thoughts and perceptions about his work may have changed.

JE: Ten years on from our initial interview your thoughts have obviously changed. You have written and illustrated nine more books, including *Willy's Pictures, The Shape Game, Into the Forest, My Dad, My Mum, My Brother, Silly Billy* and your latest, *Little Beauty*. *You and Me* will be your tenth book – which, when counted, shows you write and illustrate on average a book a year. How do you feel about your work and the ways in which it has changed and developed over the last ten years?

AB: Overall, I am pleased with my work over the last ten years, but I don't think that my output has been affected by a different approach. Without changing my overall attitude to picturebooks, there have been a number of projects that have represented new territory for me.

Perhaps the most historic gesture I've made is making a positive book about a father. Before I wrote *My Dad*, I came under a lot of criticism for my succession of incompetent or unaffectionate fathers. Some people thought that children would read about the failings of these men and imagine that they applied to their own fathers, and, although I didn't agree with this – I think that most children are astute enough to discern between fictional characters in books and people in real life – I knew that they had a point. The fathers in *Hansel and Gretel, Gorilla, Piggybook* and *Zoo* all have pronounced weaknesses. For a long time I couldn't understand why my attitude to fathers was so negative, nor how I could write a book that would reverse the trend. The natural answer seemed to be to write about my own Dad. I thought for a long time about how to do it, but couldn't think of a suitable approach until, one day, I found an old suitcase of my mother's. Among the photographs, birth certificates and family relics was Dad's old dressing gown. I hadn't seen it for years but it was powerfully familiar. Although I hadn't consciously thought about it all this time, I recognised the dressing gown from cameos in my books, and realised what an impression it must have made on me. I took it out of the case and held it, and was instantly transported back to the age of five. For the first time in decades I remembered what it was like to be a young boy who thought that his Dad could do anything. It was a breakthrough, for I suddenly knew exactly what format the book would take. *My Dad* owes everything to the dressing gown! (See Figure 54.)

My Mum followed soon after, but I found it much more difficult. Although I based the mother loosely on my own, I didn't feel that I had so much of a personal relationship with the book's character. I found it harder to take the mickey out of mums. As a father myself, I was comfortable portraying 'My Dad' as silly, overweight and a show-off, but it seemed like more of a risk to apply the same treatment to a woman. So I approached the book carefully, taking care to make the protagonist more admirable than clownish. I am quite pleased with the result, but I can still see the self-consciousness that went into the book's creation.

My Brother completed the trilogy. Unsurprisingly, I based the story on the way that I'd viewed my older brother as a child, but unlike the two prequels, I had a little help with the inspiration. I was visiting a school in the Netherlands, and the children showed me the work they'd been doing with *My Dad* and *My Mum*. They had studied the two books and subsequently produced their own version of *My Brother*. I flicked through the book and was impressed by the drawings, but I wasn't surprised to see that the story was written using the template that I'd laid down in my two books. I turned to the last page, expecting the text to continue the pattern that I'd initiated – 'I love him and he loves me too'– but they had changed the ending brilliantly. Instead of my prosaic formula, they had written the words 'And do you know what? I'm cool too.' I loved it, and it was just the spark of inspiration that I needed to ignite enthusiasm for the project.

Another prominent feature of my work in recent times is the celebration of great paintings. I have always referenced existing works of art in my books, but the last ten years have seen the creation of *Willy's Pictures* and *The Shape Game*, both of which are based entirely on great paintings and how they can be

Figure 54 My Dad: the hug

re-imagined. I had already introduced the idea of bringing works of art to the foreground in *Willy the Dreamer* – a book that pays homage to the surrealists. *Willy's Pictures* is really an extension of the ideas expressed in this book, only this time it is Willy's sketchbook that the reader is shown, as opposed to his dreams. The book has no narrative. Instead, it simply exhibits Willy's own interpretations of his chosen masterpieces. At the back of the book is a foldout page, bearing small reproductions of the original paintings. My intention was for children to compare the originals with Willy's interpretations and see how he has altered them – much like the 'spot-the-difference' puzzles that I loved as a child. *Willy the Dreamer* and *Willy's Pictures* represent a move away from conventional narrative-based picturebooks, for they rely almost entirely on the story-telling qualities of the illustrations alone. For me it is a luxury just to paint a series of pictures, without having to consider the boundaries that are imposed by the demands of the text.

The Shape Game was also about looking at paintings, but this time it was in the context of a family day out at an art gallery. The book involved a very different approach for me, which I found both intimidating and liberating. I was approached by Colin Grigg, who was the coordinator of an organization developed by Tate Britain called Visual Paths. He asked me if I would like to be the artist in residence at the Tate Britain for a period of nine months. He proposed that during this time I would work with a thousand children from inner-city schools, teaching them literacy in the context of the gallery. I would direct a series of workshops, at which the children would offer their responses to the works of art. When I finished my term at the gallery, I would be required to create a picturebook that was influenced by the experience. I was very flattered to be asked and accepted straight away, and it was only later that I became anxious about the fact that I was contracted to produce a picturebook based on a specific experience. In the past I had always allowed ideas to come to me naturally, in their own time. Never had I thought that I would ever be obligated to produce an idea within strict limitations of time and subject matter. I needn't have worried, because the project ended up being a fantastic experience. The workshops were tremendous and the children were extremely helpful. I learned to view the project as an opportunity to advance what I'd been trying to do for years: encourage children to appreciate fine art. The book is about the same family that featured in *Zoo*, on a day trip to the Tate Britain. When they enter the gallery, all but the mother are bored and resentful, but one by one they learn to engage with the paintings. They eventually leave feeling enlightened and happy. It was based on the experiences of the children I'd worked with in the gallery, for many of whom the paintings had 'opened up' once they learned how to use their imaginations.

Animal Fair was something of a novelty, because it was my first pop-up book. Thankfully I didn't have to perform any of the mechanics myself, but it was a challenge nonetheless to consider the 3-D aspect. As I painted the illustrations, I only had a vague idea of what the book would look like once the various flaps, wheels and cogs were in place, and this made the process quite exciting. I was pleased with the result. The book is for young children, and for the theme I chose a rhyme that my own children used to sing when they were young. It seemed just right for the pop-up treatment, because it is light, funny, rhythmical and it involves a monkey performing all sorts of tricks and escape acts.

Into the Forest is part of my ongoing flirtation with the fairy-tale genre. For years I have been attracted to the idea of illustrating a book of fairy tales, but for some reason this ambition has never been completely fulfilled. Instead I have produced several books that are fairy-tale-like in nature, and include numerous allusions to existing stories. *Into the Forest* is one such book, and it is very much influenced by another modern fairy tale that I produced earlier in my career, *The Tunnel*.

In recent years my work-related trips have become more frequent and exotic. The success that I've had in Latin America, particularly Mexico, has meant that I've spent a lot of time in that part of the world, and fallen in love with every aspect of its culture. *Silly Billy* – although based partly on the worried nature that has pervaded my family for generations – is largely influenced by my experiences in Latin America. On one of my visits to Mexico, I was given a box of tiny dolls. I was told that they were worry dolls. If you tell them all your worries before you go to sleep and leave them under your pillow overnight, the worries will have vanished by the morning. The gift could not have been more appropriate, and when I returned home, I passed the dolls on to the greatest worrier in my family: my mother. The dolls worked for several nights, greatly reducing her worries during the day. But then one morning she came downstairs with a worried look on her face. When I asked her what was wrong, she said 'I'm worried, Our Tony.'

'What about?' I asked.

'I've lost the worry dolls.'

With *Silly Billy* I wanted to pay tribute to my mother, the worrier, and Latin-American culture at the same time. The story is based on her experience with the worry dolls, and the illustrations are infused with the colours and spirit of Mexico.

Looking at my work over the last ten years, it is evident that my books have all been very different. I haven't consciously tried to be more experimental, and I have relied on the same organic development of ideas that I always have. If there has been any sort of change in my work I suppose it is this increase in the diversity of ideas, which seems to have happened without me thinking about it. Whatever the reasons, I am pleased with the results and I hope that my work continues to evolve in this way.

JE: This book is about responding to picturebooks; children of all ages should be given the opportunity to read, share, think and talk about picturebooks. In our last interview you were asked 'Do you see your books as being primarily for children?' Your short answer was 'Yes'. Now it is evident that many followers of your work are adults: they love your books, reading and enjoying them, of course, but also studying, writing about, deconstructing and reconstructing them and genuinely respecting them for many different reasons. Do you still see your books as being primarily for children?

AB: Yes! Of course they are for children. I am delighted that anybody reads them, and it is very pleasing to think that parents appreciate my books as they read them with their children. I am happy that teachers and librarians use them as educational resources, and that academics find them worthy of study, but my main aim is certainly to entertain the children. To be honest I don't really think about it much at all. I just want my books to be engaging, and when I paint the pictures I don't have a distinction in my head between what is likely to interest a child and what is likely to interest an adult. I suppose I just paint what interests me. It's true that I put a lot of detail into my books, and some of the references to paintings, films and other areas of adult culture I don't always expect children to identify, but I don't think that these damage the overall value of the books. Just because a child can't recognize that a particular image refers to a Magritte painting isn't to say that he or she can't derive some pleasure from the image in other ways. The connection might be identified and explained to the child by a teacher, a parent or an older sibling, or perhaps even the child him- or herself will make the connection years later when he or she comes across the painting. Even the mystery – the sense of not understanding what something means – can have a positive impact on the child's enjoyment of the book. Similarly, adults may enjoy the more childlike aspects of the books, even though they aren't specifically aimed at them.

The hidden clues and references in my pictures are extremely hidden at times, and it may seem unlikely that children will notice them, but I think a lot of adults don't realize quite how switched on children are. I have been talking to children about my books for years and it is astonishing how much they do notice. In many ways, they are more visually aware than adults. Recently, some people I know told me that they had been reading *Little Beauty* with their three-year-old granddaughter. It was she who told her grandparents to look very carefully at the two roses on the last page (see Figure 55). When they did, they saw what she had already identified: the flowers bear the faces of a gorilla and a kitten. It was also she who saw the connection with Beauty and the Beast. I think that the visual alertness of children shouldn't be underestimated.

Everyone laughed.

And do you know what happened?

Beauty and the gorilla lived

happily ever after.

Figure 55 Little Beauty: the two roses

Of course I am very pleased that academics take the time to look at my books and find things to discuss, but in the majority of cases they are simply seeing what the children already see. It is great that adults enjoy them, but my books are still primarily for children.

JE: It has been said that picturebooks afford many possibilities for children to detach themselves from their immediate world and enter the symbolic world of pretend play as they read alone or share books with friends and adults (Goswami & Bryant, 2007). What are your thoughts about this observation in relation to your books?

AB: I agree with this, but I don't think it's confined to just children and picturebooks. I think that we all detach ourselves from our immediate world whenever we read a book or watch a film or look at a painting. It is one of the main reasons that human beings immerse themselves in art. In relation to my books, it is evident that my stories often begin in the 'real world' and depart into the world of the imagination as the story develops, in a way replicating the reader's experience of opening the book and starting to read. Creating the book involves a journey into my own imagination, and by developing my stories this way I am encouraging the child to take the journey with me.

JE: Ten years ago you were asked what you thought about your books being described as postmodern. Then it wasn't something that a lot of people thought about, but now many readers, including young readers, are much more aware of picturebooks being multimodal, polysemic texts making use of many postmodern, metafictive devices to tell the story and engage the reader. Your books certainly make use of many of these devices. What are your current thoughts about your books being described as postmodern?

AB: Exactly the same as they were then. I am delighted that people talk about my books as postmodern and that such words as 'metafictive' and 'intertextuality' are used in relation to my work, but it's not something that I think about. It's just the way I have always worked. If people want to categorize it, that's fine, but if I allowed such devices to enter my consciousness as I tried to create my books I would be absolutely crippled. That's not how creativity works … At least not for me.

JE: Your work is read, studied and responded to by many researchers: Arizpe (2001), Arizpe & Styles (2003), Doonan (1999), Evans (1998), Pantaleo (2004), Saltmarsh (2007) and Serafini (2005), to name but a few. What are your thoughts about your work attracting so much attention from academics in the field of picturebook research?

AB: I am very pleased and fascinated. It is always interesting to read interpretations of my work, whether I agree with them or not. What is particularly fascinating is when somebody makes an observation that I wasn't aware of myself, for it offers me an insight into the way my subconscious works when I create. Very occasionally academics go a bit too far and over-analyse my work to the point where I am horrified or amused by my perceived intentions, but I can never really argue with somebody's interpretation.

I am pleased to hear of adults in general taking picturebooks seriously. All too often I see parents steering their children away from the picturebook section in the book shop: 'Come away, Robert, there aren't enough words in those books. Let's find you a proper book!'

Parents are trying to introduce their children to novels earlier and earlier these days, but they forget that picturebooks offer a lot for the child's development that novels can't provide. Reading a good picturebook can be a very cerebral process and I am glad that academics acknowledge this with their study.

JE: Sometimes you take ages to complete a book for various reasons. *Voices in the Park* was one such book, and when you had finished it and your publishers were pleased, you commented 'I was delighted. I still haven't worked out why it works, and in a way I don't want to, but it does show that quite often the best decisions I make are more to do with instinct rather than intellect.' (Browne & Evans, 1998: 203.) Do you still work a lot through instinct or do you deliberate and wrestle with thoughts as you work on your texts?
AB: I do both. Some parts of my books are the results of very careful consideration, whilst others are entirely improvised and spontaneous. The best way to describe the process is to use the example of a picture from *Voices in the Park* that demonstrates both approaches.

The illustration at the end of Mrs Smythe's 'voice' shows the narrator, her son Charles and their dog leaving the park (see Figure 56). She is angry because she believes that Charles has misbehaved by wandering off and playing with a rough girl. The main features of the illustration were carefully considered and plotted in my preliminary dummy version of the book. One element that was arrived at very much via an intellectual process was the positioning of the figures. Charles is almost entirely obscured by his mother. This was very consciously intended to symbolize how he is stifled by her officious, over-protective parenting. In the same illustration is an example of the instinctive process. When I make an illustration, I transfer the main parts of the picture on to watercolour paper so that an outline is created, but I always try to leave the hidden background jokes and details until I actually come to paint. This means that these parts of the picture are improvised at the last minute. I find this a much more exciting and creative process than to plan every tiny detail in advance.

I began painting the final picture of the Mrs Smythe sequence in this mindset, knowing that something would happen as I allowed my mind and my paintbrush to wander. For this illustration, I indulged in the goldenness of the autumnal colours, making things glow wherever I could. Everything in the picture is imbued with an orange blush: the dog's coat, the path that the characters have recently trod, the top of the lamp post, the windows of the buildings in the background and the leaves on the trees. My original motive behind this was purely to evoke the spirit of autumn, but there was something else that influenced my treatment of the trees. The vividness of the orange that made it seem as if they were burning, and this was partly what influenced my

Figure 56 Voices in the Park: Mrs Smythe, Charles and their dog leaving the park

decision to paint one of the trees actually ablaze. But when I look back at the picture I think that Mrs Smythe's mood also affected the decision. She herself is burning with anger as she marshals her miscreant of a son home. I have a tendency to empathize with the characters that I paint, and quite often their feelings are reflected in other parts of the illustration. It is a process that seems to be beyond my control.

Neither approach is more important than the other. I think that the combination of painful deliberation and spontaneous impulse contributes a lot to the effectiveness of my work.

JE: We now live in the rapidly changing society of the twenty-first century. Many things are happening both nationally and internationally: war; terrorism, famine, perceived breakdown of social values. In many ways nothing appears new as these things have always gone on; however, we seem to be more aware of societal changes than ever before due to the increasing ability to access information through the use of new technologies such as the Internet. Do world issues affect your work and the way you feel about the kind of books you write?

AB: Again, it isn't something that I think about. I have never written an intentionally topical book, but I believe that everything that affects me affects my work. One of the distinctive things about my books is the fact that they are all extremely personal to me, and I pour a lot of whatever I am feeling at the time into their creation. I am an artist, and even though children's books aren't always considered to be the most personal of art forms, I try to express myself every time I put brush to paper. Looking at my books, I can see that a lot is revealed about the artist: my thoughts, my feelings, my character, etc. I certainly make little attempt to conceal my passions: my books are littered with reproductions of my favourite paintings, characters from my favourite films, emblems from my favourite sports.

Everything in my life affects my work in this way. Whatever I read, whatever I see, whatever I hear: it all gets into my psyche. World events inevitably impinge on my thoughts, and although I don't make any direct references in my books to famine or terrorism, I'm sure that my views on such issues are expressed in more subtle ways.

JE: You seem to have an affinity with and an awareness of issues relating to the underdog and the injustices doled out to the underdog in real life. You also seem to be interested in animal rights. Why do you focus on these kinds of concerns?

AB: I don't intentionally focus on any concerns, so it is very difficult for me to determine why they are apparently manifested in my books. My ideas don't come to me by searching for them. They develop more like dreams, appearing gradually and hazily – not fully formed at first – accumulating more facets over time, until they finally arrive at something that is reachable. I have no control over the nature of the protagonist or the themes that will be embedded in the plot.

It's true that a lot of my characters are underdogs, but this isn't really the result of a decision. I – like most human beings – have a tendency to sympathize with the underdog, and I think this is an appropriate attitude in children's literature. Children are themselves underdogs, living in a world dominated by adults. They are smaller, weaker, more ignorant, less influential, and they spend their lives being bossed about by older brothers and sisters, parents and teachers. But it is a very common device in all forms of entertainment. One only has to look to Hollywood to see that, in many films, the protagonist is an underdog in some way; an innocent abroad. Most people identify with and support the underdog, and children perhaps have a greater justification for this than adults. Willy is the ultimate underdog, of course, and he is easily my most popular character with children all over the world (I get more letters about Willy than all of my other characters put together). He is a chimpanzee living in a world of gorillas. He is different from them in nearly every way, which makes him a total outsider. But despite the difficulties that this presents he just gets on with life, celebrating his strengths and accepting his weaknesses. Perhaps the success of Willy has influenced my decision to give many of my protagonists underdog status.

I have never been an active campaigner for animal rights, but I certainly care about the treatment of animals. If there is evidence of this view in my books then it is an example of my beliefs seeping into my work without me realizing it. It ties in with my other point, because animals are underdogs too. Certainly domestic animals and animals that are in captivity have no control over their lives. I have spent a lot of time in zoos and developed a love–hate relationship with them. I love to look at the animals, but my pleasure is always tainted by the sadness and longing that is often evident in their behaviour. The endless pacing up and down the cage of the tiger in *Zoo* is based on what I actually saw at a real zoo: it is one of the saddest things I have ever witnessed. I have a great sympathy for animals in this condition, and – without ever deciding to create a book that promotes animal rights – these feelings have clearly found an outlet in my work.

JE: Your last book, *Little Beauty*, has now been published. Would you share the thought processes that led to *Little Beauty* being written?
AB: *Little Beauty* was based on a true story that I heard about a gorilla. Some years ago a female gorilla at a zoo in California was taught sign language. She developed a vast repertoire of signs and was able to communicate many of her feelings with the keepers at the zoo. One day a keeper came to her cage to discover that she had ripped a washbasin away from the wall, and it lay broken on the floor. The keeper knew about her special talent, so he signed to her 'What happened?'

Without hesitation, she signed back to him 'The keeper did it' (see Figure 57).

Whatever the gorilla's motive for her answer, it is fascinating. If she was lying to him to avoid a reprimanding, that proves that a gorilla's mind is sophisticated enough to capacitate the social inclination to lie. If she was telling a joke, then it proves that she has a sense of humour. Incredible.

There was another story about the same gorilla. She was given a kitten to see how she would respond to the idea of a pet. She loved the kitten dearly, and for a long time she cared for it, played with it, and was as tender an owner as could be imagined. But then one night she rolled over in her sleep and crushed the kitten to death. It isn't such a light-hearted story as the other, but it does show even further just how much like human beings gorillas are (see Figure 58).

I came to learn the details of these two stories later, but the creation of *Little Beauty* was in fact the result of me misremembering them and confusing them in my head. The book is consequently a combination of the two stories, with certain altered elements. My male gorilla is versed in sign language and has a

The keepers rushed in.

"Who broke the television?" said one.

"We'll have to take Beauty

away now," said another.

Figure 57 *Little Beauty*: the keepers rushed in

But

the

gorilla

loved

Beauty.

Figure 58 Little Beauty: the gorilla loved Beauty

pet kitten, which he loves. One day he destroys his television set in a fit of rage (he is watching King Kong), and when the keeper asks him what has happened he blames it on the kitten (see Figure 59).

The ending posed a problem, because a lot of people I talked to thought that it implied a casual attitude to lying: the gorilla blames his aggressive act on somebody else, but it's OK because it's funny. I actually wasn't doing anything of the sort. All I was saying was that this particular gorilla lied – or perhaps told a joke – in this particular instance, but a lot of people were uneasy about the ambiguity of my 'message'. I wrestled with the problem for a long time and it caused me much grief, but I eventually decided to have the kitten flex her muscles in response to the gorilla's answer. She has been the passive character throughout the story, and by essentially admitting that it was she who smashed the TV she makes it very clear to everybody that it is a joke. I hope that this makes the story more about friendship than dishonesty.

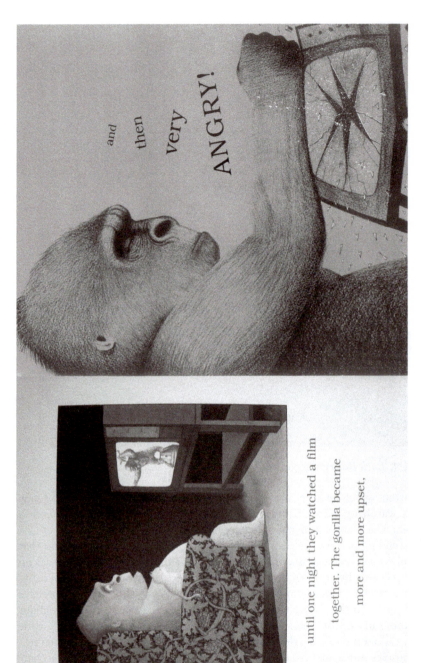

Figure 59 Little Beauty: the gorilla smashes the television

I called the book *Little Beauty* because that is the name of the kitten, but yet again it is an intentional allusion to a fairy tale, the gorilla being the implied beast. The theme of roses throughout the book substantiates this allusion.

JE: You are currently working on your latest book, *You and Me*. You have mentioned that this is one of your more complex/challenging books and that it has taken a great deal of time to think through. Why has this book been a challenge and is it different from some of your others?

AB: *You and Me* is another return to the fairy-tale genre. It is a retelling of Goldilocks and the Three Bears. I always thought that Goldilocks was a little hard done by in the story, the assumption being that she trespasses on the bears' property, steals their food and breaks their possessions for no other reason than to satisfy her own greed and selfishness. I tried to imagine a back-story to the fairy tale. Perhaps she didn't just break into their house for fun: perhaps she really was in distress and in need of food and shelter. In most retellings of the story, it is the bears with whom we are encouraged to sympa-thize, and I thought it was about time the tale was told from another perspective.

At first I decided to tell the story twice. The first half of the book was to be dedicated to the bears' interpretation. Apart from the modernization of the story, and the bears' contemporary, affluent human attire, it would be fairly traditional. The bears live a very comfortable, middle-class life and they arrive home one day to discover a 'horrible, dirty little child' fleeing their house, leaving a trail of broken chairs and empty porridge bowls behind her. They are appalled by her behaviour, and – like most people who know the story – they fail to imagine that she might be starving or distressed.

The second half of the book was to be Goldilocks's story, which would explain the circumstances under which she was forced to 'victimize' the bears. I started the book with these intentions, but soon realized that it didn't work. The whole book was far too bleak. After the opening, which focused on the bears' wealth and complacency, the book ended with Goldilocks just wandering off into the cold, wintery unknown. Yes, it was encouraging a different reading of the traditional fairy tale, but how did I expect children to respond to an ending of such futility? I also didn't like the clumsy format with the sudden transferral of narrator at the halfway point.

What to do with the book posed a big problem for a long time, but I even-tually got help from my French editor, Isabel Finkenstaedt. We decided that it would be far better to tell the two stories simultaneously, with the bears' version (specifically the baby bear's) on the right-hand page of each spread and Goldilocks's on the left (see Figure 60). Isabel suggested that Goldilocks's story be told silently, with no text accompanying the illustrations. Despite the differences of opinion, I have tried to suggest some sort of connection between Goldilocks and the baby Bear. Embedded in their parallel stories is an unspoken affinity between them. I have also decided to make the ending a lot more hopeful. Although it is ambiguous, there is going to be a suggestion in

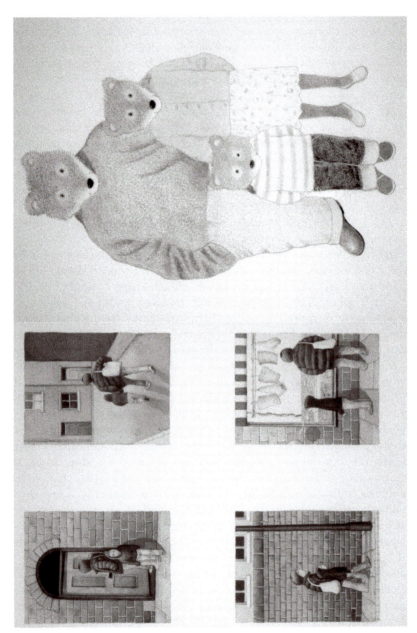

Figure 60 You and Me: Goldilocks goes to the shop with her mother ... baby bear with his family

the illustrations that Goldilocks finds her lost mother. Since I resolved these problems the book has flowed a lot better and I'm feeling much more optimistic about the project.

JE: You once said that people don't ask what your books mean ... what DO your books mean?

AB: I'm not quite sure how to answer this question. There is no constant meaning that applies to all my books. Each individual book means something different.

JE: Which other artists, illustrators and picturebook authors have influenced your work, and how?

JB: There are hundreds. Every piece of artwork I've ever enjoyed has influenced the way I work to some extent. In terms of picturebook author/illustrators, Sendak stands out hugely. I believe it was he who created the first 'true' picturebooks, in which the words and the pictures work both together and separately. Rather than the pictures being a visual reference for the events described in the text, there should be something in the illustration that the text doesn't reveal, there should be something in the text that isn't apparent in the illustration, and sometimes there should be things that are omitted from both. The gaps are to be filled in by the reader's imagination. For me it was Sendak who pioneered this concept, and every picturebook illustrator who has come since has been influenced by his ideas.

Sendak's wisdom has also given me confidence as a painter. He once said that he used to worry about the clumsiness of his illustrations. He was very critical of his own technique, and when he looked at his pictures he would cringe at the erratic cross-hatching here, or the heavily drawn figure there. But then he came to realise that it was the 'clumsiness' that made them Maurice Sendak originals. If the pictures were more precisely executed then a lot of their character would be lost, and it is the 'mistakes' (as he once thought of them) that make the pictures like nobody else's. This made me feel a lot better about the limitations of my own technique.

Another illustrator that I would like to single out is Chris Van Allsburg. I think that he has similar influences to me. He is clearly interested in surrealism and strange stories, and has a very artistic approach to children's book illustration. He is also a brilliant exemplifier of Sendak's concept of the gap between the words and the pictures. The book that demonstrates this more emphatically than any other is his *The Mysteries of Harris Burdick* (1984), for which the reader has to imagine entire stories based on a single illustration. In this sense, Sendak's gap that the child has to fill in is cavernous. It is an extraordinary idea from an extraordinary artist.

Aside from illustrators there really are too many influences to discuss, but I will mention the surrealists because it is clear what a colossal impact they've had on my work. I have been fascinated with surrealism since I discovered it during adolescence, and it has been a leading influence throughout every artistic movement in my career. Even when I was a medical illustrator I would draw tiny men clambering out of open wounds or swinging from ribcages, turning my textbook illustrations into surreal landscapes.

Thankfully, surrealism is not out of place in the children's book environment. Children themselves are natural surrealists. When children draw, they aren't bound by an adult concept of reality – they are far more imaginative. It is perfectly normal for them to draw a fish in the same scene as an aeroplane, for example. Young children's depiction of the world is so extraordinary partly because they are seeing many things for the first time: everything inspires a sense of wonder. What the surrealists tried to do was reproduce the childish state of wonder at seeing the world for the first time. By placing ordinary objects in an unusual context they created a dream-like world that was at once familiar and at the same time new and extraordinary.

JE: Thank you for sharing some of your personal responses to your own work and for giving us an insight into how you think and feel as you write and illustrate your picturebooks. You are, without a doubt, a master in your time, and each and every one of your art works – for that is what your picturebooks are – has become a masterpiece in its own right. You have incredibly diverse and creative thoughts and, thankfully for lovers of picturebooks in general, and for readers of your picturebooks in particular, you are a prolific author/illustrator whose work takes us to the edge, challenging us to think about, consider and respond to your work in ever-new and exciting ways.

References

Arizpe, E. (2001). 'Letting the story out: Visual encounters with Anthony Browne's *The Tunnel*'. *Reading* 35(3), November 2001: 115–19

Arizpe, E. & Styles, M. (2003). *Children Reading Pictures: Interpreting Visual Texts.* London: RoutledgeFalmer

Browne, A. & Evans, J. (1998). 'The role of the author/artist: An interview with Anthony Browne' in Evans, J. (ed) *What's in the Picture?: Responding to Illustrations in Picture Books.* London: Paul Chapman Publishing, pp.192–204

Doonan, J. (1999). 'Drawing out ideas: A second decade of the work of Anthony Browne'. *The Lion and the Unicorn* 23(1), January 1999: 30–56

Evans, J. (ed) (1998). *What's in the Picture?: Responding to Illustrations in Picture Books.* London: Paul Chapman Publishing

Goswami, U. & Bryant, P. (2007). *Children's Cognitive Development and Learning.* Primary Review Interim Reports: Research Survey 2/1a

Pantaleo, S. (2004). 'Young children interpret the metafictive in Anthony Browne's *Voices in the Park*'. Journal of Early Childhood Literacy 4(2), August 2004: 211–33

Saltmarsh, S. (2007). 'Picturing economic childhoods: Agency, inevitability and social class in children's picture books'. *Journal of Early Childhood Literacy* 7(1), April 2007: 95–113

Serafini, F. (2005). 'Voices in the park, voices in the classroom: Readers responding to postmodern picture books'. *Reading Research and Instruction* 44(3), Spring 2005: 47–64

Children's literature

Browne, A. (1976). *Through the Magic Mirror.* London: Hamish Hamilton Children's Books

Browne, A. (1981). *Hansel and Gretel.* London: Julia MacRae Books

Browne, A. (1983). *Gorilla.* London: Julia MacRae Books

Browne, A. (1986). *Piggybook.* London: Julia MacRae Books

Browne, A. (1989). *The Tunnel.* London: Julia MacRae Books

Browne, A. (1992). *Zoo.* London: Julia MacRae Books

Browne, A. (1997). *Willy the Dreamer.* London: Walker Books

Browne, A. (1988). *Alice's Adventures in Wonderland.* London: Julia MacRae Books

Browne, A. (1998). *Voices in the Park.* London: Random House Children's Books

Browne, A. (2000). *My Dad.* London: Random House Children's Books

Browne, A. (2000). *Willy's Pictures.* London: Walker Books

Browne, A. (2002). *Animal Fair.* London: Walker Books

Browne, A. (2003). *The Shape Game.* London: Random House Children's Books

Browne, A. (2004). *Into the Forest.* London: Walker Books

Browne, A. (2005). *My Mum.* London: Random House Children's Books

Browne, A. (2006). *Silly Billy.* London: Walker Books

Browne, A. (2007). *My Brother.* London: Random House Children's Books

Browne, A. (2008). *Little Beauty.* London: Walker Books

Van Allsburg, C. (1984). *The Mysteries of Harris Burdick.* New York: Houghton Mifflin Company

Index

Page numbers in italics denotes an illustration/table

Printed in Australia
AUHW010541110919
317142AU00002B/14